TOP 10
ORLANDO

RICHARD GRULA
JIM & CYNTHIA TUNSTALL

EYEWITNESS TRAVEL

Left **Mennello Museum** Center **Drag queen diva** Right **Merritt Island National Wildlife Refuge**

LONDON, NEW YORK,
MELBOURNE, MUNICH AND DELHI
www.dk.com

Produced by Departure Lounge, London
Printed and bound in China

First published in Great Britain in 2002 by
Dorling Kindersley Limited
80 Strand, London WC2R 0RL
A Penguin Company

15 16 17 10 9 8 7 6 5 4

**Copyright 2002, 2014
© Dorling Kindersley Limited**

**Reprinted with revisions
2004, 2006, 2008, 2010, 2012, 2014**

A CIP catalogue record is available
from the British Library.

ISBN 978-1-40938-287-4

Within each Top 10 list in this book, no
hierarchy of quality or popularity is
implied. All 10 are, in the editor's
opinion, of roughly equal merit.

MIX
Paper from
responsible sources
FSC
www.fsc.org   FSC™ C018179

Contents

Orlando's Top 10

The information in this DK Eyewitness Top 10 Travel Guide is checked regularly.
Every effort has been made to ensure that this book is as up-to-date as possible at the time of
going to press. Some details, however, such as telephone numbers, opening hours, prices,
gallery hanging arrangements and travel information are liable to change. The publishers
cannot accept responsibility for any consequences arising from the use of this book, nor for
any material on third party websites, and cannot guarantee that any website address in this
book will be a suitable source of travel information. We value the views and suggestions of
our readers very highly. Please write to: Publisher, DK Eyewitness Travel Guides,
Dorling Kindersley, 80 Strand, London, WC2R 0RL, or email travelguides@dk.com.

COVER: Front - **Alamy Images**: Greg Balfour Evans, Main; **Dorling Kindersley**: Stephen Whitehorn clb.
Spine - **Alamy Images**: Ian Dagnall b. Back - **Alamy Images**: Dennis MacDonald ca; **Dorling Kindersley**:
Stephen Whitehorn cra; **Getty Images**: Stone / Doug Armand cla.

Left **One Ocean™ show at SeaWorld®** Center **Universal Studios®** Right **Gatorland**

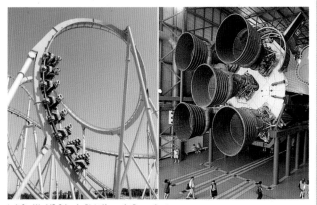

Left **SeaWorld® Orlando** Right **Kennedy Space Center**

Key to abbreviations
Adm *admission charge payable* **DA** *disabled access*

ORLANDO
TOP 10

ORLANDO'S TOP 10

TOP 10 Orlando's Highlights

One word describes Orlando's transformation in the last three decades: stunning. The city and its suburbs have gone through a Cinderella-like metamorphosis, where plain Jane has become a worldly beauty. Millions of tourists are seduced every year by sophisticated resorts, a wide range of theme parks, must-see attractions, happening nightclubs, and winning restaurants. Here are the Top 10 Orlando sights – Orlando's best of the best.

1 The Magic Kingdom® Park
The park that started Disney's Florida empire combines fantasy, adventure, and the future in a package of rides and shows that focuses on Disney movies and TV programs. *See pp8–11.*

2 Epcot®
Inquiring minds love this Disney park, which features technology in Future World and the culture, architecture and enticing food of 11 nations in World Showcase. *See pp12–15.*

3 Disney Hollywood Studios®
Lights, camera, action! Movies, TV shows and stomach-churning thrill rides come together in a theme park that sometimes also serves as a working studio. *See pp16–17.*

4 Disney's Animal Kingdom® Park
Visitors are brought face to face with the wild world of animals, but this kingdom's spacious environmental design doesn't always offer a front-row seat. *See pp18–19.*

5 Islands of Adventure®
Universal's star theme parks recreate the exciting worlds of Harry Potter, Transformers, and the Simpsons' Springfield. Be warned that 9 of its 13 rides have height or health restrictions, so it's not for the young, weak of stomach, or squeamish. *See pp20–23.*

Previous pages **Incredible Hulk Ride, Islands of Adventure®**

6 Universal Studios Florida®

What Disney can do, Universal can equal. The movie and TV themes here can make people's wildest dreams come true or worst nightmares (special effects) a reality. From Transformers to Terminator, the silver screen comes to life. *See pp24–7.*

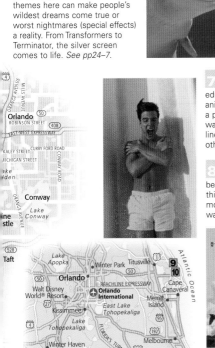

7 SeaWorld® Orlando

Its laid-back pace, educational angle, and animal actors make this a popular stop for those wanting a break from the lines and stifling crowds at other parks. *See pp28–31.*

8 Wet 'n Wild®

Some say it's hard to beat Disney's water parks, but this rival has the most thrills money can buy on the city's water scene. *See pp34–5.*

9 Merritt Island

Located at the Kennedy Space Center, this wildlife refuge is great for learning about local and migrating animals, while also enjoying a bit of fishing or hiking. *See pp36–7.*

10 Kennedy Space Center

The appeal of man in space has turned America's No. 1 space center into a stellar attraction complete with live rocket launches and exhibits. *See pp38–41.*

For more on the Top 10 sights in Orlando **See pp42–85**

Top10 The Magic Kingdom® Park

Walt Disney's first Florida theme park opened in 1971, envisaged as a place where dreams could come true, even if only for a little while. It took six years and $400 million to create "Disneyland East," which has surpassed Walt's own dream: instead of being a spin-off of California's Disneyland® Park, it has become the USA's most popular theme park, attracting more than 17 million visitors every year (some 40,000 each day). Although little has changed in 40 years, with more than 40 major attractions and countless minor ones, this is a true fantasy land for the young and young at heart.

○ A smoked turkey leg at Tomorrowland's Lunching Pad makes a good quick bite, but it's cheaper to bring your own snacks and water (bottles can be filled at the park's numerous fountains).

✈ FastPass *(see p132)* cuts the amount of time spent standing in line for the park's most popular rides and shows.

Guests of Disney resorts get extra time in the parks with the "Extra Magic Hour" program: each day one park opens an hour earlier or closes 3 hours later.

Visit midweek, as the park is at its busiest on weekends and early in the week.

Smoking is only allowed in designated outside areas.

◉ World Drive • Map F1 • 407-824-4321 • www. disneyworld.com • Open at least 9am–7pm daily, call for seasonal hours. • Adm (1-day ticket): adults $101.18, children (3–9) $89.47 (including tax). Children under 3 go free.

Top 10 Attractions

1. Splash Mountain®
2. Big Thunder Mountain Railroad
3. Peter Pan's Flight
4. Space Mountain®
5. Stitch's Great Escape™
6. Buzz Lightyear's Space Ranger Spin
7. The Many Adventures of Winnie the Pooh
8. Prince Charming Regal Carousel
9. Seven Dwarfs Mine Train
10. Pirates of the Caribbean®

Splash Mountain®
1 Disney's 1946 film *Song of the South* inspires this wildly popular flume ride, with Brer Rabbit leading the way through swamps, caves, and "the Laughing Place." Expect twists, turns, and a 52-ft (16-m), 45-degree, 40-mph (64-kmph) climax.

Big Thunder Mountain Railroad
2 Not the raciest of coasters, but the turns and dips, and realistic scenery, combine to make this an exciting trip on a runaway train through gold-rush country *(above)*.

Peter Pan's Flight
3 A flying pirate galleon soars over the sights of London and arrives in Never Land, where Peter Pan battles Captain Hook to save Wendy and her brothers.

Space Mountain®
4 Orlando's first in-the-dark roller coaster is a ride on a rocket that shoots through hairpin turns and drops at what feels like breakneck speed, although top speed is only 28 mph (45 kmph). The cosmic effects and detail enhance this thrilling ride.

Stitch's Great Escape™
5 This family-friendly adventure is based on the mayhem of Stitch's experiment in outer space. The ride uses sophisticated technology, with sights, sounds, and smells to add to the pandemonium.

Buzz Lightyear's Space Ranger Spin

Use the laser cannons on the dashboard to set off sight-and-sound effects as you hurtle through the sky and help *Toy Story's* most famous hero save the world.

The Many Adventures of Winnie the Pooh

Pooh, Eeyore, and a whole host of A. A. Milne's lovable characters come to life in this tranquil ride through the Hundred Acre Wood.

Magic Kingdom® Park Plan

Prince Charming Regal Carousel

This wonderfully refurbished 1917 carousel is a real beauty. It has handsome wooden horses and an organ that plays Disney classics. Kids love it, and adults love reminiscing about the rides of yesteryear.

Park Guide

Due to the crowds and distance involved, it takes around 20 minutes to get from the parking lots (via tram, boat, or monorail) to the park's attractions. Once inside, the Tip Board at the end of Main Street USA has the latest information on the length of lines and times of shows. Park maps are available from Guest Services to the left of the entrance. You'll need at least a day or parts of several to get the most out of the Magic Kingdom®.

Seven Dwarfs Mine Train

An exciting addition to Fantasyland®, Seven Dwarfs Mine Train is a twisty, high-speed rollercoaster trundling through the Enchanted Forest and the dwarves' deep diamond mines.

Pirates of the Caribbean®

Timbers are a-shiver as your boat cruises past a town under siege from a band of rum-soaked, Audio-Animatronic buccaneers. Dank dungeons, yo-ho-ho's, and brazen wenches – all scurvy pirate life is here.

Attraction number		1	2	3	4	5	6	7	8	9	10
Minimum height:	(inches)	40	40	–	40	40	–	–	–	–	–
	(cm)	102	102		102	102					
Recommended age group		8+	9+	all	9+	9+	all	all	all	3+	3+
Duration (minutes)		10	4	3	3	15	5	4	2	3	8

For information on Disney's tour options **See p129**

It's a Small World

🔟 Shows & Next Best Rides

1 Wishes Nighttime Spectacular

This explosive show runs nightly during summer and holidays (occasionally at other times of the year). Liberty Square, the main gates, and Frontierland® are the best areas in the park to take in the fabulous display. If you want to view from outside the Magic Kingdom®, Disney's Grand Floridian, Polynesian, Contemporary, and Wilderness Lodge resorts all have good views from upper floors.

2 Walt Disney World® Railroad

The antique steam-driven trains that travel this 1.5-mile (2-km) perimeter track offer a good overview of the park's sights, but more importantly allow you to get from A to B without the legwork. The 20-minute ride stops at City Hall, Main Street USA®, and Frontierland®.

3 Cinderella Castle

Standing 185 ft (56 m) high, this park icon is a sight to behold. Complete with Gothic spires, it's the quintessential fairytale castle, reminiscent of Neuschwanstein, mad King Ludwig of Bavaria's creation. Inside, there's only one thing of interest to visitors, the Cinderella's Royal Table restaurant, where guests can partake of a character breakfast (see p71).

4 The Magic Carpets of Aladdin

This four-passenger carpet ride lets the rider glide gently up and down and from side to side around a giant genie's bottle. Watch out for the sneaky, water-spitting camels.

5 It's a Small World

The insidious theme song will eat at your brain for months

after you visit, but small kids adore this slow-boat cruise through "lands" where small, Audio-Animatronic, costumed characters sing *It's a Small World After All* in their Munchkin-like voices.

Hall of Presidents
Every US president has an Audio-Animatronic likeness in this fascinating educational show that really highlights the wizardry of Walt Disney Imagineers (designers). The presidents nod and wave, and Abe Lincoln is the keynote speaker.

Mickey's PhilharMagic
Disney magic meets Disney music in a 3-D film spectacular starring Mickey Mouse, Donald Duck, and other favorite Disney characters animated in a way never seen before. Set in the PhilharMagic concert hall in Fantasyland®.

Haunted Mansion
A corny yet fun special-effects show with a cult follow-ing. It's a slow-moving, slightly scary ride-in-the-dark that passes a ghostly ball, graveyard band, and weird flying objects.

Monsters Inc. Laugh Floor
"Monster of Ceremonies" Mike Wazowski brings his furry comedian friends to the digital stage in this kid-friendly comedy club. Audience members help power the city of Monstropolis with their laughter.

Magic Kingdom® Park Plan

Country Bear Jamboree
Audio-Animatronic bears croon and bellow songs in this knee-slapping revue. The finale has the audience hooting and clapping for an encore.

Magic Kingdom® Parades
During summer (and occasionally at other times of the year) a key park event is the evening parade (times vary). The original show was the Main Street Electrical Parade, which was christened at California's Disneyland® Park before moving to the Magic Kingdom® in 1977. Its replacement is the bigger, better, and brighter SpectroMagic. This electri-fying, 20-minute extravaganza brings fountains, creatures, and floats filled with Disney characters to "light". It has no less than 204 speakers cranking out 72,000 watts, uses 75 tons of batter-ies (enough to power 90 houses for the duration), and 100 miles (160 km) of fiber-optic cable. The whole show is powered by 30 mini-computers. Arrive early and try to find a spot in front of the castle. If you can't stay until dark falls, there's a 15-minute Share the Dream Come True Parade (3pm daily) where guests can see their favorite Disney characters in a procession that leaves from Frontierland® to finish off down Main Street USA®.

Attraction number	1	2	3	4	5	6	7	8	9	10
Recommended age group	all	all	all	3+	3+	8+	all	8+	all	all
Duration (minutes)	20	20	–	3	11	30	15	8	–	17

🔟 Epcot®

Walt Disney imagined Epcot® (Experimental Prototype Community of Tomorrow) as a futuristic township where people could live, work, and play in technologically enhanced splendor. After his death in 1966, the idea changed dramatically, and Epcot® opened in 1982 as a park of two halves: Future World focuses on science, technology, and the environment, while World Showcase spotlights the cultures of several nations. The pairing works because both sections are educational and appeal to curious adults and kids alike. Be warned, the park is vast, a fact that has led some to joke that its name is an acronym for "Every Person Comes Out Tired."

Future World: the Coral Reef in the Living Seas Pavilion is way better than most in-park restaurants (see p95). Book ahead. World Showcase: Try fresh pastries at the Patisserie in the French Pavilion.

Use FastPass (see p132), a ride reservation system.

Save time and energy by using the shuttle boats to cross from Future World to the World Showcase.

This theme park is best toured in two days, if not more.

*⊕ Epcot Center Dr, Walt Disney World® Resort • Map G2
• 407-824-4321
• www.disneyworld.com
• Future World: Opens 10am–7pm daily; World Showcase: Opens 11am–9pm daily. Hours are often extended during holidays and in summer months.
• Adm: adults $95.85, children (3–9) $89.46 (including tax). Children under 3 go free.*

Top 10 Future World Exhibits

1. Test Track
2. Innoventions East
3. Innoventions West
4. The Seas with Nemo & Friends
5. Ellen's Energy Adventure
6. Journey into Imagination with Figment
7. Soarin'
8. Mission: SPACE®
9. Spaceship Earth
10. Living with the Land

Test Track
This ride takes you through the tests carried out on automobile prototypes before they hit the consumer market. Riders get to experience brake tests, S-curves, and a 12-second, 65-mph (104-kmph) burst of speed. You must be at least 40 inches (102 cm) tall.

Innoventions East
A refrigerator that can compile a grocery list and a toilet seat with a built-in warmer are among the "smart" furnishings in the House of Innoventions exhibit. Kids like this pavilion's Internet Zone with games such as virtual tag.

Innoventions West
Few can resist Video Games of Tomorrow, a Sega presentation that lets visitors try out next generation games. In the same pavilion, Medicine's New Vision is an exhibit that offers video games along a medical theme.

The Seas with Nemo & Friends
Board a "clamobile" and join your undersea pals to find Nemo. In the same pavilion is the interactive show "Turtle Talk with Crush," also inspired by the same Pixar film.

Ellen's Energy Adventure
A show-and-ride focusing on themes from "fossil fuel" dinosaurs to future energy concerns.

Journey into Imagination with Figment

An open house at Dr. Channing's Imagination Institute is turned inside out by Figment, a playful purple dragon who causes chaos and leads the tour through his upside-down house.

Soarin'

Feel the exhilarating rush of this free-flying hang-gliding adventure over the magnificent landscapes of California *(below)*. You must be 40 inches (102 cm) tall to take this ride.

Epcot® Park Plan (Future World)

Mission: SPACE®

This popular thrill ride takes you on a journey to space with a crash landing on Mars. It is intense and not for anyone prone to motion sickness, or sensitive to tight spaces, loud noises or spinning. If you don't go on the "Mission" you can enjoy interactive games at the "Advance Training Lab."

Park Guide

The main entrance is convenient for Future World, where nine pavilions encircle Spaceship Earth. Getting to World Showcase Lagoon and the 11 nations beyond requires a longer trek, though handy boat shuttles run from Showcase Plaza to the pavilions of Germany and Morocco. A second entrance, at International Gateway, is accessible from Disney's Yacht Club, Beach Club and BoardWalk Inn resorts. Maps that give up-to-date show information are available at both entrances.

Spaceship Earth

The ride inside is nothing to write home about. But this giant golf ball – actually a 180-ft (55-m) geosphere– is an engineering marvel, made of 11,324 triangular aluminum panels that absorb the rain rather than letting it run off.

Living with the Land

The best of the vast Land Pavilion's exhibits involves a boat ride through rain forest, desert, and prairie biomes. It's followed by a look at agricultural experiments including hydroponics and growing plants in simulated Martian soil.

Attraction number	1	2	3	4	5	6	7	8	9	10
Recommended age group	8+	8+	8+	all	all	all	8+	12+	all	all
Duration (minutes)	5	–	–	30	32	6	5	45	17	13

For science on a smaller scale at the Orlando Science Center **See p60 &p113**

Overview of World Showcase Pavilions

World Showcase Pavilions

Canada

The star attraction here is the inspirational 360-degree CircleVision film, *O Canada!*, which reveals some of the country's scenic wonders. You also get to experience traveling by dogsled. Outside, Canada's rugged terrain is convincingly re-created. Gardens that are based on Victoria's Butchart gardens, a replica of an Indian village, and the Northwest Mercantile store, selling items such as tribal crafts and Canadian maple syrup, can be explored.

China

The CircleVision movie, *Reflections of China*, is a fascinating journey through China's natural and man-made riches. The pavilion features a 15th-century Ming dynasty temple, a ceremonial gate, and tranquil gardens. The Yong Feng Shangdian Department Store *(see p92)* is a wonderful treasure trove of Asian goodies. Try not to miss the dynamic Dragon Legend Acrobats who perform several times each day.

Morocco

Look for the Koutoubia minaret, a copy of the tower from a 12th-century mosque in Marrakesh, and you've found this exotic pavilion. Inside, the typical souk architecture is embellished by beautiful carvings and mosaics. The Casbah marketplace *(see p92)* is bursting with hard-to-resist crafts sold by "merchants," and you can see carpets being woven on looms. "Local" cuisine such as couscous is available in the Pavilion's restaurant *(see p95)*.

American Adventure

Enhance your knowledge of US history in a 30-minute dramatization featuring Audio-Animatronic actors. Mark Twain and Benjamin Franklin are the narrators who explain key events, including the writing of the Declaration of Independence, and Susan B. Anthony speaks out for women's rights. The Voices of Liberty singers perform in the main hall of the pavilion, which is modeled on Philadelphia's Liberty Hall.

Japan

A breathtaking five-story pagoda, based on Nara's 8th-century Horyuji temple, forms the centerpiece of this architecturally amazing pavilion. The traditional Japanese gardens are pretty impressive, too, and a perfect spot to escape the throngs. The peace and quiet is only occasionally broken by the beat of drums: go investigate: the Matsuriza troupe is one of the best shows in Epcot®.

Norway

Norway's Maelstrom ride takes you on a 10-minute journey through fiords and fairy-tale forests in a dragon-headed vessel. You land in a 10th-century Viking village, where a short film portrays Norway's natural treasures. The realistic replica of Oslo's 14th-century Akershus Castle houses the restaurant (see p95).

United Kingdom

Examples of typical British architecture through the ages line the quaint cobblestone streets here. Apart from shops selling quintessential British merchandise

Epcot® Park Plan (World Showcase)

(teas, china, crystal, and more), there's also a park with a bandstand and a roaming improv troupe providing entertainment.

Mexico

El Rio del Tiempo (River of Time) is an eight-minute multi-media boat ride that explores Mexico's past and present, from the Yucatan's Mayan pyramids (the pavilion is housed in a replica of one) to the urban bustle of Mexico City life. Mariachis entertain, and there's a *plaza* with stalls selling colorful souvenirs such as sombreros, *piñatas*, and leather goods.

France

This pavilion sports scale replicas, including the Eiffel Tower, and shops selling French products. The 18-minute, five-screen film, which sweeps through glorious landscapes accompanied by the music of French composers is a highlight.

Germany

In this cartoon-like, archetypal German village, you'll find a miniature model railroad, including a wonderfully detailed Bavarian Village. The Biergarten restaurant (complete with brass band) serves traditional food, and shops sell everything from Hummel figurines to wines and cuckoo clocks.

IllumiNations

Created to celebrate the millennium, Epcot®'s stunning fireworks and laser show is still thrilling visitors every night at 9pm. It is a grand half-hour, sound-and-vision nightcap which also brings the World Showcase Lagoon fountains into the act. There are scores of good viewing places all around the edge of the Lagoon.

🔟 Disney Hollywood Studios®

Like Universal Studios®, Disney Hollywood Studios® underscores Orlando's standing as a small, but growing, film production center and offers an up-close look at the world of "Lights! Camera! Action!". The park cost $300 million to create and the result is an effective fusion of fun and information; the attractions tend to be complex, involving rides, shows, and educational commentary, so there really is something for everyone. Nostalgic references to Hollywood's heyday are balanced by high-tech trickery, making this a must for anyone with even a remote interest in the movies.

🍦 A hand-dipped ice-cream cone at Hollywood Scoops slides down a treat, but for more substantial refreshment, try the Sci-Fi Dine-In Theater, serving diner fare in a 1950s retro setting, where guests can watch B-movie clips.

🎟 Use FastPass *(see p132)*, a ride reservation system, to cut the amount of time spent standing in line for the most popular rides and shows.

As in all Disney parks, smoking is only allowed in designated outdoor areas.

Backstage Magic Tour, a 6–8-hour tour behind the scenes at Disney Hollywood Studios®, Epcot®, and Disney World®, is available by calling 407-939-8687.

🌐 *Epcot Resorts Blvd*
• *Map G2*
• *407-824-4321*
• *www.disneyworld.com*
• *Open at least 9am–7pm, sometimes later*
• *Adm: adults $95.85, children (3–9) $89.46 (including tax), children under 3 go free.*

Top 10 Attractions

1. Rock 'n' Roller Coaster® Starring Aerosmith
2. Twilight Zone Tower of Terror™
3. Fantasmic!
4. Indiana Jones™ Epic Stunt Spectacular
5. Muppet™ Vision 3-D
6. Studio Backlot Tour
7. The Legend of Captain Jack Sparrow
8. Star Tours
9. Beauty and the Beast Live on Stage
10. Voyage of the Little Mermaid

1 Rock 'n' Roller Coaster® Starring Aerosmith
A sign warns, "prepare to merge as you've never merged before," but by then it's far too late. Your limo zooms from 0 to 60 mph (97 kmph) in 2.8 seconds and into multiple inversions as Aerosmith blares at 32,000 watts *(above)*.

2 Twilight Zone Tower of Terror™
The spooky surroundings are a facade in front of the real terror, a gut-tightening, 13-story fall. To many, it's Disney's best thrill ride.

3 Fantasmic!
Lasers, fireworks, waterborne images, and a sorcerer mouse are the stars of this end-of-day extravaganza that pits the forces of good against Disney villains such as Cruella De Ville and Maleficent. Performance times vary seasonally.

4 Indiana Jones™ Epic Stunt Spectacular
Indy's action-packed day is full of thrills and spills, and near-death encounters. A stunt co-ordinator explains how it's all done.

5 Muppet™ Vision 3-D
Miss Piggy, Kermit, and the rest of the crew star in a show celebrating both Henson's legacy and Disney's special-effects wizardry and audio-animatronics.

16   *For another movie-flavored theme park* See pp24–7

Studio Backlot Tour
What begins as a tram tour through movie sets and the prop department ends at Catastrophe Canyon. Here, explosions, floods, and fire give riders a bit of a shake-up before getting to see behind the Canyon's scenes.

The Legend of Captain Jack Sparrow
Tour Davey Jones' Locker, the deck of the Black Pearl, and other highlights from all four *Pirates of the Caribbean* movies with animatronic characters and a disembodied pirate skull as a guide.

Entrance

Disney Hollywood Studios® Park Plan

Star Tours
Climb in and swallow hard: your 40-seat spacecraft is going on a journey riddled with dips, bumps, and laser fire. The *Star Wars*–inspired show is presented in digital 3-D video with a flight-motion simulator.

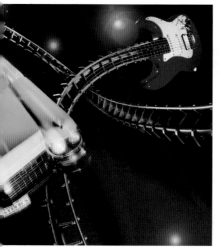

Park Guide
Pick up a map from Guest Services, to the left of the entrance. Staff are on hand to help you find your way around and provide information. The tip board at Sunset and Hollywood boulevards lists up-to-the-minute information on show schedules, wait times, visiting celebrities, and ride or show closures. This park tends to be less busy at the beginning of the week, when many visitors hit the Magic Kingdom® or Epcot®, and it can easily be tackled in one day.

Beauty and the Beast Live on Stage!
The music from the animated film alone is enough to sell this Broadway-style show. The sets, costumes, and production numbers are pretty spectacular, too.

Voyage of the Little Mermaid
This show uses cartoons, live characters and Audio-Animatronics, as well as special effects with lasers and water to create an underwater grotto. Young children may find the lightning storm scary.

Attraction number		1	2	3	4	5	6	7	8	9	10
Minimum height:	(inches)	48	40	–	–	–	–	–	40	–	–
	(cm)	122	101						101		
Recommended age group		9+	9+	all	all	all	all	all	8+	all	all
Duration (minutes)		3.5	4.5	30	40	25	35	15	10	30	17

Disney's Animal Kingdom® Park

As the name implies, wildlife rules at the latest addition to Disney's empire of fun, which is home to over 1,700 animals and around 250 species spread across 500 acres (200 hectares) of lush landscape. Here, the serious issue of conservation is combined with the playfulness of a theme park, though critics complain that the landscaping makes it hard to see the animals, especially in the hottest parts of the day. There's compensation in the fact that the park has some enthralling shows, rides, and attractions reflecting conservation and nature at Disney.

○ **Restaurantosaurus** *(see p71)* serves up kid-friendly fast food for lunch and dinner.

◐ **The best times to see the animals are** as soon as the park opens and within an hour of it closing, especially during the hot months (May–Sep).

Use FastPass *(see p132)*, a ride reservation system that helps cut the amount of time spent standing in line for the most popular rides and shows.

As in all Disney parks, smoking is allowed only in designated outdoor areas.

⊛ *Savannah Circle, Walt Disney World Resort*
• *Map G1*
• *407-824-4321*
• *www.disneyworld.com*
• *Open at least 8am–6pm, sometimes 7am–7pm. Call for seasonal hours.*
• *Adm: adults $95.85, children (3–9) $89.46 including tax. Children under 3 go free.*

Top 10 Attractions

1. Kilimanjaro Safaris®
2. Pangani Forest Exploration Trail®
3. Festival of The Lion King
4. Kali River Rapids®
5. Maharajah Jungle Trek®
6. The Tree of Life
7. It's Tough to Be a Bug!®
8. Finding Nemo – The Musical
9. DINOSAUR
10. The Boneyard®

1 Kilimanjaro Safaris®
The park's most popular ride *(right)* puts you on a large safari jeep to bump along dirt tracks looking for black rhinos, lions, zebras, and more. You're reminded that it's a theme park, though, as a staged adventure unfolds – guests have to save the elephants from "poachers". The animals are real, but that baobab tree was made by Disney's Imagineers.

2 Pangani Forest Exploration Trail®
As you're surrounded by thick vegetation, it's sometimes hard to see the animals on this walk-in-the-woods with a difference. The gorillas are the main attraction, but if the stars of the show prove shy, there are also hippos, exotic birds, and weird-looking mole-rats.

3 Festival of The Lion King
One of Orlando's best shows won't fail to throw you into the spirit of things when it gets going. This production uses singers, dancers, and *The Lion King*'s popular score to emphasize nature's diversity.

4 Kali River Rapids®
The park's conservation message is evident on this exciting raft ride, which passes from a lush landscape to one in the process of being scorched for logging. You need to be 38 inches (96 cm) tall or more to ride, and like to get wet!

For other Disney sights and attractions **See pp88–91**

Maharajah Jungle Trek®

The giant Old World fruit bats, some with man-sized wingspans, are easily spotted, but the Bengal tigers are elusive when it's hot. You might also see Komodo dragons, tapirs, and deer on this atmospheric Asian stroll.

The Tree of Life

The park's symbol is this 145-ft (44-m) tall tree created by Walt Disney Imagineers. Look carefully: there are 325 mammals, reptiles, amphibians, insects, birds, dinosaurs, and Mickeys carved into its trunk, limbs, and roots.

Disney's Animal Kingdom® Park Plan

It's Tough to Be a Bug!®

Located inside the Tree of Life's 50-ft (15-m) base, this 3-D, effect-filled show offers a view of the world from an insect's perspective. The climax is sure to make an impression.

Finding Nemo – The Musical

The Theater in the Wild is transformed into an enchanted undersea world for this original stage show, which merges puppetry with live performances. The show lasts for 30 minutes.

Park Guide

The park, which is Walt Disney World® Resort's largest, is divided into six zones: Oasis (the entrance area); Discovery Island (with the Tree of Life at its center); and the lands of Camp Minnie-Mickey (the main children's zone), Africa, Asia, and Dinoland USA® radiating out from it. Maps are available at Guest Relations, at the entrance to the park.

DINOSAUR

Expect to be shaken up on this wild ride, which takes you back 65 million years. Convincing animatronic dinosaurs lurk in the darkness. There's a 40-inch (102-cm) minimum height requirement.

The Boneyard®

Possibly the best of its kind in any of the Disney parks, this playground is a perfect place for kids to burn off surplus energy. The play area is built around the "remains" of dinosaurs. It's both educational and fun.

Attraction number	1	2	3	4	5	6	7	8	9	10
Recommended age group	all	all	all	8+	all	all	all	all	9+	3 to 12
Duration (minutes)	14	–	28	5	–	–	7	30	4	–

For another conservation-oriented park See pp28–31

🔟 Islands of Adventure®

Orlando didn't have a lot to offer adrenalin junkies until Universal unveiled its second Central Florida park in 1999. Billed as the "world's most technologically advanced theme park," no local rivals can touch Islands of Adventure®'s (IOA) thrill power and innovation (although Tampa's Busch Gardens [see p82] is also highly rated by thrill-seekers). With terrifying roller coasters, three heart-stopping water attractions, and stunningly creative rides, it is the place to head for those who like to live dangerously.

Green Eggs and Ham Café

🟢 Go on. Try a green eggs and ham sandwich at the Green Eggs and Ham Café.

🟠 The Universal Express system *(see p132)* cuts the amount of time spent standing in line for the most popular rides and shows.

Some of the park's rides have shorter lines for single guests and couples willing to split up.

During thunderstorms, the park's plentiful outdoor rides close.

🟤 *Hollywood Way*
• Map T1 • 407-363-8000 • www.universal orlando.com
• Open at least 9am–7pm, call for seasonal hours.
• Adm: adults $97.98, children (3–9) $91.59 (including tax), children under 3 go free.
• One-day tickets can be upgraded to a two-day pass if you find you want to spend another day in the park.

Top 10 Attractions

1. Incredible Hulk Coaster®
2. The Amazing Adventures of Spider-Man®
3. Doctor Doom's Fearfall®
4. Pteranodon Flyers®
5. Jurassic Park River Adventure®
6. Flight of the Hippogriff™
7. Harry Potter and the Forbidden Journey™
8. Dragon Challenge®
9. Poseidon's Fury®
10. The Cat in the Hat™

Incredible Hulk Coaster®
You blast out of the darkness at 40 mph (64 kmph), go weightless, and endure seven inversions and two drops during this white-knuckle ride *(below)*.

The Amazing Adventures of Spider-Man®
Slap on 3-D glasses and battle the baddies while fireballs and other high-definition objects fly at you. The experience is amazing *(below)*.

Doctor Doom's Fearfall®
This ride climbs 200 ft (61 m), before dropping and pausing at several levels to maximum thrilling effect.

Pteranodon Flyers®
Eye-catching metal gondolas swing from side to side on this prehistoric bird's-eye tour around the park's Jurassic Park zone.

Jurassic Park River Adventure®
This ride starts slowly but quickly picks up speed as some raptors get loose *(below)*. To escape you will have to take an 85-ft (26-m), flume-style plunge.

Flight of the Hippogriff™

This family-friendly Harry Potter-themed coaster introduces you to the Hippogriff and takes you on a training flight over the Forbidden Forest, Hagrid's Hut, and Hogwarts grounds.

Harry Potter and the Forbidden Journey™

Walk through the gates of Hogwarts to board this ride and encounter a horde of Dementors and a quidditch match.

Islands of Adventure® Park Plan

Park Guide

Despite the elevators and moving sidewalks, it can still take 20 minutes to get to the attractions from the parking lot. Try to arrive early; if you are staying in a Universal Resort, you can get in before other visitors and enjoy the benefits of free Universal Express access, which allows you to skip long lines by showing your room key. Other visitors can buy a Universal Express Plus Pass from as little as $20 plus tax.

Dragon Challenge™

These two floorless coasters do five rollovers and come within 1 ft (30 cm) of each other no less than three times. If you are really courageous, go for seats in the front row.

Poseidon's Fury®

Visitors tour the ruins of the ancient Temple of Poseidon before passing through a swirling vortex of water and looking on as all hell breaks loose when Poseidon and Zeus have an almighty battle.

The Cat in the Hat™

Hold on as your couch spins and turns through 18 Seussian scenes. The Cat, Thing One, and Thing Two join you on a ride through a day that's anything but ordinary.

Attraction number		1	2	3	4	5	6	7	8	9	10
Minimum height:	(inches)	54	40	52	36	42	36	48	54	–	–
	(cm)	137	102	132	91	107	92	122	137	–	–
Recommended age group		9+	8+	10+	7+	9+	9+	9+	9+	all	8+
Duration (minutes)		2	4	0.5	1.5	6.5	2	5.5	2.5	6	5

Left **One Fish, Two Fish....** Center **Dudley Do-Right** Right **Jurassic Park® Discovery Center**

Gentler Attractions

One Fish, Two Fish, Red Fish, Blue Fish™
Fly your fish up, down, and all around on an aerial carousel ride just 15 ft (4 m) off the ground. If you don't do what the song says, you'll get sprayed with water.

Caro-Seuss-El™
This merry-go-round replaces the traditional horses with interactive versions of Dr. Seuss's cowfish, elephant birds, and mulligatawnies. Regular carousels will never seem the same again.

If I Ran the Zoo
The 19 interactive stations in this Seussian playground use features such as flying water snakes, caves, and water cannons, and include a place to tickle the toes of a Seussian critter.

Jurassic Park® Discovery Center
See through a dinosaur's eyes, match your DNA to theirs, and watch an animatronic velociraptor "hatch" in the laboratory. There are several interactive stations, where kids can brush up on their dinosaur facts.

The Mystic Fountain
Make a wish at this fountain in Sinbad's Village. This wonderful fountain is interactive and is surprisngly playful, asking questions of and teasing guests. Watch out that it doesn't spray you, so don't stand too close.

Camp Jurassic
Burn off energy in an adventure playground full of places to explore, including dark caves where "spitters" (small dinosaurs) lurk. See if you can find out how to make dinosaurs roar.

Triceratops Discovery Trail

Me Ship, The Olive
The play area here is full of interactive fun, while Cargo Crane offers an alternative hands-on experience: a chance to fire water cannons at riders on Popeye & Bluto's Bilge-Rat Barges (see p21).

High in the Sky Seuss Trolley Train Ride!™
Follow the story of the Sneetches™ on this gentle ride above the attractions of Seuss Landing.

The Eighth Voyage of Sinbad Stunt Show
This show is filled with stunts, giant flames, and explosions, as Sinbad hunts for lost treasure.

Storm Force Accelatron®
Dizziness is the name of the game as you and X-Men superhero Storm spin your vehicle fast enough to create electrical energy that will send the evil Magneto to the great beyond.

Top 10 Facts

1 Steven Spielberg produced the 3-D films shown in Spider-Man.

2 Spider-Man's screens are up to 90 ft (27 m) wide.

3 The 15-Hz square audio wave shock used in Spider-Man is a frequency low enough to make humans sick.

4 Each "Scoop" on the Spider-Man ride actually only moves 12 inches (30 cm) up or down.

5 Dragon Challenge™'s two dragons travel at up to 60 mph (96 kmph) and 55 mph (88 kmph) respectively.

7 Dragon Challenge™'s structure is 3,200 ft (975 m) long and can handle 3,264 riders per hour.

8 At 3,180 ft (969 m), the Dragon Challenge™ line is the longest in the world.

9 The Hulk is 3,700 ft (1.1 km) long and can handle 1,920 riders per hour.

10 The Hulk's G-force is the same as that experienced in a F-16 fighter jet attack.

IOA's "State-of-the-Future" Rides

Guests at Islands of Adventure® (IOA) get a first-hand demonstration of some of the most technologically advanced coasters and attractions ever created. At the top of the list is The Amazing Adventures of Spider-Man® (see p20), which took half a decade and more than $100 million to develop and was then upgraded in 2012. New digital film technologies had to be invented for the convincing floor-to-ceiling 3-D images that are projected to a moving audience. The "Scoop" motion simulator, wind cannons, and pyrotechnics are precision-synchronized by a vast computer network. Computers also play a big part in the Dragon Challenge™ (see p21). They calculate the weight of every passenger load, then adjust the speed and departure sequence in order to maximize thrills on this dual coaster. Unique to the Incredible Hulk Coaster® (see p20) is a thrust system that blasts cars out of a tunnel instead of the usual long, slow haul to the top of an incline. But even with all these high-tech innovations, some low-tech touches can't be avoided. Just below the Hulk stretches a huge net designed to catch personal belongings that fall from screaming riders.

The Incredible Hulk
Riders experience zero-gravity inversions as they are spun upside down at 110 ft (33 m) above the ground before dropping 105 ft (32 m) at more than 60 mph (96 kmph).

The Amazing Adventures of Spider-Man®

🔟 Universal Studios Florida®

Universal's first park in Florida opened in 1990, with movie-themed rides and shows, and a mission to steal some of Disney Hollywood's limelight. But it is only since a revamp that the park has really taken off, due largely to the runaway success of the hugely popular Men in Black™ Alien Attack, Terminator 2®: 3-D, and the child-friendly Woody Woodpecker's KidZone.

The Universal globe

🅰 Don your movie star shades and grab a pastry and a cappuccino at the Beverly Hills Boulangerie.

🅱 The Universal Express ticket *(see p132)* lets you cut the amount of time spent in lines for the most popular rides and shows.

VIP tours *(see p129)* help beat the crowds during peak periods.

Note that some rides don't open until around 11am.

⊛ 1000 Universal Studios Plaza
• Map T1
• 407-363-8000
• www.universalorlando. com
• Open at least 9am–7pm but call to check seasonal hours.
• Adm: adults $97.98, children (3–9) $89.46 (including tax), children under 3 go free.

Top 10 Attractions

1 Terminator 2®: 3-D
2 The Simpsons Ride™
3 Men in Black™ Alien Attack
4 Twister – Ride It Out®
5 Shrek 4-D™
6 Transformers: The Ride-3D
7 Disaster!
8 Despicable Me
9 Hollywood Rip Ride Rockit®
10 Revenge of The Mummy®

Men in Black™ Alien Attack

You and your "alienator" must keep the intergalactic bad guys from taking over the world as you spin through the streets, looking to shoot the monstrous bugs *(below)*.

Twister – Ride It Out®

The special effects make you feel as if a tornado is sucking the air out of the room as a 5-story funnel cloud really does make cows fly. Rated PG-13.

Terminator 2®: 3-D

Live stage action, six 8-ft (2.4-m) robots, and an amazing three-screen, 3-D film *(below)* combine for a stunning, action-packed show (PG-13).

The Simpsons Ride™

Swoop, soar, and smash your way through Krustyland on a motion simulator ride with Bart and the rest of the US's favorite cartoon family.

Shrek 4-D™

See, hear, and feel the action in "OgreVision" as Shrek and Donkey set off to rescue Princess Fiona from Lord Farquaad.

For Universal's sister park, Islands of Adventure, See pp20–23

Universal Studios Florida® Park Plan

6 Despicable Me
Explore the lair and secret lab of super-villain Gru in this interactive 3-D digital adventure. Laugh as riders are transformed into minions and taken to a minion-inspired dance party.

7 Disaster!
This interactive ride gives visitors a walk-on role in some of the world's worst disasters, from fires and floods to earthquakes and subway accidents.

8 Transformers: The Ride-3D
Be a part of the smashing, explosive action of this thrilling ride, based on the popular Transformers movies, which includes 60-ft (18-m) tall high-definition 3D robots.

9 Hollywood Rip Ride Rockit®
Riders choose their own music soundtrack for this 65-mph (105 km/h) coaster, Orlando's tallest, towering 17 stories above Universal, and can buy a dvd of their ride to take home.

10 Revenge of The Mummy®
This high-speed rollercoaster propels guests through Egyptian tombs to face their fears. "Dark ride" scenes and a revolutionary induction track ensures its popularity.

Park Guide

It takes about 20 minutes to get from the parking lot to the attractions. Once inside, if you feel disoriented, park hosts can advise you on how best to get from A to B. If you are staying at a Universal hotel, make use of the early admission perk; if you haven't got that option, try to arrive an hour before the park opens and hit the major rides first. The park tends to be quietest midweek, and the crowds seem to evaporate when it rains, so this park is a good bet in bad weather. While it's mostly a built up mix of soundstages, backlots, sets, and shops, there are some green areas in which to take time out.

Attraction number		1	2	3	4	5	6	7	8	9	10
Minimum height:	(inches) (cm)	–	40 102	42 107	–	–	40 102	–	–	51 130	48 120
Recommended age group		all	8+	8+	8+	8+	8+	8+	8+	13+	8+
Duration (minutes)		23	4	4	18	20	5	5	4	2	4

For more attractions in the International Drive area See pp96–9

25

Left **A Day in the Park with Barney™** Right **Beetlejuice's Graveyard Revue™**

Shows & Kids' Stuff

1 Fear Factor Live
Do you have the nerve to participate in this extreme audience participation show? Perform all kinds of stunts as you compete against other guests. Unscripted and unpredictable.

2 Beetlejuice's Graveyard Revue™
Dracula, Wolfman, Frankenstein, and Beetlejuice rock the house with music and pyrotechnic special effects in an 18-minute show. Rated PG-13.

3 Curious George Goes To Town
Follow in the footsteps of that mischievous monkey Curious George at this interactive playground, which offers water-based fun and an arena with thousands of soft sponge balls.

4 Blues Brothers
Non-purist fans of this film, who don't need to see John Belushi and Dan Ackroyd in the key roles, will enjoy this foot-stomping 20-minute revue.

5 Animal Actors on Location
This creative animal show features wild, wacky, and occasionally weird live and video animal action. Expect plenty of audience participation.

6 Woody Woodpecker's Nuthouse Coaster®
Very similar to the Barnstormer ride in Disney's Magic Kingdom® *(see p8)*, this 55-second ride for the young (and timid adults) has just one corkscrew curve.

7 E. T. Adventure®
Everyone's favorite extra-terrestrial takes guests on a bike ride to save his planet. Peddle through strange landscapes to meet Tickli Moot Moot and other characters that Steven Spielberg created for this ride.

8 A Day in the Park with Barney™
The puffy purple dinosaur is adored by preschool kids, so this 25-minute sing-along show is guaranteed to get small fans into a frenzy. Everyone else should probably steer clear.

9 Fievel's Playground®
This partially hidden water playground has a house for kids to explore and a mini water slide, for which the line is often painfully slow.

Fievel's Playground®

10 Universal Orlando®'s Horror Makeup Show
A hilarious and educational look at special effects makeup used in the movies. Explore the secrets with movie-clips, props, and demonstrations.

For Orlando's best dinner shows **See pp80–81**

Top 10 TV Shows and Films made at Universal Studios Florida®

1. Family Feud
2. Ace Ventura Jr: Pet Detective (2009)
3. Beethoven's Big Break (2008)
4. Psycho IV (1990)
5. Problem Child 2 (1991)
6. Matinee (1992)
7. The Waterboy (1998)
8. Hoover (1998)
9. House on Haunted Hill (1999)
10. Held for Ransom (2000)

Behind the scenes

Universal Studios Florida® is more than just a tourist attraction. Since opening in 1990, it has also been the production site for thousands of television shows, commercials, music videos, and movies. While TV and film production has been scaled back in favor of theme park rides and live entertainment (such as Blue Man Group at the Sharp Aquos Theatre), there are still five working sound stages, two broadcast studios, casting and makeup services, post-production editing facilities, and various backlot film sets, including re-creations of New York streets, Hollywood Boulevard, a fishing village, and many others. Though these areas are not normally open to the public, if park guests want to be part of some camera action, they can join the studio audience when TV shows shoot episodes at Universal. Tickets for these productions are typically distributed free of charge on the day of taping. Visitors can check in advance with Guest Services to find out if special-event TV shows will be taped during their visit. There are also regular presentations that give a behind-the-scenes look at the movie-making process.

Star Spotting

Universal Studios doesn't just allow you to "ride the movies." Here, you get to meet the stars, too. Actors playing a whole host of silver-screen and TV legends – including Marilyn Monroe, Scooby-Doo, SpongeBob SquarePants, and the Simpsons – can be seen around the park (especially in the Front Lot) and are always willing to pose for photos.

Hollywood Boulevard, Universal Studios Florida®

10 SeaWorld® Orlando

Opened in 1973, SeaWorld® Orlando is the city's third major attraction. But its unique marine wildlife focus and educational goals puts it in a league all of its own. Guests can get up close and personal with killer whales, sea lions, manatees, rays, and a host of other watery creatures. During 2012 and 2013, SeaWorld® is undergoing a major redevelopment, so some attractions may not be open.

Journey to Atlantis® ride

🍴 For lunch, head to **Sharks Underwater Grill.** This upscale restaurant offers fish and seafood and allows diners to eat under water, surrounded by creatures of the deep.

🎫 Get a **Quick Queue** ticket for special access *(see p132).*

Beat the heat with mid-day visits to air-conditioned indoor attractions.

Didn't bring a stroller? Rent one at the Children's Store. Two-way radios can also be rented at the maps & education building.

🌐 7007 SeaWorld Dr
• Map T5
• 407-351-3600
• www.seaworldorlando.com/seaworld/fla
• Opens 9am, closes between 5pm and 10pm (depending on the season)
• Adm: adults $97.98, children (3–9) $89.46 (inclusive of tax). Children under 3 go free.

Top 10 Attractions

1. Dolphin Cove
2. Wild Arctic®
3. Kraken®
4. Journey to Atlantis®
5. One Ocean™
6. Shark Encounter
7. Antarctica
8. Pacific Point Preserve
9. Manta
10. A'Lure

Wild Arctic®

2. An impressive and chilly re-creation of the Arctic, with ice walls nearly a half-inch thick. See polar bears *(below)*, beluga whales, harbor seals, and walruses. Guests can opt to "arrive" by a simulated helicopter ride, but the line will be longer.

Kraken®

3. Billed as the "tallest, fastest, longest, and only floorless roller coaster in Orlando," Kraken® is a fearsome thrill. It takes riders up 15 stories, spins them upside down seven times, and plunges under water, all at speeds up to 65 mph (104.6 kmph).

Dolphin Cove

1. The joyful spirit of "Flipper" lives on with these playful bottlenose dolphins *(below)*, which romp at the edge of the lagoon where they can be petted.

Journey to Atlantis®

4. The big draw of this flume ride is a 60-ft (18-m) drop, but the surprise bonus is the twisting roller coaster section near the end. Everyone should expect to get wet, especially those in the front of the car.

One Ocean™

5. This show features SeaWorld®'s majestic killer whales playing, leaping, and interacting with each other and their trainers, all set to an original musical score.

For more watery fun in Orlando See pp48–9

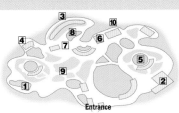

SeaWorld® Orlando Park Plan

Shark Encounter

Here, thanks to the world's largest underwater acrylic tunnel, you can stand six inches (15 cm) from a toothy shark and glide on a people-mover through a world of slithery eels, pufferfish, and sleek barracuda.

Antarctica: Empire of the Penguin

Explore the world of penguins in vehicles over the 4-acre (2-ha) "South Pole". You can see the birds up close.

Pacific Point Preserve

On the surf-drenched rocks of this re-created California coast, hundreds of sea lions and seals cavort and squall in a deafening, endless request for lunch.

Park Guide

Upon arrival, grab a map/event schedule at the Information Counter, and plan your visit according to the live shows you wish to see. The thrill rides – Wild Arctic®, Kraken®, and Journey To Atlantis® – have the longest lines, so visit those when major live shows are taking place. Finally, consider visiting in the late afternoon and evening. Lines vanish, temperatures cool, and the park takes on a different character under the evening sky.

Manta

This thrilling ride combines education and fun, with floor-to-ceiling aquariums and a unique roller coaster *(left)* that allows you to spin, glide, and soar like a manta ray.

A'Lure

Taking place at the Nautilus Theater, this exciting show features flying performers, aerial tumblers, and silk yo-yo artists. It narrates the tale of the mythical sea sirens, who were said to use their hypnotic song to lure sailors to a watery grave by causing them to shipwreck.

Left **Dolphin Nursery** Right **Shamu's Happy Harbor**

TOP 10 Shows & Other Attractions

1 Pets Ahoy!
A multi-species cast of 18 cats, a dozen dogs, a flock of birds, a den of rats, three little pigs, and one horse prove their stage savvy in this humorous display of skills and tricks.

2 Shamu Rocks
The underwater viewing area for SeaWorld®'s killer whales offers an ongoing show of its own. This spot gives the best glimpse of adult whales tending their young.

3 Turtle Trek
Find out all about a turtle's lifecycle and the hardships it has to overcome from the turtle's point of view in this 3D, 360-degree undersea ride and attraction.

4 Blue Horizons
This show is a breakthrough theatrical spectacular that show-cases graceful dolphins and false killer whales, a rainbow of exotic birds, and a cast of world-class divers and aerialists in elaborate costumes.

5 Stingray Lagoon
Lean over this waist-high lagoon and pet the velvety hides of stingrays. The ever-hungry rays flock to those offering fish – feeding times are displayed next to the booth selling fish.

6 Dolphin Nursery
When park dolphins give birth, they're brought to this shaded outdoor pool to be with their young calves. Just ask, and the staffer on duty will provide lots of fascinating information.

7 Sky Tower
For a marvelous view of the park and its backstage areas, take a guided trip to the top of the 450-ft (137-m) revolving Sky Tower. The once-extra admission fee is now included.

8 Manta Aquarium
Floor-to-ceiling aquariums present thousands of tropical fish, octopus, rare leafy sea dragons, and more than 300 rays. Kids can get a 360-degree underwater view through the pop-up observation dome.

9 Shamu's Happy Harbor
Kids can only focus for so long. After that, bring them to this huge playground, complete with slides, roller-coaster rides, a mini-waterpark, a four-story maze of nets, steel drums, and a separate sandbox for smaller guests.

10 Turtle Point
Here you can see endangered and threat-ened species of sea tur-tles in a natural lagoon complete with beach, dunes, and indigenous plant life.

Stingray Lagoon

*For information on Discovery Cove®, SeaWorld®'s sister park **See p97***

Top 10 Rescued Animals at SeaWorld® Orlando

1. Sea turtles (Cheloniidae)
2. Manatees (Trichechus)
3. Pygmy sperm whales (Kogia breviceps)
4. Dwarf sperm whales (Kogia simus)
5. Pilot whales (Globicephala)
6. Bottlenose dolphins (Tursiops truncatus)
7. Killer whales (Orcinus orca)
8. Sandhill cranes (Grus canadensis)
9. Herons (Ardeidae)
10. Grackles (Quiscalus)

SeaWorld®'s Rescue & Rehabilitation Program

Park staff do more than teach killer whales to splash the audience on command. As part of their commitment to conservation, animal experts at all SeaWorld® parks in Orlando, Texas, and California are on call 24 hours a day to rescue sick or injured sea mammals, birds, and turtles. These animals are sheltered at the parks, nursed back to health, and – whenever possible – released into the wild. Endangered Florida manatees are regular beneficiaries of the rescue program. As a result of motorboat propellers, tangled fishing lines, and dangerous toxins, numerous manatees are injured or killed each year. When the call goes out, SeaWorld® responds with a specially equipped animal rescue unit, which can begin emergency treatment on the spot. Manatees on the mend, along with those that wouldn't survive in the wild, are housed in the park's Manatee exhibit (see p29). Since SeaWorld® Orlando started its rescue program in 1976, it has been responsible for saving more than 270 manatees, with more than 100 released back into the wild. By the end of 2000, SeaWorld® Orlando's entire program had rescued and cared for 3,251 animals, including those from animal shelters, and released 735 back into the wild.

Breeding program

SeaWorld® also has a hugely successful breeding program: baby penguins, seals, and no less than 10 killer whale calves have been born at SeaWorld® Orlando.

SeaWorld® staff conducting a triple manatee release

Following pages **Kraken® Ride, SeaWorld® Orlando**

🔟 Wet 'n Wild®

Opened in 1977 by George Millay, the founder of SeaWorld®, Wet 'n Wild® boasts an awesome collection of rides, family activities, and a beach party atmosphere that visitors of all ages enjoy. There is a refreshing lack of merchandise tie-ins here, even though the park is now owned by Universal Studios®. The focus is on original thrill rides that leave guests breathless and grinning. Despite strong challenges by Disney World in the form of Blizzard Beach and Typhoon Lagoon, Wet 'n Wild® remains the region's best water park, and one of the area's top attractions.

The central Surf Lagoon

🍴 Bubba's Bar-B-Q & Chicken is a good bet for lunch. The park's food outlets accept cash, as well as all major credit cards.

⏱ Steps to rides and asphalt walkways can get very hot in high temperatures. Be sure to wear non-slip footwear as protection.

Hi-speed rides can leave you uncovered! Ladies, avoid bikinis or consider adding a T-shirt.

Rides have a 36-inch (91-cm) minimum height requirement for kids riding solo.

• 6200 International Dr
• Map T2
• 407-351-1800
• www.wetnwildorlando.com
• Open 10am–5pm daily, call to check seasonal hours • Adm: adults $58.58, children (3–9) $53.25 (including tax), children under 3 go free. Afternoon discounts are available year-round.

Top 10 Features

1. Der Stuka/The Bomb Bay
2. The Storm
3. Black Hole
4. Disco H2O
5. Mach 5
6. The Flyer
7. Lazy River
8. Bubba Tub
9. The Blast
10. Brain Wash

Der Stuka/The Bomb Bay

The park's scariest ride has two options. Der Stuka is a six-story free fall down a 78-degree incline; the steeper Bomb Bay *(below)* is just as high but even more terrifying.

The Storm

Hurtle down a shoot filled with mist, thunder, and (at night) lightning, then swirl into an open bowl before dropping into a lower pool. Thrilling.

Black Hole

Two people in a raft hang on for dear life as they travel 500 ft (153 m) of twisting tubes in pitch-black darkness *(right)*.

Disco H2O

Board a four-passenger tube and head toward a watery nightclub, complete with groovy disco hits from the 1970s.

Mach 5
A solo flume navigated by riders on a foam mat. On tight turns, ride the flowing water as far up the wall as possible.

Entrance

Wet 'n Wild® Park Plan

The Flyer
On this watery toboggan run, four riders mount one raft and plow through 450 ft (137 m) of banked curves and racing straight runs.

Lazy River
A mile-long (1.6-km) circular waterway *(left)*, which gently winds past swaying palms, tropical flowers, and waterfalls. Perfect for slowly floating along in an inner tube or for a refreshing swim that takes you back to where you started.

Bubba Tub
This six story-high slide *(left)* offers three big drops during its descent. The large circular rafts hold up to four, making it perfect for getting the whole family screaming.

Park Guide

Wet 'n Wild®'s aquatic center is the giant Surf Lagoon, which is encircled by various rides. On entering the park, bear right and head to the Tube, Towel & Locker Rental counter to get a locker for your belongings. You can return to it whenever you need to during the day. Guest Services is located on the left as you go into the park. If you plan to do some tanning or lying around, try to reserve a beach chair with your towel before hitting the rides, and make sure you've got sunscreen. After that, just see which ride has the shortest line.

Brain Wash
Hold on to your inflatable two- or four-person ride *(above)* as it hurtles down an extreme six-story tube, eventually dropping 53 ft (16 m) into a giant domed funnel. Riders must be at least 48 inches (122 cm) tall.

The Blast
A two-person tube ride through a "broken" pipeline. Riders zip through sharp turns, raging rapids, and churning waves, passing colorful machinery and exploding pipes, while the swirling colors and sound effects twist and turn into a waterfall plunge at the end.

TOP10 Merritt Island

Thanks to the U.S. government's race into space, Merritt Island National Wildlife Refuge at the Kennedy Space Center has become the second-largest reserve in Florida. Founded in 1963 to serve as a security buffer zone for NASA, its 140,000 acres now serve as an important habitat for endangered species and a vital stop-over along the migration path of hundreds of birds. The manatees are the refuge's most popular attraction.

Wildlife drive starting point

🍴 Grab a bite to eat at Paul's Smoke House located directly across the Indian River Lagoon before setting out to the island.

🕐 The best times to spot wildlife on the Black Point Wildlife Drive are one to two hours after sunrise and one to two hours before sunset. At these times, the animals make their way to the impoundments for feeding.

🔎 Located just east of Titusville on SR 402. From I-95, take exit 220 and head east for four miles on SR 402 (Garden Street).
• 321-861-0667
• http://fws.gov/merritt island or www.nbbd. com/ godo/minwr
• Open year-round.
• Closed federal holidays and 4 days prior to spacecraft launches.
• No admission charge ($5 daily pass for boat ramps).

Top 10 Attractions

1. Manatee Observation Point
2. Black Point Wildlife Drive
3. Fishing
4. Boating
5. Bird Tours
6. Hiking
7. Waterfowl Hunting
8. Visitor Center
9. Migrations
10. Beaches

1 Manatee Observation Point

Though more common in spring and fall, manatees (sea cows) frequent the refuge year-round. Visitors can see these herbivorous animals up close in Banana River or from the viewing platform at Haulover Canal.

2 Black Point Wildlife Drive

The best places to spot wildlife here are linked by an easy access drive. Follow the seven-mile, one-way loop to see a variety of waterfowl, wading birds, and raptors.

3 Fishing

With both Florida State and Refuge fishing permits, you can cast your line on the Indian River, Banana River, and Mosquito Lagoon. Red drum, spotted sea trout, and snook are the most common catches.

4 Boating

Boating or canoeing is still the best way to get close to the wildlife. In season, the waterways are filled with wading birds in migratory pit stops and manatees in the depths.

Bird Tours
For those with no bird-watching experience, the reserve offers birding tours for beginners. A well-trained park volunteer teaches visitors to identify many of the different types of birds in the refuge, such as this snowy egret.

Merritt Island Plan

Hiking
There are six hiking trails on offer. Most are quite wet, but none are too strenuous. They range from a quarter of a mile (0.4 km) to five miles (8 km).

Waterfowl Hunting
So large are the numbers of birds involved in the seasonal migration that hunting for ducks and coot is allowed from November to January. Permits and safety cards are required, and all expeditions must return by early afternoon.

Visitor Center
In addition to a 20-minute video of the refuge, the center has wildlife exhibits and educational displays providing a good introduction to the Island. The ponds behind the center are favorite spots for alligators.

Migrations
Throughout the year, the refuge plays host to migrating animals. The birds return in May, and during June and July turtles lay their eggs on the beaches. In September waterfowl are plentiful in the rivers.

Beaches
Visitors to the refuge spend more time on land than in water, but Playalinda Beach provides access, parking, and other facilities for swimmers. However, beware of alligators on the road to the beach.

Audio Guide
The Visitor Center sells CDs and tape guides for the Black Point Wildlife Drive. You can also pick up a self-guiding brochure near the entrance to the drive. This provides information on the best places to spot wildlife along the route. Unless you want to keep the brochure, you are encouraged to leave it in the box at the end of the drive for other visitors to use.

Kennedy Space Center

More than any other Florida attraction, the Kennedy Space Center highlights and celebrates the fruits of human inquiry and imagination. Built in 1967, the center's Visitor Complex has become one of Florida's most popular tourist destinations. Each year, it offers a fascinating window on life beyond Earth to more than 1.5 million visitors, and is the site of many dramatic spacecraft launches.

Vehicle Assembly Building

○ Grab a hot dog and sit next to a chunk of real moon rock at the Moon Rock Café.

✪ Kennedy Space Center Tours provides tickets and transportation to the Visitor Complex, with several pick-ups in Orlando and Kissimmee. Call 888-838-8915 or visit www.kennedyspace centertours.net

◉ Rte 405, Titusville • Off map • 321-449-4444 • www.kennedy spacecenter.com • Open 9am–5pm daily. • Adm: $50; children (3–11) $40. Children (0–2) free. • Rocket launch tickets must be purchased in advance. Call 321-449-4400 for information on launch viewing tickets. Visit www.kennedyspace center.com for more information. • Call for details of inclusive tour.

Top 10 Attractions

1 Spacecraft Launches
2 Cape Canaveral: Then & Now Tour
3 Shuttle Launch Experience
4 Astronaut Encounter
5 Atlantis
6 IMAX Theaters
7 International Space Station Center
8 Apollo/Saturn V Center
9 Rocket Garden
10 Early Space Exploration

Spacecraft Launches
Watching this, the ultimate Florida thrill ride *(below)*, is a once-in-a-lifetime experience. Check the website for up-to-date rocket launch schedules.

Cape Canaveral: Then & Now Tour
This three-hour tour visits historic launch pads and the US Air Force Space & Missile Museum.

Shuttle Launch Experience
This exciting simulation ride *(above)* allows visitors to experience the unique sights, sounds, and feel of a space shuttle launch.

Astronaut Encounter
The Kennedy Space Center is the only place on earth where guests can meet a real astronaut every day *(right)*. Children and adults alike find these 30-minute question-and-answer sessions inspiring.

Atlantis
This is the new permanent home of the space shuttle, Atlantis. The $100-million exhibit tells the story of the space shuttle's achievements over its span of 30 years.

6 IMAX Theaters

The Center's twin, back-to-back, 5.5-story theaters show two films: *Space Station – 3D* and *Hubble 3D*, offering an inspiring look into the far reaches of the universe, and the legacy of the Hubble Space Telescope, the world's first orbiting observatory.

Entrance

Kennedy Space Center Plan

7 International Space Station Center

Here, visitors can explore detailed, full-scale models of the International Space Station's compartments and see actual components being prepared for use.

8 Apollo/Saturn V Center

Visitors relive the historic launch of Apollo 8 in the Firing Room Theater and get to walk underneath one of only three Saturn V rockets *(above)* left in existence *(see p40)*.

9 Rocket Garden

Unlike any other garden you have seen, this area *(right)* houses eight actual rockets, including a Mercury Atlas similar to the one that was used to launch astronaut John Glenn. Red, white, and blue lighting adds drama and patriotic flair to these historic spacecraft.

10 Early Space Exploration

This exhibit offers visitors the opportunity to look at the actual Mercury Mission Control consoles used for the first American manned flights. It also highlights the Mercury and Gemini space programs and features artifacts from the first manned flights.

Center Guide

About a 45-minute drive from Orlando, the Center forms part of the Merritt Island National Wildlife Refuge *(see p52)*. Admission includes a bus tour to exhibits located away from the Visitor Complex; it's worth renting the tour's audio guide. Boarding areas for the bus tours are just inside the complex, once you pass through the information center. Except for launch days, the center is rarely overcrowded.

Left **Saturn V** Center **X-15** Right **Gemini VII capsule lauched by Titan II**

Rockets: Past, Present, & Future

Jupiter C
1 This early variation of the Mercury Redstone rocket *(see below)* was developed by a team headed by the German scientist Wernher von Braun. The Jupiter C carried the USA's first satellite, Explorer I, which launched on January 31, 1958.

X-15
2 The X-15 rocket plane flew 199 missions from 1959 to 1968, carrying a who's who of astronauts, including moon-walker Neil Armstrong. It reached altitudes of 354,200 ft (107,960 m) and speeds of 4,520mph (7,274 kmph).

Mercury Redstone
3 This rocket carried the first American into space. Alan B. Shepard Jr.'s 15-minute, 22-second ride aboard the Freedom 7 capsule in 1961 was one of six flights in the Mercury program.

Mercury Atlas
4 When the six-flight Mercury program graduated from sub-orbital to orbital flights, the Atlas replaced the Mercury Redstone. This rocket took John Glenn, Scott Carpenter, Wally Schirra, and Gordon Cooper into space in 1962–3.

Titan II
5 When a larger capsule was needed for two-person crews, this rocket earned its place in NASA history. It was used for 10 manned flights (Gemini Titan expeditions) in 1965 and 1966.

Saturn 1B
6 The Saturn 1B launched Apollo lunar spacecraft into Earth orbit in the mid-1960s to train for manned flights to the moon. Later, it launched three missions to man the Skylab space station (1973) as well as the American crew for the Apollo/Soyuz Test Project (1975).

Saturn V
7 At 363 ft (110 m), this was the largest launch vehicle ever produced. The highlight of its career was Apollo 11, the 1969 mission that landed Buzz Aldrin and Neil Armstrong on the moon.

Titan Centaur
8 The Titan Centaur rocket launched Voyager I and II in 1977 on a mission to explore Jupiter and Saturn, Uranus, and, 12 years after its launch, Neptune.

Mercury Redstone

Pegasus
9 Today's version of this winged wonder is capable of flying small communications satellites into a low Earth orbit from the bellies of mother ships such as the L-1011.

X-43A Launch Vehicle
10 These diminutive rockets may one day boost small, unmanned jets at high speeds and altitudes, improving the safety of manned flights.

Top 10 US Crewed Space Program Events

1. **May 5, 1961** Alan B. Shepard, Jr. becomes the first American in space.
2. **Feb 20, 1962** John H. Glenn, Jr. becomes the first American to orbit the Earth.
3. **Jun 3, 1965** Edward H. White, Jr. becomes the first American to walk in space.
4. **Jul 20, 1969** Neil A. Armstrong becomes the first person to walk on the moon.
5. **Apr 11–13, 1970** An explosion nearly causes disaster for Apollo 13.
6. **Apr 12, 1981** The first shuttle is launched.
7. **Jan 28, 1986** Seven astronauts die in the Challenger space shuttle explosion.
8. **May 27–Jun 6, 1999** The space shuttle docks for the first time on the International Space Station.
9. **Feb 1, 2003** Columbia explodes on re-entering Earth's atmosphere, killing seven astronauts.
10. **Jul 21, 2011** The shuttle program ends with the landing of Endeavour at Kennedy Space Center.

The Space Shuttle

The space shuttles were the first fully reusable spacecraft and the best recognized of NASA's vehicles. Five of them ventured into space: Columbia, Challenger, Discovery, Atlantis, and Endeavour. Once in orbit, the shuttles were capable of cruising at 17,500 mph (28,163 kmph), and their cargo bays could hold a fully loaded tour bus, yet the engineless orbiters could glide to a runway more gracefully than a pelican landing on water. Despite the loss of two of the spacecraft and their crews – Challenger in 1986 and Columbia in 2003 – the shuttles were a remarkable success. They were pivotal in building the International Space Station and extending the life of the Hubble Space Telescope, and their crews carried out valuable cutting-edge research while in orbit.

The 100th space shuttle launch

Investigations in Space
The shuttles allowed astronauts to conduct a wide range of experiments. Here, mission specialist Kathryn P. Hire undergoes a sleep study experiment in the Neurolab on board the Earth-orbiting space shuttle Columbia (April 20, 1998).

Left **Dragon Challenge**™ Right **Incredible Hulk Roller Coaster**®, both **Islands of Adventure**®

🔟 Thrill Rides

Splash Mountain®
Prepare to get wet on this deep-drop ride. In summer, it's a cooling trip; at any time of year it's one to enjoy as a spectator from the bridge between Frontierland® and Adventureland®. Even in that relative safety you may get drenched. *See p8 (Magic Kingdom®).*

Twilight Zone Tower of Terror™
Take the plunge on the phantom elevator that crosses into the Twilight Zone at the Hollywood Tower Hotel. According to legend, in 1939, five passengers on the eleva- tor disappeared during a violent thunderstorm, never to be seen again. Not suit- able for young children. *See p16 (Disney Hollywood Studios®).*

Rock 'n' Roller Coaster®
This ride accelerates like a military jet. If that isn't enough to make heads spin, each 24-passenger "stretch limo" has 120 speakers that blare Aerosmith hits at a teeth-rattling decibel level. *See p16 (Disney Hollywood Studios®).*

Incredible Hulk Coaster®
Possibly the ultimate inver- sion ride – it's a zero-G-force, multi-looping ride of a lifetime. The net catches personal items riders should have stashed in a locker. *See p20 (Islands of Adventure®).*

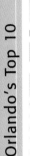

Dr. Doom's Fearfall®

Dragon Challenge™
The ride climbs 12.5 stories above the ground before you real- ize it's too late and you're locked in for the duration. To increase the adrenaline rush, try to get one of the two outside seats in the first eight rows of either dragon. Centrifugal force will steal some of your courage. *See p20 (Islands of Adventure®).*

The Amazing Adventures of Spider-Man®
More high-tech than Uni- versal Studios' Back to the Future, but tamer than the Dragon and Hulk coasters. Still, it's not for those with heart problems or motion sickness tendencies. Use the single line if alone or split from your group – it's quicker. *See p20 (Islands of Adventure®).*

Doctor Doom's Fearfall®
This is a bit like free-falling in a metal harness. As your legs dangle free and you bob to a

Kraken®, SeaWorld®

Many thrill rides are not suitable for young children.

stop, you'll probably be screaming at the top of your lungs. *See p20 (Islands of Adventure®).*

Hollywood Rip Ride Rockit®

The tallest (167 feet/51 m) and one of the fastest (65 mph/105 km/h) coasters in Orlando lets you pick a soundtrack and buy a recording of your ride to edit into your own music video later. *See p25 (Universal Studios®).*

Kraken®

Think pure speed as Poseidon's mythological underwater beast breaks free and without warning pulls your 32-passenger train 151 ft (46 m) closer to heaven, then dives 144 ft (44 m) back toward hell at speeds of 65 mph (105 km/h)! If you survive, expect seven loops on a 4,177-ft (1,273-m) course. This may just be the longest 3 minutes, 39 seconds of your existence. *See p28 (SeaWorld®).*

Summit Plummet

No water park ride will tangle up your bathing suit faster than this 120-ft (36-m), partial-darkness ride. It starts slow, but ends in a near vertical drop that has you plummeting at 60 mph (96 km/h). It's not for the weak of heart or those under 48 inches (122 cm). *See p89 (Blizzard Beach).*

Top 10 Thrill Rides for Children

1 Peter Pan's Flight
Fly over London and on to Never Land with Peter and the Lost Boys. *See p8.*

2 Prince Charming Regal Carousel
A 100-year-old beauty with an engaging fairy-tale theme. *See p9.*

3 The Many Adventures of Winnie the Pooh
Pooh created controversy when he replaced Mr. Toad's Wild Ride in 1999, but he's since won converts. *See p9.*

4 The Magic Carpets of Aladdin
A gentle ride for all ages aboard a flying carpet. *See p9.*

5 Flight of the Hippogriff™
Like the Barnstormer and Woody's Nuthouse, this one's corkscrew action is a blast. *See p21.*

6 Pteranodon Flyers®
A neat aerial adventure, but it can make some riders queasy. *See p20.*

7 The Cat in the Hat™
This ride's dizzying, 24-ft (7-m) tunnel can leave your head and tummy in a spin. *See p21.*

8 Caro-Seuss-El™
Seussian characters make this carousel ride truly unique. *See p22.*

9 E.T. Adventure®
You may have to wait in line a while before pedaling your bicycle past fantastic scenery and characters. *See p26.*

10 Woody Woodpecker's Nuthouse Coaster®
The banked turns of this mini coaster are absolutely exhilarating. *See p26.*

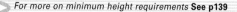

For more on minimum height requirements See p139

Left **Titanic – The Experience** Right **Ripley's Believe It Or Not!® Odditorium**

Smaller Attractions

Gatorland®
This park is chock-full of around 800 lurking alligators, honking for mates, and sometimes performing tricks. The gators don't sit up and beg, but they do jump for food – raw chicken, to be exact, dangled over their ponds by a brave employee. Two hundred or so crocodiles are here to add diversity, as are snakes and other reptiles. There is also a fun water park, Gator Gully Splash. *See p107.*

The Holy Land Experience
Ancient Jerusalem comes to life at this attraction, which has reconstructions of Jesus' tomb, the temple, and the caves where the Dead Sea scrolls were found. Make no mistake: this is a "Christ-centered ministry," but guests of any religion can get a kick out of cast members acting out biblical scenes and telling stories from both testaments. A café serves up "Goliath burgers" among other fare. *See p98.*

Ripley's Believe It or Not!® Odditorium
Cunningly designed, this building looks like it's about to slip into the ground. Inside, kids might squeal – and adults might cringe – over the replicas of human and animal oddities on display. Two-headed cat, anyone? A movie shows people swallowing coat hangers, light bulbs, and more. There are also plenty of quirky displays, such as a rendition of the *Mona Lisa* made out of toast. *See p98.*

Titanic – The Experience
The spirit of Leonardo DiCaprio lingers around this impressive recreation of the doomed Titanic. Guided tours by actors playing crew members and passengers bring the displays to life. Among the 200 or so exhibits are life jackets salvaged from the ship, which add a solemn touch. *See p99.*

Fun Spot America
Looking for life in the fast lane? The Fun Spot's thrilling go-kart tracks and the huge ferris wheel are especially designed for adrenalin enthusiasts. The addition of two giant roller coasters and the world's biggest SkyCoaster have only made it more attractive to visitors. *See p97.*

Gatorland®

iFLY Orlando

If you've always wanted to try sky-diving but don't like the thought of stepping out of a plane, this vertical wind tunnel is for you. More than 100,000 visitors each year immerse themselves in the high adventure of skydiving without ever having to pack a parachute. There are certain weight restrictions and you

iFLY Orlando

have to be more than three years old, but other than that no experience is necessary. The price includes a class, gear and equipment, and two 1-minute jumps, which is usually more than enough to exhaust a novice skydiver. ✎ *6805 Visitors Circle* • *800-759-3861* • *Map T2* • *Open 10am–9:30pm daily* • *Adm* • *www.iflyorlando.com*

Zip Orlando

Fly over untouched Florida's wilderness choosing from a range of day or night excursions. Take a moonlit or a zipline tour, or opt for the guided ATV tour through the backcountry in search of native animals. *See p107*

WonderWorks

Gimmicks abound inside this building, which, like Ripley's, is sinking into the ground, only this time it's roof first. Inside, there's an interactive arcade of some mild scientific educational value. Among the more than 85 hands-on activities, the curious can experience an earthquake or virtual hang gliding, and test their reflexes. For simple fun, the huge laser-tag field is a blast. *See p99.*

Reptile World Serpentarium

This unique and educational attraction gives visitors the opportunity to watch a snake handler in action as he extracts poisonous venom from deadly snakes. It also contains the largest reptile exhibit in Florida. *See p108.*

Winter Park Scenic Boat Tour

Glide through three of Winter Park's lakes on a pontoon boat for this hour-long tour. Nature-lovers can spot birds such as ospreys and herons. The more materialistic can swoon over huge lakeside mansions, sometimes getting close enough to peek in a window. The architecture of Rollins College, and the secluded feel of the canals, make this tour a popular option for the kitschweary. *See p119.*

Left **Swan Boats, Lake Eola** Right **CityWalk®**

🔟 Ways to Have Fun on the Cheap

The Peabody Ducks
It all began in the 1930s when a couple of inebriated sportsmen returning from a weekend hunting trip thought it would be funny to put live ducks in the Peabody Hotel's lobby fountain. The joke stuck and now the original ducks' descendants are local celebrities. They march down from their penthouse at 11am, via the elevator, and return at 5pm. ✆ *9801 International Dr • Map T4 • 407-352-4000 • Free • www.peabodyorlando.com*

HOB Blues Bar
The main room at House of Blues is one of the best spots in town to catch big-name acts *(see p74)*. But the HOB Blues Bar, next door, is an intimate stage for small-scale blues bands that are generally unknown but excellent. Guests ordering dinner get priority for table seating. ✆ *Downtown Disney Westside • Map G2 • 407-934-2583 • Open 11am–11:30pm Sun–Wed (to 1:30am Thu–Sat) • Free*

The Peabody Ducks

Silver Spurs Rodeo
Located inside of Osceola Heritage Park, the Silver Spurs Arena seats 8,300 people. The Silver Spurs Rodeo was founded in 1944 by the Silver Spurs Riding Club to promote good horse-riding skills. The rodeo has bareback bronc riding, barrel racing, bull riding, saddle bronc, steer wrestling, team roping, and tie-down roping. It is the oldest rodeo in the Kissimmee-St. Cloud area. *See p109.*

Downtown Disney®
Undergoing renovation until 2016, the Downtown Disney® area is being rebranded as Disney Springs. It will reopen with a new multilevel shopping arcade, fresh restaurants, and the Splitsville bowling centre along with many other existing attractions. Kids, in particular, like the LEGO® Imagination Center's *(see p92)* outdoor work stations where they can make almost anything.

Disney's BoardWalk®
A recreation of a 1940's seaside resort, Disney's BoardWalk® offers many attractions to visitors, with street performers, good restaurants and bars, and even a leisurely water taxi ride to the back gate of Epcot®. It is a great place to watch Disney's nightly fireworks for free. The ESPN Club is a perfect venue to catch a major league game of any kind on giant TV screens. *See p93.*

Center for Birds of Prey

Founded by the Florida Audubon Society, and off the beaten tourist track, this center's primary function is to rescue and rehabilitate wounded and orphaned raptors. Birds of prey that can't be released back into the wild, however, are kept and used to educate the public about wildlife conservation. With knowledgeable staff and the opportunity to stand close to birds such as eagles and vultures, the center is a captivating treat for a handful of dollars. See p120.

Silver Spurs Rodeo

Universal's CityWalk® & Portofino Bay Boat Ride

By day, visitors stroll through this area of restaurants and shops on their way to Universal Studios® and Islands of Adventure® (see pp20– 27). In the evening, CityWalk® becomes its own sparkling destination, a swinging Downtown with outdoor entertainment and pulsating crowds to rival Disney's BoardWalk®. For 15 minutes of quiet romance, take the free boat ride (which runs until 2am) between CityWalk® and the Portofino Bay Hotel (see p142). In the moonlight, the Portofino's *faux* Italian paint job looks even more convincing. ◎ Map T1

Swan Boats In Lake Eola

Tucked under the blossoming skyline of downtown Orlando, Lake Eola Park is a charming city oasis (see p52). Those seeking some (inexpensive) time alone can rent a two-person Swan Boat (propelled by pedal power) and cruise about on the lake. See p114.

Fort Wilderness Petting Farm

For kids who want to ride a pony (for a small charge) or get to pet miniature donkeys, goats, and other farmyard creatures, this splendid little park can't be beaten. ◎ Walt Disney World • Map F2 • 407-824-2900 • Open 8am–5:30pm daily • Free

Orlando Speedworld Speedway

This racetrack, 17 miles (30 km) east of Orlando, sees eight divisions of highly modified stock cars race each week. However, the most entertaining evenings are those with destructive, madcap races like Schoolbus Demolition Derbys, and Boat and Trailer Races. The price depends on what's on, but it's always a cheap night out. ◎ Highway 50 (at the 520 Cocoa cutoff), Bithlo • Map F1 • 407-568-1367 • Open 8pm Fri Apr–Nov • Adm • www.orlandospeedworld.org

Left **Wet 'n Wild®** Right **Discovery Cove®**

Places to Cool Off

Wet 'n Wild®
Orlando's best water park is full of rides and slides to keep the most hardened thrill-seeker's adrenalin pumping. But it's not all action – there are kids' rides and chill-out areas, too. *See pp34–5.*

Discovery Cove®
Need to unwind on a tropical beach, swim with dolphins, or snorkel over coral reefs? Well, if you check into Discovery Cove®, you can. This exclusive (daily entry is limited to 1,000 people) and inspired Orlando attraction offers the features and personalized services of an upscale island resort. Admission is not cheap, but includes everything from lunch to wet suits and sun block. Reservations two months in advance are suggested. *See p97.*

Lakefront Park

Blizzard Beach
In the battle for water park supremacy, Wet 'n Wild®'s main competitor is this sizeable Disney park. It's what a ski resort would be like if it started to melt, with water slides replacing ski runs. Geared to teens and young adults, the park offers seven water slides and excellent rides, a wave pool, and kids' areas. If park capacity is reached early (as it often is), it closes to new admissions until later in the day. *See p89.*

Lakefront Park
The Lakefront Park is very family orientated. The park includes a marina with 143 boat slips, a children's playground, picnic areas with pavilions and grills, a performing arts pavilion for concerts and special events, walking and biking trails, a white sand beach, beach volley ball courts and a water fountain playground, which has a great view of picturesque East Lake Tohopekaliga. *See p108.*

Typhoon Lagoon
This Disney water park is an enthralling mix of slides, tubes, and the largest wave pool in the US. It's well-suited to families with pre-teen children who'll appreciate the gentle nature of the attractions here. One stand-out is Shark Reef, a short snorkel course over a coral reef teeming with tropical fish and live sharks. Wannabe surfers *(see p57)* can pay an extra fee to use the wave pool outside of regular opening hours. *See p89.*

Orlando Dive & Snorkel Tours
Dive at Florida's most spectacular crystal clear inland springs and rivers, which boast 200 ft (61 m) visibility and a wide variety of marine life. Swim with manatees,

turtles and catfish or enter the 'grand ballroom' 100 ft (30 m) below the surface in a cavern dive. Gear rental, transportation, and lessons are available. ⓢ 13800 S.R. 535 • Map G3 • 407-466-1668 • Open daily • www.diveorlando.com

Sammy Duvall's Watersports Centers

These Disney World-based centers were founded by four-time world champion water-skier Sammy Duvall. The Contemporary Resort branch offers parasailing, water-skiing, wake-boarding, knee-boarding, and tubing. Guests can either rent a boat and driver or take lessons. The slalom course is geared to more hardcore water-skiers. Guests can bring their own gear or rent it. ⓢ Map F1 & G2 • 407-939-0754 • Open winter: 10am–5pm daily; summer: 8am–6pm daily • Adm • www.sammyduvall.com

Buena Vista Watersports

This friendly facility, offers water-ski lessons, water-ski and wake-boarding charters, and rentals of personal watercraft (such as Waverunners and Seaddoos). The center, on the shores of Lake Bryan, is geared to beginners, and kids as young as three can join in. Non-skiers can enjoy the use the lakeside beach, volleyball net, and picnic area.
ⓢ 13245 Lake Bryan Rd • Map G3 • 407-239-6939 • Open 9.30am–6pm daily (weather permitting) • Adm • www.BVwatersports.com

Aquatica®

SeaWorld®'s unique waterpark allows you to swim with, under and through sealife, with high-speed tube slides and half-pipes,

Jet skiers, Buena Vista Watersports

competitive mat races, giant wave pools, and the Dolphin Plunge, which zooms along through enclosed slides into a dolphin pool ⓢ 5800 Water Play Way • Map U5 • 888-800-5447 • Opening hours vary seasonally • Adm • www.aquaticabyseaworld.com

Makinson Aquatic Center

On the eastern edge of Kissimmee, this center offers three pools – one for laps, one for kids, and another for the water slide. It's perfect for families with toddlers or youngsters for whom a major water park could be a bit overwhelming (and admission is far cheaper). ⓢ 2204 Denn John Lane • Map H4 • 407-870-7665 • Open Tue–Sun Mar–Sep (times vary) • Adm • www.kissimmee.org

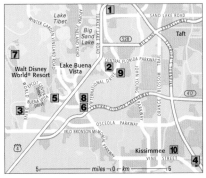

Left **Canaveral National Seashore** Right **Turkey Lake Park**

10 Parks & Preserves

1 Canaveral National Seashore & Merritt Island National Wildlife Refuge

These two federal preserves bordering the Kennedy Space Center are home to scores of species, including endangered ones such as sea turtles, manatees, dolphins, alligators, bald eagles, and ospreys. Explore Canaveral's beaches (including a naturist one, Playalinda) and Merritt Island's trails, driving route, and observation deck *(see pp36–7)*. ◈ *Titusville • Off map • Seashore open at least 6am–6pm daily; refuge open at least 9am–5pm daily • Adm (seashore), free (refuge) • www.nps.gov/cana*

Lake Eola Park

2 Lake Eola Park

Burn a few calories on the 0.9-mile (1.4-km) trail that circles the lake here. Less energetic pursuits include feeding the birds and cruising Lake Eola in the swan-shaped rental boats *(see p47)*. This 43-acre (17-ha) park is also home to several annual and seasonal events, including the 4th of July fireworks show. See p114.

3 Wekiwa Springs State Park

These springs provide a fertile habitat for such species as white-tail deer, gray foxes, bobcats, raccoons, and black bears. They also provide some of the best places for paddling in a boat in central Florida. Canoe rentals, and picnic, grilling, camping, and volleyball areas are also available. ◈ *1800 Wekiwa Circle, Apopka • Map A3 • 407-884-2008 • Open 8am–sunset • Adm • www.floridastateparks.org/ wekiwasprings*

4 Lake Louisa State Park

You can fish, swim, or paddle a canoe, but you'll have to bring your own equipment. The beach has a bathhouse with showers, and there's a picnic area. White-tail deer, wild turkeys, marsh rabbits, opossums, and raccoons are common, and don't be surprised if a polecat (also known as a skunk!) cuts across your path. ◈ *State Park Dr, Clermont • Off map • 352-394-3969 • Open 8am–sunset • Adm • www.floridastateparks.org/lakelouisa*

5 Lake Kissimmee State Park

This park is one of the best bird-watching areas in the state. You might see bald eagles and snail kites, as well as whooping and sandhill cranes. Other residents include otters, wild turkeys, deer, and fox squirrels. On weekends, the park has a re-created 1876 cattle camp. ◈ *Camp Mack Rd, Lake Wales • Off map • 863-696-1112 • Open 7am–sunset • Adm • www.florida stateparks.org/lakekissimmee*

Bill Frederick Park at Turkey Lake

Unlike many state parks with spartan amenities, this 300-acre (120-ha) city retreat has a swimming pool, picnic pavilions, a lake full of fish, nature and jogging trails, three playgrounds, and a farm-animal petting zoo. It also has camping areas if the call of the wild is too strong to leave. ◈ *3401 S. Hiawassee Rd • Map D3 • 407-246-4486 • Open 8am–5pm daily (to 7pm Apr–Oct) • Adm*

Big Tree Park

Though the Senator, a 3,500-year-old cypress tree, burned down in 2012, its companion the 2,000-year-old Lady Liberty, still stands along with Phoenix, a Senator clone, which was planted in 2013. The park has picnic tables and a boardwalk through the cypress swamp. ◈ *General Hutchison Pkwy, Longwood • Off map • 407-665-2001 • Open 8am–sunset • Free*

Tosohatchee State Reserve

Swamps dotted with hardwood hammocks (tree islands) and a 19-mile (30-km) stretch of the St. John's River combine to make this one of Central Florida's prettiest and most primitive parks. Photographers will appreciate the scenic locales, some with wild orchids and other flora. Hawks, eagles, fox squirrels, and songbirds can sometimes be seen from the park's trails. ◈ *Christmas, 18 miles (29 km) NE of Orlando • Off map • 407-568-5893 • Open 8am–sunset • Adm*

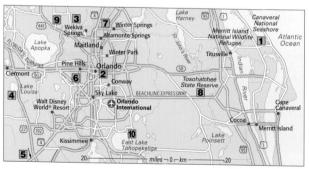

Wekiwa Springs State Park

Wheatley Park

This city park is more urban oasis than rustic countryside retreat. It features lots of facilities such as basketball, tennis, and sand volleyball courts, and picnic areas with grills for a barbecue. Kids will appreciate the well-equipped playground. ◈ *18th & Central Ave, Apopka • Off map • 407-886-1441 • Open sunrise–sunset • Free*

Ralph V. Chisholm Park

This shady park, on the shore of East Lake Tohopekaliga, has various amenities including a beach, swimming area, horse trails, children's playground, softball and baseball fields, sand volleyball courts, and picnic areas. Bring your own equipment, food, and drinks. ◈ *4700 Chisholm Park Trail, St. Cloud • Off map • 407-343-7173 • Open sunrise–sunset • Free*

➤ *For more on day trips out of the city See pp82–5*

Left **Clubhouse, Champions Gate** Right **Falcon's Fire**

🔟 Golf Courses

1 Disney's Osprey Ridge
Arguably the most challenging of Disney's five 18-hole courses, the Tom Fazio-designed Osprey Ridge features native woodlands, elevated tees, fairly large greens, nine water holes, and more than 70 bunkers. *Golf Digest's* "Places to Play" ranks it among Florida's best public and resort courses. (Max yds: 7,101 [6,493 m]. USGA rating: 74.4.) ⊗ *Golf View Dr • Map F2 • 407-938-4653 • www.disneyworld.com*

2 Grand Cypress Golf Club
Jack Nicklaus designed these highly rated 45 holes; the New Course was actually inspired by the Old Course at St. Andrews in Scotland. The club is semi-private with some public tee times. (Max yds: 6,906 [6,315 m]. USGA rating: 74.4.) ⊗ *1 N. Jacaranda • Map F2 • 407-239-4700 • www.grandcypress.com*

3 Waldorf Astoria Golf Club
Rees Jones designed this challenging 18-hole course to follow the contours of a wetland preserve. Impressive stands of pine and cypress trees line the fairways, and a 5-tee system accommodates players of all skill levels. (Max yds: 7,108 [6,500 m]. USGA rating: 74.6.) ⊗ *14200 Bonnet Creek Resort Ln • Map G2 • 407-597-5500 • www.waldorfastoriaorlando.com*

4 Disney's Magnolia
Here's a course with forgivingly wide fairways that let you hammer the ball. But don't get reckless: 11 of the 18 holes contain water and the course has 97 bunkers, with many waiting to gobble your miss hits. Part of the PGA's Funai Golf Classic *(see p57)* is played here. (Max yds: 7,190 [6,574 m]. USGA rating: 73.9.) ⊗ *Palm Dr • Map F1 • 407-938-4653 • Lessons available • www.disneyworld.com*

5 Celebration Golf Club
The father-and-son team of Robert Trent Jones, Sr. and Jr. came up with a course that has water on 17 of 18 holes thanks to natural wetlands, so bring an extra ration of balls. There's also a three-hole junior course for 5- to 9-year-olds. (Max yds: 6,786 [6,205 m]. USGA rating: 73.) ⊗ *701 Golf Park Dr • Map G2 • 407-566-4653 • Lessons available • www.celebrationgolf.com*

6 Champions Gate
Greg Norman created two 18-hole courses (the National and the International)

Villas of Grand Cypress

→ Make reservations at more than 40 Orlando-area golf courses with Tee Times USA 800-465-3356 or Florida Golfing 866-833-2663.

located in this resort community southwest of Disney, featuring woods, wetlands, and open land. Between them they have 13 water holes, and share double greens at the 4th and 16th holes. (Max yds: 7,048 [6,445 m] and 7,407 [6,773 m], respectively. USGA rating: 75.1 & 76.3.) ✪ *1400 Masters Blvd • Map H1 • 407-787-4653 • Lessons available • www.championsgategolf.com*

Orlando Area Golf Course

Orange County National – Panther Lake

The elevation changes as much as 60 ft (18 m) in places on this 18-hole course, one of *Golf Digest's* top "Places to Play". It also gets high marks for course condition and pace of play. The course is surrounded by woodlands, while adjoining wetlands and lakes yield 13 water holes. (Max yds: 7,295 [6,670 m]. USGA rating: 75.7.) ✪ *16301 Phil Ritson Way • Map E1 • 407-656-2626 • Lessons available • www.ocngolf.com*

Disney's Palm

This jewel of a course is surrounded by woodlands. Half of its holes have water,

and its 94 bunkers create headaches for those whose shots stray. The 18th hole is one of the toughest on the PGA Tour. (Max yds: 6,957 [6,391 m]. USGA rating: 73.) ✪ *Palm Dr • Map F1 • 407-939-4653 • Lessons available • www.disneyworld.com*

Disney's Lake Buena Vista

This tight course with its heavily bunkered fairways and greens also uses dense pine forest to challenge golfers. Its most unusual feature is an island green on the seventh hole. Perennially rated as one of Florida's Top 20 in *Golfweek*. (Max yds: 6,819 [6,325 m]. USGA rating: 72.7.) ✪ *Buena Vista Dr • Map F2 • 407-938-4653 • www.disneyworld.com*

Falcon's Fire

With just three water holes, the first nine may convince you to let your guard down, but seven of the last nine holes give you a chance to submerge a ball in two large lakes. This Rees Jones course opened in 1993 and hosts the Senior PGA Tour's qualifying school. (Max yds: 6,901 [6,310 m]. USGA rating: 72.5.) *See p110.*

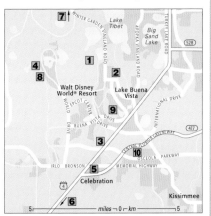

Left **Playing tennis, Grand Cypress Raquet Club** Right **Cycling along scenic country trails**

Sports & Outdoor Activities

1 Horseback Riding
Tri-Circle-D Ranch at Disney's Fort Wilderness Resort offers 45-minute guided trail rides on horseback or carriage through the woodlands. Smaller children can tour the stables and take a pony ride. ® *Walt Disney World • Map F2 • 407-824-2900 • Open 8:30am–4pm daily • Adm • www.disneyworld.com*

Tri-Circle-D Ranch, Fort Wilderness

2 Tennis
Disney's Contemporary Resort has six hydrogrid courts and its Grand Floridian Resort & Spa has two clay ones. The nearby Grand Cypress Raquet Club has 12 courts, four of them all-weather. ® *Disney • Map F1 • 407-939-7529 • Open 9am–10pm daily • Adm* ® *Grand Cypress • 1 N. Jacaranda • Map F2 • 407-621-1991 • Open 8am–5pm daily • Adm*

3 Cycling
Get away on Disney's scenic bike trails. You can rent single, multi-speed, and kids' bikes at the Fort Wilderness Resort's Bike Barn. Tandems and cycles with baby seats and training wheels are also available. ® *Walt Disney World • Map F2 • 407-824-2900 • Open at least 9am–5pm daily • Adm*

4 ESPN Wide World of Sports
Kids and the young-at-heart can play video sports on 40-inch televisions, watch semi-pro baseball, soccer, basketball, and volleyball. Take part in the runDisney marathon and collect merchandise from selected locations. ® *Walt Disney World • Map G2 • 407-828-3267 • Open 9:30am–5pm daily • Adm*

5 Swimming
Most of Orlando's hotels have their own pools, but for a change of scene and a place to swim serious lengths, try an aquatic center. *See p49.*

6 Boating
The man-made lakes around Walt Disney World are perfect for idling away an afternoon. Several of the resorts have small motorboats and pontoon boats for hire. There are also paddle-boats for people who like a more rigorous work-out. ® *Map F1–G2 • Open at least 9am–5pm daily • Adm*

7 Watersports
Test your water-skiing legs at one of Sammy Duvall's Water Sports Centers (which also offers parasailing and wake-boarding). Buena Vista Watersports (which also charters and rents boats) is another option. *See p49.*

Surfing

In land-locked Orlando? You bet. According to the state's surf addicts, who sometimes rent the park after hours, Disney's Typhoon Lagoon *(see p48)* has wave-making down to a fine art. But you don't have to be a pro to give it a try. Carroll's Cocoa Beach Surfing School puts on a twice-weekly class for beginners. *Walt Disney World • Map G2 • 407-939-7873 • Open 6:45–9:30am Tue & Fri • Adm*

Fishing

Land your dinner (and a good fish story) with Pro Bass Guide Service, a Winter Garden outfit that specializes in guided bass-fishing. Local and regional trips to some of Central Florida's most picturesque rivers and lakes are on offer (pick-up can be arranged), as are offshore expeditions for saltwater species, such as redfish and sea trout. *407-877-9676 • Open daily • Adm*

Freshwater fishing, Central Florida

Hayrides

For something a little more unusual in the way of outdoor fun, try a 45-minute hay wagon ride around Disney's Fort Wilderness Resort. Expect some singing and dancing, and a good-time atmosphere that makes for a relaxing end to the day. One of Disney's most popular campground experiences. *Walt Disney World • Map G2 • 407-824-2900 • evenings daily • Adm*

Sporting Events

Florida Citrus Bowl
The annual college football showdown between the No. 2-ranked teams from the Southeastern and Big Ten conferences; preceded by a huge parade. *407-849-2020 • Jan 1*

Walt Disney World Marathon
A 26.2-mile (42.6-km) race with entrants from around the world. *407-824-4321 • Early Jan • www.disneyworld.com*

Speedweeks
Two weeks of motor action at Daytona Beach, ending with the Daytona 500. *866-761-7223 • Early Feb*

Silver Spurs Rodeo
Twice a year rodeo events for cowboys and girls in Kissimmee. *407-677-6336 • Oct • www.silverspursrodeo.com*

Arnold Palmer Invitational
Golf legend host Arnold Palmer, plus players like Tiger Woods, are the draw. *407-876-2888 • Mar*

Atlanta Braves Spring Training
Catch baseball's Braves in pre-season training. *407-939-7712 • Mar • www.braves.com*

Orlando Predators
Grab a chance to support the local arena football team. *407-648-4444 • Apr–Aug*

Orlando City Soccer
Watch professional sports teams in action here. *407-478-4007 • Feb–Aug*

Orlando Magic
Don't miss the NBA team if it's the season. *407-440-7000 • Oct–Apr*

Children's Miracle Network Classic
Disney hosts tour pros in a week of golfing events. *407-939-4653 • Mid-Oct*

For more Orlando area events **See pp64–5**

Left **nèu lotus spa at Renaissance Orlando Resort** Right **Massageworks Salon & Day Spa**

🔟 Spas

1 Spa at the Buena Vista Palace

Just around the corner from Disney's parks, the Buena Vista Palace offers an upscale experience that's from another world. This full-service, European-style spa has various styles of massage; body treatments (mud masks, wraps, and polishes); facials; and hydrotherapy treatments. It has steam rooms, saunas, and a health-and-fitness center. ✆ 1900 Buena Vista Dr • Map G2 • 407-827-2727 • Usually open 9am–6pm daily

2 Mandara Spa at the Portofino Bay Hotel

A state-of-the-art fitness center with a full-service spa (massages, saunas, facials, a couple's treatment room, and more) are on offer at this Universal resort. If you are a guest, you can choose to have your massage in your room. ✆ 5601 Universal Blvd • Map T1 • 407-503-1000 • Open 9am–6pm daily

3 Grand Floridian Senses Spa & Health Club

The spa at Disney's Victorian-style resort has a whole range of services including water and massage therapies, aromatherapy, body wraps, and masks. There's a couple's treatment room and a well-equipped health club. The Grand Floridian also offers nutrition and fitness counseling. ✆ 4401 Floridian Way • Map F1 • 407-824-2332 • Open 8am–8pm daily

4 Relâche Spa at Gaylord Palms

This full-service spa offers hair styling along with a range of relaxing treatments including aromatherapy massage with essential oils, organic facial treatments tailored to your skin's needs, moisturizing manicures, and exfoliating pedicures. ✆ 6000 W. Osceola Pkwy, Kissimmee • Map G3 • 407-586-4772 • Open 9am–8pm daily

Relâche Spa

5 nèu lotus spa at Renaissance Orlando at SeaWorld®

There's a full line of traditional spa services here, including massages (Swedish, deep tissue, and reflexology); body treatments (polishes and wraps); and a full line of facials, one of which is designed to introduce teenagers to the basics of skin care. In-room massages are available for an extra charge. ✆ 6677 Sea Harbor Dr • Map T5 • 407-248-7428 • Open 8am–8pm

6 Disney's Saratoga Springs Resort

The spa at this resort has a range of massage therapies (including hydromassage), body treatments, facials, pedicures and manicures. Treatments can be selected individually or as part of a full-day package, and the staff are happy to design personal treatment programs. Reservations must be made by phone in advance. ◈ *1920 Magnolia Dr • Map G2 • 407-827-4455 • Open 8am–8pm • www.relaxedyet.com*

Spa at the Buena Vista Palace

◈ *216 Broadway • Map H4 • 407-932-0300 • Open 8am–7pm Mon–Sat • www.massageworksdayspa.com*

Ritz-Carlton Spa

A day spent in this spa is time well spent. Start your day with a facial in one of the Spa's 40 treatment rooms. Go for a swim in the private 4,000-sq ft (375-sq m) heated outdoor lap pool or enjoy a relaxing massage followed by a visit to the boutique. End your outing with dinner at Norman's. ◈ *4012 Central Florida Pkwy • Map F4 • 407-393-4200 • Open 9am–7pm daily • www.ritzcarlton.com/en/Properties/Orlando/Spa*

7 Omni Orlando Resort at Champions Gate

This beautiful resort has a first-class spa with state-of-the-art treatments and a deluxe fitness facility. From aromatherapy facials to sports massages, clients can take a break from the crowds at this luxurious secret resort and have a day of pampering. ◈ *1500 Masters Blvd, Championsgate • 407-390-6603 • www.omnihotels.com*

8 Poseidon Spa at Grand Bohemian

The AAA Four Diamond Grand Bohemian is a landmark luxury hotel, and the Poseidon Spa only adds to the acclaim. This relaxing spa offers several therapeutic treatments including facials, manicures, pedicures, and massage. ◈ *325 S. Orange Ave • Map P3 • 407-313-9000 • Open 9am–6pm daily • www.grandbohemianhotel.com*

9 Massageworks Salon & Day Spa

Located in a 100-year-old Kissimmee schoolhouse, this spa has an air of yesteryear. Treatments include massages (Swedish, neuromuscular, reflexology, and sports); therapies (salt scrubs, aroma steam, and mud-aloe); wraps (oil, marine algae, and sea clay); and colonic irrigation. There are sauna, teeth-whitening, and power nap facilities available. It's possible to combine treatments in three- to six-hour packages.

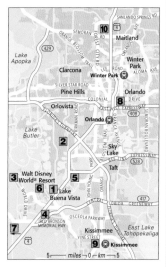

Left **Exhibit, Mennello Museum of American Folk Art** Right **Orlando Science Center**

Museums

Orlando Museum of Art

Following a multi-million dollar makeover in 1997, the Orlando Museum of Art (OMA) has earned a reputation as one of the southeast's top arts museums. The fine permanent collection is dominated by pre-Columbian art and American artists such as Georgia O'Keefe, George Inness, and Robert Rauschenberg. These works are supplemented by touring exhibitions from major metro-politan museums, and numerous smaller shows of regional or local significance, although curators tend to avoid overtly controversial works.
See p113.

Orlando Science Center

This huge, attention-grabbing, explora-torium-style museum boasts hundreds of interactive, child-friendly exhibits that are designed to introduce kids of all ages to the wonders of science. The center's four floors are divided into 10 themed zones. These deal with subjects ranging from mechanics to math, health and fitness to lasers, making this an educational and fun break from the usual Orlando theme park distractions. Don't miss the CineDome, which houses the planetarium and the world's largest Iwerks® theatre.
See p113.

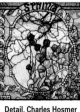

Detail, Charles Hosmer Morse Museum of American Art

Orange County Regional History Center

Given the region's relatively short history, this museum has wisely ignored geographic limitations. Exhibits not only feature local photographs and memorabilia, but a re-created Victorian parlor, a 1926 fire station, and fascinating tempo-rary shows that cover themes relating to other parts of Florida, such as pirates and space travel.
See p113.

Charles Hosmer Morse Museum of American Art

Here rests the world's most comprehensive collec-tion of work by Ameri-can artist Louis Comfort Tiffany, best known for his Art Nouveau stained-glass pieces. The museum's high-lights are a spec-tacular chapel Tiffany made for the 1893 World's Columbian Exposition and a re-creation of Tiffany's grand New York home. *See p119.*

Cornell Fine Arts Museum

Located on the campus of Rollins College, the small but stylish Cornell is Florida's oldest art collection. It showcases Euro-pean and American paintings, sculpture, and decorative arts ranging from the Renaissance and Baroque periods to the 20th century. Among the highlights

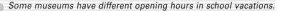

Albin Polasek Museum and Sculpture Gardens

are *Madonna and Child Enthroned* (c.1480) by Cosimo Rosselli, and *Reclining Figure* by Henry Moore (1982). *See p119.*

Mennello Museum of American Folk Art

This small, lakeside museum houses an unusual and charming collection of paintings by obscure curio-shop owner and Floridian folk artist, Earl Cunningham (1893–1977). In addition to his own work are traveling exhibitions featuring the works of other "outsider" artists. *See p113.*

Holocaust Memorial Resource & Education Center

It was founded in 1980 by survivors and witnesses of the Holocaust. It aims to inculcate the value of compassion and generosity in future generations. The museum conducts lectures, hosts a film series, and has a permanent exhibition of remembrances. ◎ *851 N. Maitland Ave • Map J3 • 407-628-0555 • Open 9am–4pm Mon–Thu, 9am–1pm Fri, 1–4pm Sun • www.holocaustedu.org*

Albin Polasek Museum and Sculpture Gardens

Czech-American Polasek (1879–1965) was a sculptor who specialized in European figurative technique. In semi-retirement, he moved to this self-designed house and studio, where he continued working until his

death. The beautiful gardens are filled with his sculptures, as are four galleries within the house, which also hold a few pieces from other artists. *See p119.*

Zora Neale Hurston National Museum of Fine Arts

Eatonville – the first incorporated African-American municipality in the USA – was the childhood home of Zora Neale Hurston (1903–1960), writer, anthropologist, and folklorist. This modest museum offers exhibitions centered on Hurston and the Eatonville of days gone by. *See p120.*

Maitland Historical & Telephone Museums

Artifacts, textiles, and photos from Maitland's pioneer days through to the heydays of the citrus and lumber industries are the focus here. In the same building, the Telephone Museum has vintage phones and memorabilia. ◎ *221 W. Packwood Ave • Map J4 • 407-644-2451 • Open 12–4pm Thu–Sun • Free (donation) • www.maitlandhistory.org*

Left **Orlando Philharmonic** Right **The Orlando Shakespeare Theater**

Cultural Venues & Organizations

Orlando Shakespeare Theater

This nationally recognized theater company performs the Bard's works as well as modern classics and Broadway hits. Their productions can be seen in an 8-month-long season at their state-of-the-art theater at Loch Haven Park. ⊗ *812 E. Rollins St • Map M3 • 407-447-1700 • Adm • www.orlandoshakes.org*

Orlando Repertory Theatre

Founded as the Orlando Little Theatre in 1926, the Repertory has grown into Orlando's version of a Broadway theater. It has three stages and puts on classic and contemporary plays alike. The year-round schedule is packed with high quality shows. The Theatre for Young People perform educational plays for school children. ⊗ *1001 E. Princeton St • Map M3 • 407-896-7365 • Adm*

Theatre Downtown

Named as Orlando's Best Local Repertory Company, this volunteer organization has been producing first-rate shows since 1984. In 1989, it moved to a former appliance store, and in this casual setting has presented an array of classics, contemporary works (such as David Mamet's *American Buffalo*), and new plays by local writers. ⊗ *2113 N. Orange Ave • Map M3 • 407-841-0083 • Adm • www.theatre-downtown.net*

Enzian Theater

Central Florida's only full-time art-house cinema is a unique venue – its single-screen, 250-seat house is arranged like a dinner theater, with waiters serving food and drinks (including beer and wine). Featuring foreign and American independents, and with regular special-interest festivals, plus the Florida Film Festival *(see p65)*, this is a place for true cinephiles. *See p121.*

SAK Comedy Lab

A downtown favorite, SAK is Orlando's home of improvisation comedy. Shows are always funny and inventive, and there are two per night. The 8pm shows are usually family-friendly, while the later ones get a bit edgier, although obscene material is strictly avoided. Of particular interest are the series shows, such as *Foolish Hearts*, an ongoing, improvised soap opera. ⊗ *29 S. Orange Ave • Map P3 • 407-648-0001 • Adm • www.sak.com*

Orlando Ballet

Orlando Philharmonic

Orlando's resident orchestra boasts more than 80 conservatory-trained musicians. Venues vary, and include the Phil's home at Symphony Square, Leu Gardens (for outdoor concerts), and even SeaWorld®. Its best-known showcase is the "Phil at Carr", an eight-concert series (Sep–May) at the Bob Carr Performing Arts Center, with guest artists in both classical and pop concerts. ✆ *Symphony Square, 812 E. Rollins St • Map M3 • 407-896-6700 • Adm • www.orlandophil.org*

Orlando International Fringe Festival

The 14-day Orlando Fringe follows in the footsteps of the grand-daddy of fringe: the Edinburgh (Scotland) Fringe Festival. Like Edinburgh, the Orlando Fringe presents uncensored, unjuried music, dance, and other perfomances, and pays 100 percent of box office sales to the artists. The Orlando Fringe is held at the Lowndes Shakespeare Center, the Orlando Rep, and other nearby sites. *See p64.*

Orlando Ballet

This small, but growing, company presents four major productions annually, including a version of *The Nutcracker*, choreographed by company artistic director Fernando Bujones. Smaller shows are held on community stages, but the major productions are at the Bob Carr Performing Arts Centre. ✆ *1111 N. Orange Ave • Map P3 • 407-426-1739 • Adm • www.orlandoballet.org*

Osceola Center for the Arts

Kissimmee's home of high culture offers a theater, art gallery, and special events. The Osceola Center for the Arts (OCFTA) has an engagingly diverse schedule, eagerly offering a little bit of everything, from Broadway to Barbershop, storytelling to sculptures. ✆ *2411 E. Irlo Bronson Memorial Hwy • Map P3 • 407-846-6257 • Adm • www.OCFTA.com*

Mad Cow Theatre

A favorite among local actors, this mainstay theatrical group has developed a reputation for small, high-quality shows. With a passion for both classic and contemporary productions, the theater represents the best from American and World literature. Past plays have ranged from Chekhov to Neil Simon. ✆ *54 W Church St • Map P3 • 407-297-8788 • Adm*

Mad Cow Theatre

Left **Orlando International Fringe Festival** Right **Blue Skies Balloon Festival**

Festivals & Events

1 Renninger's Antique Extravaganzas

From Victorian furnishings to vintage political campaign buttons, you can find all things old and valuable sold at the 1,400 antique stalls spread across a meadow here. The prime goods go fast, so get here early (it opens around 9am). ◈ Renningers Antique Center, Hwy 441 • Off map • 352-383-8393 • 3rd weekend of Jan, Feb, & Nov

2 Blue Skies Balloon Festival

Over 20 exotic hot air balloons, some in the shape of animals or even a space shuttle, can be seen taking to the skies at this festival. Capture this view on camera from below. You can also take a ride on one of the hot air balloons which will take you over the theme parks and untouched Florida territory. ◈ Formosa Gardens, 7836 W. Irlo Bronson Memorial Hwy • Map G1 • 800-831-1844 • Jun

Poster, Florida Film Festival

3 Central Florida Fair

This massive 11-day shindig takes place close to Downtown Orlando, but its cowpoke attitude is a world away. The country-style attractions include carnival rides, livestock shows, country music, farming exhibits, and more fried food than you'll ever care to eat. ◈ 4603 W. Colonial Dr • Map C3 • 407-295-3247 • Early Mar • www.centralfloridafair.com

4 Winter Park Sidewalk Arts Festival

For three days, this prestigious outdoor festival sees hundreds of artists exhibit on sidewalk stalls. Traffic comes to a standstill as the crowds mill around. ◈ Cranes Roost Park, Altamonte Springs • Map A5 • 407-592-0002 • Mid-Feb • www.uptownartexpo.com

5 Uptown Art Expo

This fine art and craft expo enjoys a pretty setting on the shore of Cranes Roost Lake, and showcases the juried work of 125 artists. There are also children's activities, and a chalk street art competition for adults and teens ◈ Cranes Roost Park, Altamonte Springs • Map A5 • 407-592-0002 • Mid-Feb • www.uptown artexpo.com

6 Orlando International Fringe Festival

With over 500 performances in 14 days, the Fringe offers improvised comedy, drag shows, stand-up, and more. Inspired by the Edinburgh festival, this premier event draws enthusiastic local crowds. ◈ Various venues • 407-648-0077 • May • www.orlandofringe.org

7 Zellwood Sweetcorn Festival

Eat as much sweetcorn as you can while listening to excellent country bands. A huge machine, Big Bertha, cooks up to 1,650 ears of corn every 9 minutes. There are also some fairground rides and a crafts fair. ◎ *4253 Ponkan Rd • Off map • 407-886-0014 • Mid-May • www.zellwoodcornfestival.com*

Florida Film Festival

This 10-day festival is packed with more than 100 features, documentaries, and shorts. Filmmakers introduce their works, and a few Hollywood names make guest appearances. ◎ *Enzian Theater, 1300 S. Orlando Ave, and other venues • Map D4 • 407-629-1088 • Apr • www.floridafilmfestival.com*

Gay Days

Gay Days is a week-long blowout of parties and theme park visits for more than 130,000 gay and lesbian guests. By day, gay and straight mix in the parks; at night, parks and clubs are rented for evening raves. ◎ *Various venues • 888-942-9329 or 407-896-8431 • www.gaydays.com • Early Jun*

Anime Festival Orlando

This gathering of "Japanimation" fanatics has screenings, Japanese video games, dance and costume contests, and dozens of dealers offering hard-to-find collectibles. ◎ *Renaissance Orlando at Seaworld® • Map F3 • 3 days in Jun, Jul or Aug • www.animefestivalorlando.com*

Gay Days

Attraction Events

1 Mardi Gras at Universal
The ultimate "Big Easy" party, with parades, music, and lots of beaded necklaces. ◎ *Universal Studios® • Feb–Mar*

2 Disney Hollywood Studios Star Wars Weekends
Four consecutive weekends of *Star Wars*-inspired frolics. ◎ *Disney Hollywood Studios® • May*

3 Night of Joy
A two-night showcase of contemporary Christian music. ◎ *Disney World® • Early Sep*

4 Bands Brew & BBQ
Combines beer, grilled food, and top musical acts. ◎ *SeaWorld® • Feb–Mar*

5 Halloween Horror Nights
Universal is transformed into a ghoulish home for the undead. ◎ *Universal Studios® • Oct–Nov*

6 Epcot® International Food & Wine Festival
Disney chefs and sommeliers strut their stuff. ◎ *Epcot® • Oct–Nov*

7 Epcot® International Flower & Garden Festival
Meet master gardeners and HGTV stars. ◎ *Epcot® • Mar–May*

8 Disney World Festival of the Masters
Daytime art exhibits and nighttime big-name jazz shows. ◎ *Downtown Disney® • Nov*

9 Mickey's Very Merry Christmas Party
Evening seasonal fun complete with snow and enchanting parades. ◎ *Magic Kingdom® • Dec*

10 Grinchmas
Enjoy a live performance of *How the Grinch Stole Christmas* at Seuss Landing. ◎ *Islands of Adventure® • Dec*

Left **Downtown Disney Store** Right **Nike Factory Store, Orlando Premium Outlets International**

Places to Shop

Orlando Premium Outlets
This terrific 150-store complex is located just across I-4 from the east entrance of Disney World. It boasts high-end designer outlets by Versace, DKNY, and Barney's New York, as well as a mix of popular brands including Nike, Timberland, and Banana Republic. ◉ *8200 Vineland Ave • Map F3 • 407-238-7777 • www. premiumoutlets.com*

Orlando Premium Outlets International
This 180-store mall offers upscale shopping from stores such as Eddie Bauer, Betsey Johnson, Perry Ellis, Lacoste, Juicy Couture, Hugo Boss, Coach, Kate Spade, Ugg, Movado, and Le Creuset. ◉ *4951 International Drive • Map U2 • 407-352-9600*

Mall at Millenia
Upscale and slightly uptown, the Mall at Millenia offers luxury retailers including Tiffany & Co., Louis Vuitton, Neiman Marcus, and Jimmy Choo, as well as mid-price stores like Macy's, Pottery Barn, and Gap. Valet parking and currency exchange are available, and there's also a US Post Office in the mall, which is handy for mailing purchases home or sending gifts. Special events at the mall include fashion expos and interactive children's activities. Central Florida's only IKEA store is across the road from Millenia. ◉ *4200 Conroy Road • Map E4 • 407-363-3555*

Florida Mall
Sure, it's a big enclosed suburban mall, but it's also one of the best in Central Florida and hugely popular with visitors and locals. Stores include Dillard's, JC Penney, Macy's, Saks Fifth Avenue, Sears, Nordstrom, Lord & Taylor, and more than 200 others. ◉ *8001 S. Orange Blossom Trail • Map E4 • 407-851-6255 • www.simon.com*

Park Avenue

Park Avenue
This eight-block stretch of downtown Winter Park retains a times-gone-by quality. A canopy of live oak trees shades the brick-paved street, which is surrounded by low buildings and flanked by relaxing Central Park. Many of the stores on this upscale avenue are independents, but there are some national chains too, such as Williams & Sonoma and Lilly Pulitzer. There's no food court, but the sidewalks are lined with places for lunch or dinner. ◉ *Park Ave bet Fairbanks Ave & Swoope Ave • Map L4*

Factory outlets – which sell last season's stock and imperfect goods at discounts of at least 30 percent – generally open 9am–9pm daily.

Pointe Orlando

Pointe Orlando is a complex of shopping, dining, and entertainment venues. It offers something for everyone – a 21-screen cinema, a Wonderworks entertainment center, several upscale restaurants, plus more than 20 retail stores, including Victoria's Secret, Armani Exchange, and lots of specialty stores. The landscaped outdoor layout makes this a pleasant place for a shopping spree. § 9101 International Dr • Map T4 • 407-248-2838 • www.pointeorlando.com

Downtown Disney®

There are two shopping options in Downtown Disney®. On the glittery West Side is the massive RideMakerz car shop and the House of Blues store. The more serene Marketplace is highlighted by World of Disney (the planet's largest Disney store) and the LEGO® Imagination Center, an enormous superstore. § Downtown Disney • Map F2 • 407-824-4321 • www.disneyworld.com

Flea World

Claiming to be America's largest flea market, Sanford's Flea World is a Byzantine maze of more than 1,700 sales booths, which are bursting with bargains every weekend. The mostly new goods are already cheap, but you can haggle to lower prices still. In addition to an A to Z list of goods for sale, Flea World also has live bands, bingo, and an old-style amusement park, Fun World, for the kids. § 4311 S. Hwy 17/92, Sanford • Off map • 407-330-1792 • Open 9am–6pm Fri–Sun

Ivanhoe Row

Renninger's Antique & Flea Markets

Spread across a bucolic country meadow, Renninger's offers a large, folksy flea market, and a diverse indoor and outdoor antique market. The flea market offers everything from clothing to vinyl. The antique market has permanent dealers who specialize in excellent furnishings and jewelry. Renninger's also hosts the massive Antique Extravaganzas (see p64). § 20651 Hwy 441, 1 m (1.6 km) E. of Mount Dora • Off map • 1-352-383-8393

Ivanhoe Row

This stretch of antique shops has thinned out due to rising rents, but there are still more than a dozen stores offering vintage linens, clothing, jewelry, and various collectables. Imported furniture from Bali and vintage LPs can also be found here. § N. Orange Ave • Map N3

Factory outlet stores often have sales at the same times of the year as regular shops (Mar–Apr and Aug–Oct).

67

Left **The Boheme** Right **Park Plaza Gardens**

High-End Restaurants

Victoria & Albert's
The high price can limit this to very special occasions, but trust the first-class food, fine wine, and faultless staff to make a memorable visit. It's decorated like Queen Victoria's dining room, and each table gets its very own Victoria and Albert as servers. Changing menus offer seven courses of international dishes, including apple-smoked Colorado bison and black bass with couscous. Take advantage of the wine-pairings (a glass with each of the five courses); it's cheaper and more varied than buying a bottle. *See p94.*

Primo
Housed in the sprawling J.W. Marriott Hotel, Primo has an elegant and warm dining area. Chef Melissa Kelly creates delicious dishes with Mediterranean accents using fresh local ingredients, including herbs and vegetables from the garden behind the hotel.

Emeril's of Orlando

Sit on the outdoor patio and sample the chargrilled Moulard duck for a special treat. ○ *4040 Central Florida Pkwy • Map T6 • 407-393-4444 • Dinner only • No kids' menu • Pre-arrange vegetarian entrées • $$$$*

California Grill
The 15th-floor vista here gets top marks from both critics and diners. The redesigned kitchen and menu has only helped further that general opinion. Popular choices are seared grouper in a noodle bowl with ginger-crab salad and some of the most inventive sushi in town. They also offer an interesting menu for people who prefer vegetarian. It's hard to get a table on weekends. *See p94.*

Emeril's of Orlando
Famous US TV chef Emeril Lagasse owns this place, but only appears once a month, leaving the day-to-day cooking of the creole-inspired menu to his chefs. They create treats such as quail stuffed with Louisiana oyster dressing, andouille-crusted redfish, and a kosher salt and cracked black pepper rib-eye steak. This lofty place has a 12,000-bottle wine cellar. Book well in advance for dinner; there's a similar lunch menu at two-thirds of the price. ○ *CityWalk • Map T1 • 407-224-2424 • $$$$$*

Norman's
A high-end restaurant located in the Ritz-Carlton, Norman's specializes in a fusion of Latin,

Todd English's bluezoo

European, and Floridian cuisine. World-renowned chef Norman Van Aken holds court when in town, but the kitchen turns out his New World cuisine regardless. The highlights here are the Brazilian conch chowder and barbequed veal chops.
◈ 4012 Central Florida Pkwy • Map F4 • 407-343-4333 • Pre-arrange vegetarian entrées • $$$$$

Fiorella's Cucina Toscana
Inside the Westin Hotel, this is hand-crafted Tuscan and northern Italian cuisine with a modern flair, served in a relaxed atmosphere. The striking dining room features colorful contemporary art glass, and has views of the open kitchen. Specialties include seafood dishes based on seasonal local produce, and the signature "Globo" brownie in a chocolate dome. *See p105.*

The Boheme
The signature restaurant of the Westin Grand Bohemian Hotel is a key business venue and a prime romantic destination. Serving classic dishes with a modern twist, menu highlights range from Southern crab cakes to filet mignon and rack of lamb. Sip a Martini before dinner in the hip Bösendorfer Lounge. *See p117.*

Todd English's bluezoo
Celebrate the "blue zoo" of the ocean in a glass-accented dining room that feels like an underwater scene. Asian, Tuscan, and American touches appear in innovative dishes created with superb fish selections. Meat dishes are also available.
◈ Dolphin Hotel, 1500 Epcot Resorts Blvd, Lake Buena Vista • Map G2 • 407-934-1111 • Dinner only • No kids' menu • Pre-arrange vegetarian entrées • $$$$$

Park Plaza Gardens
For a touch of class, book a table at the exquisite Park Plaza Gardens. The glorious cuisine (such as blackened deep sea grouper with red lentils and curry vinaigrette) is enjoyed in a divine garden, much like a French courtyard. Take your pick from one of the best wine lists in Orlando, and finish off with towering desserts such as the triple chocolate cake. *See p123.*

Napa
This California-themed upscale restaurant in the Peabody Orlando Hotel *(see p143)* includes superb seafood, local and seasonal organic ingredients, and a wide-ranging international wine list. The restaurant overlooks the inviting, palm-ringed Grotto Pool.
◈ 9801 International Dr • Map T3 • 407-345-4570 • $$$$$

Unless stated, all restaurants advise reservations, are non-smoking, take credit cards, and have DA, kids' menus, A/C, and vegetarian dishes.

Left **Outback Steakhouse** Right **Café Tu Tu Tango**

🔟 Family Restaurants

Rainforest Café

1 This jungle-themed restaurant provides noisy fun and a California-style menu. The mixed grill includes barbecued ribs, soy-ginger steak skewers, chicken breast, and peppered shrimp. Kids get their own special menu, the cartoon-like decor is good fun, and a "volcano" erupts every now and then. *See p95.*

Romano's Macaroni Grill

Romano's Macaroni Grill

2 Despite being part of a chain, Romano's has a neighborhood feel. The modestly priced Italian menu includes thin-crust pizzas cooked in a wood-burning oven, sauteed salmon scaloppini, and chicken marsala. Paper tablecloths and crayons will keep kids happy for hours. ◈ *12148 Apopka-Vineland Rd • Map F2 • 407-239-6676 • $$$*

Coral Reef Restaurant

3 A 600,000-gallon (272,600-liter) floor-to-ceiling aquarium is a calming backdrop to this themed restaurant. Despite the high-brow, mainly fish and seafood menu, it's very child-friendly. Try the sauteed rock shrimp in a lemon cream sauce. *See p95.*

Outback Steakhouse

4 Tasty seared steaks are the headliners here; choose from rib-eyes, strips, fillets, and porter-houses. The Outback also serves good smoked ribs, shrimp and chicken over fettucine, rib-and-chicken combos, pork chops, and hamburgers. ◈ *4845 S. Kirkman Rd • Map D3 • 407-292-5111 • $$$*

Restaurant Marrakesh

5 Mosaic tiles and a painted Moorish ceiling set the Moroccan scene. The food is flavorsome, with delights such as roast lamb *au jus* with couscous, and marinated beef shish kabobs. A belly dancer shimmies around and kids love to join her. *See p95.*

Café Tu Tu Tango

6 The menu in this lofty space is Spanish tapas in name but more international in flavor, with such diverse nibbles as baked goat's cheese, tuna sashimi, alligator bites, and snapper fingers. Performers (from sword eaters to artists at work) provide the entertainment. *See p105.*

Boma – Flavors of Africa

7 This all-you-can-eat, African-themed restaurant is in Disney's Animal Kingdom® Lodge. Dishes from more than 50 African countries are served from the open kitchen for breakfast and dinner. There's a good selection of fire-grilled meats, salads, and African pastries for dessert. The dinner

Unless stated, all restaurants advise reservations, are non-smoking, take credit cards, and have DA, kids' menus, A/C, and vegetarian dishes.

buffet is a family-friendly option. ⊗ 2901 Osceola Parkway • Map G1 • 407-939-3463 • $$$

8 Baja Burrito Kitchen
The draw here is the fresh and healthy Californian and Mexican cuisine, such as tacos, quesadillas, fajitas, and burritos, stuffed with lean meat and sour cream and cheese. ⊗ 2716 E. Colonial Dr • Map N4 • 407-895-6112 • $$

9 Panera Bread
There are no preservatives in the dough used in the sandwiches and baked goods here available to eat in or take away; there's everything from whole-grain to focaccia and sourdough. Soup is also available. ⊗ 7828 Sand Lake Rd • Map F3 • 407-226-6992 • $

10 Chili's Grill & Bar
This international Tex-Mex chain serves scrumptious Cajun chicken sandwiches, margarita-grilled chicken topped with lime shrimp, and Cadillac fajitas with black beans and rice. See p105.

Chili's Grill & Bar

Dining with Disney & Universal Characters

1 Chef Mickey's
Mickey hosts American buffet breakfasts and dinners in the Contemporary Resort.

2 Restaurantosaurus
Donald Duck and pals host the Breakfastosaurus in the Animal Kingdom every morning.

3 Wonderland Tea Party
Every weekday at 2pm, Alice in Wonderland characters join guests in the Grand Floridian resort for tea and cakes.

4 1900 Park Fare
Have breakfast with Mary Poppins or a sit-down dinner with other Disney favorites at the Grand Floridian Resort.

5 Mickey's Backyard BBQ
Disney characters keep you entertained at this hoedown and all-you-can-eat American buffet dinner in Fort Wilderness.

6 Cinderella's Royal Table
A whole host of Disney characters join you for the "Once Upon a Time" breakfast in Magic Kingdom®'s Cinderella castle (park adm required).

7 Circus McGurkus
The Cat in the Hat, the Grinch, Thing One, and Thing Two turn up at Seuss Landing in Islands of Adventure at 2:45pm daily for a late lunch.

8 The Crystal Palace
Meet Pooh and his cohorts for American buffet breakfasts, lunches, and dinners in Magic Kingdom (park adm required).

9 Liberty Tree Tavern
Mickey and Goofy host the sit-down dinner "Liberate your Appetite" in the Magic Kingdom (park adm required).

10 Cape May Café
Join Goofy for a breakfast buffet at the Beach Club Resort.

For character meals, call seven days in advance (Disney: 407-939-3463; Universal: 407-363-8000). Expect to pay $ for kids, $$–$$$ for adults.

Left **Bösendorfer Lounge** Right **Downtown bar scene**

🔟 Places to Have a Drink

1 Lucky Leprechaun
A lively, welcoming Orlando institution. As its name suggests it has Irish connections and a friendly Irish flair. They offer a huge selection of great beers, including all the Irish beers you could hope for, and also food. There is karoke every night, live entertainment, and big-screen televisions showing all the important sporting events. Very popular hangout with the locals. *See p104.*

2 Independent Bar
A relaxed and hip place where you can dance to great tunes without the stuffiness of many other clubs. Fabulous mix of music from classic pop and hip hop to indie and jazz. Plenty of room at the long bar and on the spacious dance floor. *See p116.*

3 Cowboys Orlando
Kick up your heels at this popular country music dance venue, located near downtown Orlando. This huge club has four bar areas and state-of-the-art sound and lighting. It's open Thursday to Saturday to guests over 18 years old, and has nightly drink specials and dance contests. *See p116.*

4 The Bar at California Grill
This bar is a fabulous place to kick back, enjoy a bottle of wine and watch the fireworks over the Magic Kingdom®. The secret is out, though, so come early for a table. Finding a spot at other times isn't too hard as long as you avoid the dinner rush. *See p94.*

5 Fiddler's Green
A big, noisy Irish pub, Fiddler's Green has an excellent beer selection, a homey, shabby ambience, and a bartender who pours faster than anyone in town. Darts and occasional live music form the entertainment, but people come here just to down a few beers and shoot the breeze. Lunch and dinner are served. *See p123.*

Bar-B-Q Bar

Most bars tend to open betweem 4–8pm and close around 2am.

6 Bar-B-Q Bar

It's little more than an average beer joint with sticky floors and loud crowds, but Bar-B-Q is *the* place to see and be seen for the more creative set. A favorite venue with local musicians, the bar gets packed whenever there's a good band on stage. People-watch clubbers cruising the Orange Avenue strip from a sidewalk table. ◈ *64 N Orange Ave • Map P3 • 407-648-5441*

7 Sky 60

Located above The Social *(see p74)*, this rooftop bar is an Orange Avenue hotspot, attracting folks who prefer not to mingle with the masses but rather look down on them. Covered in whitewash, this airy spot is a classier option for folks who usually drink downstairs or at the Bar-B-Q Bar. Entertainment is typically provided via a DJ who leans toward refined, less aggressive grooves. *See p116.*

8 The Bösendorfer Lounge

Luxury is a tough sell Downtown, partly because the club crowd tends to be well under 30 and lacking serious funds. However, this swanky hotel bar is thriving, confirming that an older, upscale, and urbane crowd is more than willing to pay the price for a suave evening of fancy cocktails. *See p74.*

9 Dexter's of Thornton Park

A white-collar after-work crowd frequents this hugely popular bar/restaurant in a spacious, loft-like room. On fine nights, drinkers often head for the small outdoor space or spill out onto the sidewalk, jostling and juxtaposing with the congregations from the fundamentalist church and a working-class beer joint that are located on the same street. Dexter's is also known for its great New American menu, and for serving lots of wines by the glass. There's another branch in Winter Park *(see p122).* ◈ *808 E. Washington St • Map P3 • 407-648-2777*

Fiddler's Green

10 The Courtesy

This trendy, speakeasy bar serves hand-crafted cocktails concocted with local and fresh ingredients. Pick your choice of liquor from a fine collection of cocktails, absinthe, beer, and wine. Its cozy ambience, and the friendly and knowledgeable staff make the visit very pleasurable. The Courtesy also offers catering services and cocktail classes on select Saturdays. Go early to avoid crowds. ◈ *114 N. Orange • Map P3 • 407-704-9288*

The minimum age requirement for drinkers in Florida is 21 years. Be sure to bring photo ID to avoid being turned away at the door.

73

Left **Hard Rock Live** right **Blue Martini**

Live Music Venues

The Social

This intimate downtown club serves up an eclectic mix of live music from established acts to up-and-coming artists. Sounds range from alternative rock to funk, jazz, and dance, with local DJs also gracing the club's legendary stage. For years, the club's policy of booking top national touring acts meant it was the shining light of Orlando's live music scene. Competition from much larger clubs is stiffer now, but this tiny spot, with its stylishly raw decor, remains O-Town's favorite venue to enjoy live music. *See p116.*

House of Blues

Wall-to-wall original folk art gives this giant venue a funky look. But like all things in the Disney empire, the decor hides a modern, smooth-running machine. HOB books amazing acts in every genre, from hip-hop to death-metal. Unlike many clubs, shows start and end on time, and the sound system is crystal clear. The one flaw is an incredible lack of seating with stage views, so be prepared to be on your feet all night. *See p93.*

Hard Rock Live

The yin to HOB's yang, Hard Rock has a more comfortable room, with balcony seating and good stage views. The grand ballroom decor is more appropriate for acts that want to perform in an elegant setting, so it's not surprising that top R&B artists such as Maxwell and Erykah Badu play here. The Hard Rock schedule is more erratic, with fewer top name bookings. *See p104.*

Blue Martini

They sell 29 different types of Martini here, of every color and description. This vibrant spot – they have live music every night – is popular with young professionals unwinding after work as well as at weekends. Tapas and a light meal menu are also on offer. The outdoor patio bar is a good place to mix and mingle. ✆ 4200 Conroy Rd • Map M3 • 407-447-2583

The Bösendorfer Lounge

The lounge music craze that once swept the nation is now only for serious practitioners. This elegant hotel bar is a swell place to sip cocktails and dig the duo in evening dress who sing near the $250,000 Bösendorfer Grand piano. Maybe it's the heavy drapes, the dark wood, or the well-tuned ennui of some patrons, but you feel wealthy just being here. *See p116.*

Blues Bar at House of Blues

Before it evolved into a chain of mega-clubs, the original HOB concept was closer to

Almost everyone needs to show ID to get into Orlando's clubs, most of which are for over 21's only; others set higher age limits.

this casual roadhouse place, which offers bayou-inspired eats, cold beer, and live blues bands on a low stage. Though they get little promotion, the bands booked here are excellent. And even if dinner prices are inflated (*à la* everything at Disney), the cover charge is zero. *See p46.*

Live music at the House of Blues

Adobe Gilas

The downside to Gilas is that they book mostly cover bands. The upside is a young, good-looking crowd getting smashed on tequila and dirty dancing with near strangers. The band usually sets up on the patio, but it's more fun and sweaty when it rains and the band crams itself into an inside corner. Sure, the southwestern theme decor gets old fast, but if you need to relive the days of dorm parties, this is the place to go. *See p104.*

Atlantic Dance Hall

Travel back in time to the glamorous dance halls of the 1930s and '40s and dance the night away! A great venue featuring wonderfully kitsch Art Deco interiors and grown-up entertainment, Atlantic Dance Hall is ideally located for those staying at a Disney resort. Dueling DJs spin on Thursday and Friday nights, while dance-along videos play on Tuesdays, Wednesdays and Saturdays. *See p93.*

Backstage at the Rosen Plaza

This swinging nightclub is located within the Rosen Plaza Hotel on International Drive.

Dance the night away to live bands and top DJs who play popular hits from the 1970s, the 1980s and the 1990s. Valet parking is also available. ⊗ *Rosen Plaza Hotel, 9700 International Dr* • *Map F3* • *407-996-9700* • *www.rosen plaza.com*

Bongo's Cuban Café

This lively venue combines Old Havana and Miami. In addition to delicious Cuban food, Bongo's serves up furious salsa rhythms on the sound system. There is multilevel indoor and outdoor seating, dancing every night, and great live music on Fridays and Saturdays. *See p93.*

Left **Firestone Live** Right **Downtown nightlife scene**

TOP 10 Hip Clubs

Hard Rock Live
1 Located at Universal's CityWalk®, this vibrant and huge venue looks like a Roman Coliseum and offers seating for up to 2,000 people – great for a mildly decadent but definitely fun night out. The first floor has a standing-room only dance floor. Hard Rock Live's stunning sound systems are state of the art, as is its lighting technology. Emerging local musical performers, as well as big national and international touring acts, make regular appearances here. *See p104.*

Hard Rock Live

The Beacham Theater
2 Housed in a downtown Orlando building that once hosted the famous Vaudeville acts of the 1920s, the Beacham Theater is a 1,250-seat live music venue and a buzzing nightclub, with high-tech sound, and light systems and a large dance floor. National touring acts appear regularly; on other evenings, DJs set the pace. Friday night is Ladies' Night. A dress code is enforced. *See p116.*

Firestone Live
3 Once named top club in the US by *Rolling Stone* magazine, Firestone Live occupies the interior of one of Orlando's oldest buildings. Its vast size, an awe-inspiring light and sound system, and an international DJ lineup still make this the best night out in Orlando. The club attracts a mixed crowd that is very gay-friendly. The sounds run from trance to hip-hop to Latin, depending on the night of the week. *See p116.*

Revolution Nightclub
4 With more than 14,000 sq ft (1,300 sq m) of dancing space, multiple bars, and three separate rooms of music, Revolution is tailored for the alternative local crowd. Live bands and world-class DJs play Miami salsa, hip-hop, and techno until the early hours, while the Hydrate Video Bar area features giant video screens. ◈ 375 S. Bumby Ave • Map D5 • 407-228-9900 • Adm

Monkey Bar
5 A sign outside the Wall Street complex of bars and restaurants may proclaim the existence of Monkey Bar, but it takes a walk through the downstairs Tiki Bar and a ride on the elevator to enter this upstairs hideaway. Trendy and cozy, Monkey Bar offers food as well as quirky drinks and live music. Enjoy half-priced Martinis during happy hour (4–7pm Tue–Fri). ◈ 19 N. Orange Ave • Map D4 • 407-849-0471 • Closed Sun, Mon • Adm

Samba Room

This South Orlando club is upscale and hip. It's a restaurant during the week, but on Friday and Saturday nights it also has live Latin and Reggae music, and dancing until 2am. The menu features Latin fusion cuisine and there's also a cigar lounge. ⊗ *7468 W. Sand Lake Rd • Map S3 • 407-226-0550 • Adm • www.sambaroom.net*

Rok Room

A rock-themed "Ultra lounge", Rok Room is hidden in an alley behind larger and swankier nightclubs. Look for the sign on the sidewalk and be ready to climb some stairs. It plays a wide variety of music such as rock, dance, dubstep, top 40, hip-hop, and house. The service is very friendly. Wednesdays, Fridays, Saturdays, and Sundays are special nights. Over 21s only; no cover charge. ⊗ *41 W. Church St • Map P2 • 407-992-0398 • www.rokroom.com*

The Groove

The theme changes every night at this Universal CityWalk® dance club, with music from the 1970s and '80s, current dance hits, Latin, techno, and more. The club area features a giant psychedelic dance floor, but the smaller areas – the Candle Room, Blue Room, and Red Room – are great for more intimate partying. The Groove is an attractive

alternative for teens, too, with dedicated teen nights on Mondays and Wednesdays. *See p104.*

The Social

This intimate live music venue is located in the heart of Downtown's party district. It regularly features big name acts

and there's live music most nights. It also has one of the best Martini bars in town. *See p116.*

Roxy

Tucked into an after-dark desert area of town, Roxy is a big multi-floor dance club, with impressive hip-hop, Latin, and house DJs playing nightly.

Roxy

The loyal following tends to be less self-consciously trendy and more hetero than the usual Downtown club mix. For example, Monday Night Fights see amateur boxers from the crowd knock back a few beers then jump in a ring to fight each other. Well, the crowd *is* different from that found in Downtown. ⊗ *740 Bennett Rd • Map N5 • 407-898-4004 • www.roxyorlando.com*

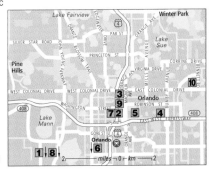

For more information on nightlife **See pp72–5**

Left **Firestone Live** Right **Carmello, the Orlando drag queen diva**

Gay & Lesbian Nightlife

1 Parliament House Resort
Parliament is one of the southeast's premier gay resorts, boasting non-stop entertainment. Beside a 130-room hotel, there's a pulsating dance club, a piano bar, a country and western bar, a video bar, lakeside beach parties, and more. ⊛ 410 N. Orange Blossom Trail • Map P2 • 407-425-7571 • Free (Adm to club)

2 The New Phoenix
Claiming to be Winter Park's oldest gay bar, Phoenix holds drag queen and king shows on weekends. It also hosts karaoke and free pool nights. ⊛ 7124 Aloma Ave • Map C6 • 407-678-9070 • Adm

3 The Brink
This downtown hotspot does not charge cover before 10:30pm which means that you need to arrive early. Located behind Firestone Live, The Brink courts a young crowd with happy hours specials, Friday night drag shows and "pants optional" nights. ⊛ 47 W. Amelia St • Map P3 • 407-388-4384

4 Revolution Nightclub
Revolution is a mega-club that combines the Revolution Nightclub, the Hydrate Video Bar, and the Majestic Theatre and Lounge under one roof. Diverse crowds hit the dance floor at Revolution, enjoy drinks and the hottest videos at Hydrate, or watch live theater, music, and female impersonators at the Majestic. There's also an outdoor patio for unwinding and relaxing, and a game room with pool tables, darts, and video games.
⊛ 375 S Bumby Ave • Map P3 • 407-228-9900

5 The Peacock Room
The Peacock's jazzy ambience is a welcome respite

The Peacock Room

from the thump of techno. This is a small, stylish lounge in the heart of Orlando's gay-friendly ViMi district. The decor is muted Art Deco and a small jazz band often plays. The cool vibe also attracts straights, making for a nice mix. ◈ *1321 N. Mills Ave • Map N4 • 407-228-0048 • Free*

Savoy Orlando
A sophisticated North Orange lounge that caters for an upscale crowd of mostly professional gay men. High bar tables, black leather stools, and crystal chandeliers give the club a classy air. ◈ *1913 N. Orange Ave • Map P3 • 407-898-6766 • Free*

Parliament House

Firestone Live
Ensconced within a former Firestone garage, this giant venue has long been rated one of the southeast's top dance clubs, particularly with gays, ravers, and all types trendy. Although gay-only nights are gone, Firestone continues to pump out house, hip-hop, and trance music for "the community." The upstairs Glass Chamber is a relaxing chill-out room with comfy couches. *See p116.*

Pulse
This is an Orlando hot spot for gays, with DJs spinning music from the 1970s and 80s. Tuesday night is Karaoke Night, while Wednesday is College Night. Hip-hop music is featured on Thursday nights, but whatever type of music you enjoy, you will find it here. This welcoming establishment is a firm favorite

for the Orlando gay crowd. ◈ *1912 S. Orange Ave • Map Q3 • 407-649-3888 • Adm*

Stonewall
Everything from leather-clad dancers to "under-wear nights" makes this a go-to for the local gay communi-ty. There are daily happy hours, bingo and poker nights, and karaoke on Fri-day nights. ◈ *741 W. Church St • Map P3 • 407-373-0888 • Free*

Hanks
Hanks has been open for over 20 years and is one of Orlando's oldest gay bars. Pool tables, darts, video games, and a juke-box make this unpretentious beer and wine bar a casual hangout. The Back Room, the adjoining adult store, is open nightly. ◈ *5026 Edgewater Dr • Map L1 • 407-291-2399 • Free*

For more on Orlando's clubs See pp76–7

Left **Medieval Times** Right **Sleuth's Mystery Dinner Theatre**

Dinner Shows

Hoop-Dee-Doo Musical Revue

Book early for Disney's most popular "chow-and-cheer" night. The jokes are silly, the stars dress in costumes from Broadway's *Oklahoma!,* and if you don't join in the sing-along fun, the actors and audience will keep on at you until you do. Dinner is all-you-can-eat fried chicken and barbecue ribs; a vegetarian menu is available with 24 hours' notice. *See p93.*

Arabian Nights

Horses steal this show. Several breeds such as chiseled Arabians and muscular Belgians thunder through a performance that includes Wild West trick riding, chariot races, a little slapstick comedy, and bareback daredevilry. Horse fans can pet the four-legged stars after the show. 🅂 *6225 W. Irlo Bronson Memorial Hwy • Map G2 • 407-239-9223 • 7:30pm nightly*

Medieval Times

Horses take a secondary role at this spectacle. Instead, the action heroes are knights who get into sword fights, joust, and otherwise raise the roof while you feast on the likes of barbecued ribs, and roasted chicken with your fingers (after all, this is the 11th century). If you arrive early, you can tour a re-created medieval village. 🅂 *4510 W. Irlo Bronson Memorial Hwy • Map G3 • 407-396-1518 • Show times vary*

Spirit of Aloha Dinner Show

High-energy performers from Hawaii, New Zealand, and Tahiti show off their hula, ceremonial, and fire-dancing in an open-air theater. Meanwhile, tuck into the all-you-can-eat meal, which includes roast pork and chicken, fried rice, vegetables, and fruit. Learn how to make *leis* and do the hula in the pre-show. 🅂 *Disney's Polynesian Resort • Map F1 • 407-824-2000 • 5:15 & 8pm nightly*

Arabian Nights

Pirates Dinner Adventure

The swashbuckling actors entertain with comedy, drama, and music, on a set that is is a full-size pirate ship on a water-filled "lagoon". The dinner buffet features roast chicken, braised beef, herbed rice, and more. After the show, there's a Buccaneer Bash

All shows charge admission, which sometimes varies depending on whether the performance is midweek or on the weekend.

Pirates Dinner Adventure

Dance Party to help you burn a few of those spare calories. 🍴 *6400 Carrier Dr • Map U2 • 407-248-0590 • 7:45pm nightly*

Titanic Dinner Event

Experience first-class dining aboard the recreated ship, Titanic, as participants re-enact the retirement dinner of Captain E.J. Smith on that fateful night when it sank. Complete with a tour of the ship, this trip will be one to remember. A three-course dinner and a theatrical evening are included. 🍴 *7324 International Dr • Map E3 • 407-248-1166 • Pre-arrange vegetarian entrées • 7pm Wed, Fri & Sat*

Sleuth's Mystery Dinner Theatre

The theater's cast stages eight different shows over the course of a month, all with a suspicious death and a twist before the mystery is uncovered. Meals include hors d'oeuvres before the show, then your choice of honey-glazed Cornish game hen, prime rib, or lasagna with side dishes, dessert, and unlimited beer, wine, and sodas. 🍴 *8267 International Dr • Map T1 • 407-363-1985 • Show times vary*

Capone's Dinner & Show

Settle into the 1930s and visit Al Capone's notorious speakeasy, a place where pseudo-mobsters and their molls entertain guests with a lot of song and dance. The all-you-can-eat buffet offers pasta, sausage with peppers and onions, baked chicken and ham, vegetables, potatoes, and whatever beer, wine, coffee, iced tea and sodas you care to drink.

🍴 *4740 W. Irlo Bronson Memorial Hwy • Map G3 • 407-397-2378 • 8pm nightly*

Outta Control Magic Comedy Dinner Show

The audience becomes a part of the show in Tony Brent's 90-minute interactive mixture of magic and fast-paced improvisational comedy. Impersonations and mind-reading are accompanied by all-you-can-eat hand-tossed pepperoni pizza, popcorn, beer, soda, and desserts. The show is suitable for all ages. 🍴 *Wonderworks, 9067 International Dr • Map T4 • 407-351-8800 • 6 & 8pm nightly*

Treasure Tavern

This adults-only alternative to the kid's Pirates show combines circus, burlesque, comedy, magic, live music, and prime rib dinner with a full bar. 🍴 *6400 Carrier Dr • Map U2 • 407-206-5102 • 8pm Tue–Sat*

There is no minimum age limit for dinner shows, although some may be unsuitable for younger children.

Left **Clearwater Beach, Gulf Coast** Right **Florida Aquarium**

🔟 Day Trips South & West

1 Busch Gardens

With six roller coasters, three water rides, and many other attractions, this park is a close second to Islands of Adventure *(see pp20–23)* on the thrill front. Roller coaster addicts rate the park's SheiKra ride very highly - it's a floorless 70-mph (120-km/h) coaster. Nature lovers will enjoy the animal interactions, of the Jungala attraction and the truck ride through the plains of the Serengeti Safari. Ask about the free shuttle from Orlando for ticketholders. ◐ *3000 E. Busch Blvd, Tampa • 813-987-5082 • Hours vary seasonally • Adm • www.buschgardens.com*

Busch Gardens

2 Florida Aquarium

Florida's native species are just a fraction of the more than 10,000 animals and plants on display in this modern attraction. Wetlands, bays, coral reefs, and their creatures are featured in several galleries, and you can watch divers feed sharks and other marine creatures. ◐ *701*

Channelside Dr, Tampa • 813-273-4000 • Open 9:30am–5pm daily • Adm

3 Lowry Park Zoo

Tampa's first zoo has 1,500 creatures, including Malayan tigers, African elephants, and Komodo dragons. It also serves as a rehabilitation center for injured manatees *(see p31)* and as a sanctuary for Florida panthers and red wolves. A free-flight aviary and petting zoo provide a chance to touch some tamer species. ◐ *1101 W. Sligh Ave, Tampa • 813-935-8552 • Open 9:30am–5pm daily • Adm • www.lowryparkzoo.com*

4 Ybor City/Centro Ybor

The Latin heart of Tampa contains the Ybor State Museum, plus trendy art galleries and lively cafés. Take the opportunity to try a Cuban sandwich, and strong *café cubano*, or to salsa and *merengue* into the small hours in one of the district's dozen or so clubs. ◐ *Seventh Ave, Tampa • Off Map • www.ybor.org*

5 Henry B. Plant Museum

In the late 1800s, railroad magnate Henry B. Plant built an opulent Moorish palace in the swamps of Tampa, attracting tourists and celebrities alike. Now part of the University of Tampa, this museum honors the life and times of Plant. Take a tour through its authentically restored rooms. ◐ *410 W. Kennedy Blvd • 813-254-1891 • Open 10am–5pm Tue–Sat, noon–5pm Sun • Adm • www.plantmuseum.com*

The Gulf Beaches

6 Western Pinellas County has more than 30 miles (48 km) of white-sand, low-surf, warm-water beaches that are highly popular throughout the year. St. Pete Beach, Treasure Island, Madeira Beach, and Clearwater Beach are among the many headliners. ◈ *St. Pete Beach to Clearwater Beach • Off Map*

Historic Bok Sanctuary

7 This National Historic Landmark has nearly 250 acres (100 hectares) of gardens and grounds surrounding a 205-ft (62-m) bell tower and Mediterranean Revival mansion. The visitor center has a museum, video, café, and gift shop. ◈ *1151 Tower Blvd, Lake Wales • 863-676-1408 • Adm • Dis. access • www.boksanctuary.org*

Salvador Dali Museum

8 The world's most comprehensive collection of Salvador Dali's work from 1914 to 1970 can be found at this world-class museum. The art on display includes oils, watercolors, and sculptures by the great Surrealist. There's a café and an interesting outdoor space, the Avant-Garden. ◈ *1 Dali Blvd, St. Petersburg • 727-823-3767 • Open 10am–5:30pm Mon–Sat (to 8pm Thu), noon–5:30pm Sun • Dis. access • www.thedali.org*

Caladesi Island State Park

9 This 3-mile (5-km) island, accessible by ferry from Honeymoon Island, is a lovely outdoor retreat traversed by a nature trail. A ban on cars helps keep it much as it was a century ago. In

Annie Pfeiffer Chapel, Florida Southern College

season, beach areas are dotted with the tracks of loggerhead turtles that nest here. ◈ *Ferry to island • 3 Causeway Blvd, Dunedin • 727-469-5918 • Ferry runs 10am–5pm daily • Adm • Off Map*

Florida Southern College

10 In the late 1930s, renowned architect Frank Lloyd Wright designed 12 campus buildings at this college – the world's largest collection. Highlights include the Annie Pfeiffer Chapel, the Roux Library, the Danforth Chapel, and the Esplanades. Pick up a walking-tour map from the visitor center. ◈ *111 Lake Hollingsworth Dr, Lakeland • 863-680-4110 • Visitors center open 11am–4pm Tue–Fri, 10am–2pm Sat, 2–4pm Sun • Free*

Left **Daytona Beach** Right **Ron Jon Surf Shop, Cocoa Beach**

TOP 10 Day Trips North & East

Kennedy Space Center

This well-conceived monument to America's space program impresses visitors with exhibits both mammoth, such as the Saturn V Rocket, and minuscule, such as antiquated space suits. Bus tours are a good way to take in the installations. *See pp38–41.*

Cocoa Beach

Just 60 miles (96 km) east of I-4 via the Beachline Expressway, Cocoa Beach is the seashore closest to Orlando. The beach is picturesque, although the surrounding town is less so (apart from the lovely Cocoa Village near US Hwy 1). Surfing is taken seriously here, due in part to the presence of the Ron Jon Surf Shop, a vast surfing mecca that sells surf wear, beach gear, boards, and every imaginable beach accessory. ◈ *Off map*

Daytona Beach

During the annual "Spring Break," this legendary beach (just 90 minutes from Orlando along I-4) is the destination for thousands of vacationing college students, who drink and party until they drop. But sun and fun isn't all that's offered. Beach Street is lined with shops, restaurants, and clubs; and of course, there's the Daytona Speedway, home to the Daytona 500 and other NASCAR races (*see p57*). ◈ *Off map • Tourist info 386-255-0415*

New Smyrna Beach

Just south of Daytona Beach, New Smyrna is a smaller, calmer town that lacks Daytona's party scene. The white sand beach is picture perfect – but as at Daytona, cars share the space with sunworshipers. For food, the place to go is JB's Fish Camp, a raucous and friendly shack beside Mosquito Lagoon, which serves some of the state's tastiest fish, seafood, and key lime pie. ◈ *Off map*

Rivership Romance on St. John's River

Cassadaga Spiritualist Camp

Buried deep in the woods near exit 54 off I-4, tiny Cassadaga was founded more than 100 years ago as a community of clairvoyants, mediums, and healers. Resident spiritualists promote the science, philosophy, and the religion of Spiritualism; offer contacts with the deceased in the Spirit World; and provide a variety of healing services for the body, mind, and spirit. Staff at the Cassadaga Camp Bookstore can put visitors in touch with on-call mediums in the area and even provide a phone to make appointments.

For information on Day Trips West See pp82–3

Crystal River Manatee Swim and Snorkel Tour

Three covered boats tour year-round down the pristine Crystal River, allowing guests to view – and swim with – endangered manatees (see p33). Sightings of these gentle creatures are most frequent from late October to late March. ⊗ Pete's Pier, 1 SW 1st Place, Crystal River • Off map • Tours daily, call for times • 352-628-3450 • Adm • www.crystalrivertours.com

Merritt Island National Wildlife Refuge

This 140,000-acre (56,000-ha) wildlife sanctuary (the second-largest in Florida) has more federally-endangered species than any other refuge in the United States. A six-mile (10-km) driving tour with shaded board-walks weaves through lush pine and oak hammocks. See p52.

St Johns Rivership Company

Operating out of historic Sanford, this 1946-built triple-decked boat offers daily cruises along the scenic St. John's River. It's a truly civilized way to catch a glimpse of the Florida that tourists rarely see. ⊗ 433 N. Palmetto Ave • 321-441-3030 • Adm • No DA • www.stjohnsrivershipco.com

Central Florida Zoo and Botanical Gardens

Beneath this zoo's dense canopy of foliage, visitors can observe the residents (from howler monkeys

Local architecture, Mount Dora

to bald eagles, llamas, and zebu) at close quarters. Some areas fall short – the pacing big cats obviously need bigger cages – but on the whole, this makes for a rewarding trip. ⊗ 3755 N.W. Hwy 17–92, Sanford • Off map • Open 9am–5pm daily • 407-323-4450 • Adm • www.centralfloridazoo.org

Mount Dora

Just 25 miles (40 km) from Orlando, charming Mount Dora seems plucked from the 1950s. The cozy downtown is unmarred by strip malls or chain stores. Instead, the local industry is antiques, with dozens of small shops on and around Donnelly Street as well as Reninger's Antique & Flea Markets (see p67) on the edge of town. Train buffs can enjoy a ride on the Mt. Dora trolley for a guided tour, and Lake Dora offers plenty of boating opportunities. ⊗ Tourist info 1-352-383-2165 • Off map

AROUND TOWN

ORLANDO'S TOP 10

Left **Lake Buena Vista** Right **Lake Buena Vista environs**

Walt Disney World® Resort & Lake Buena Vista

THERE WAS ONLY ONE *drawback to California's Disneyland, Walt Disney's first theme park, which opened in 1955: the area was prime real estate and there was no free space around the park in which to expand. So, following an aerial tour of Central Florida in 1965, Disney began covertly to buy large tracts of land. At the time, this patch of the Sunshine State was little more than cow pastures, citrus groves, and swamps, and was of little interest to anyone. Today, the 47-sq-mile (121-sq-km) Walt Disney World® Resort is a self-contained and virtually self-governing entity (call 911 here and you get a Disney employee) containing four major theme parks, two water parks, several smaller attractions, and many hotels and resorts, which also spill over into the adjoining Lake Buena Vista area. For some of the 43 million guests who visit annually, it's a once-in-a-lifetime vacation, but many can't get enough of this enchanted fantasyland and return time and again to relive the experience.*

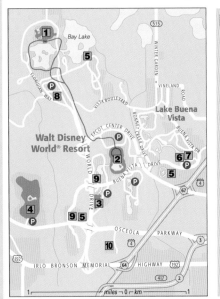

🔟 Sights

1. **Magic Kingdom®**
2. **Epcot®**
3. **Disney Hollywood Studios®**
4. **Disney's Animal Kingdom® Park**
5. **Water Parks**
6. **Cirque du Soleil**
7. **DisneyQuest**
8. **Richard Petty Driving Experience**
9. **Fantasia Gardens & Winter Summerland Miniature Golf**
10. **ESPN Wide World of Sports®**

Magic Kingdom®
Who's the leader of the theme-park pack? Disney's first Florida park is the most popular in the US. *See pp8–11.*

Epcot®
Walt Disney's guys knew something had to appeal to curious adults and techno kids. Epcot® is that something. *See pp12–15.*

Disney Hollywood Studios®
A park that combines front-of-house fun with behind-the-scenes explanation. *See pp16–17.*

Disney's Animal Kingdom® Park
Disney's fourth Orlando park is a place where elusive animals roam. *See pp18–19.*

Water Parks
Disney World has two water parks. The hugely popular Typhoon Lagoon, designed to resemble a beach resort devastated by a tropical storm, can hold more than 7,000 people at once, and has plenty of rides and attractions. Blizzard Beach's theme is a ski resort that melted and is a favorite among water slide fans. But whatever extreme weather they represent, these parks have similar features: long drops to build up speed and darkened tubes to confuse you before spilling you, laughing or screaming, into a wading pool below. The parks have seasonal opening hours, so call to check. *See p48.* ◈ Typhoon Lagoon • Map G2 • 407-560-4141 • Adm ◈ Blizzard Beach • Map G1• 407-560-3400 • Adm

Cirque du Soleil
Nowadays, circuses without animals are all the rage, and the Canadian company Cirque du Soleil is one of the best of its kind. So popular are its shows that, in addition to world tours, there are now permanent venues, too. Orlando's high-energy, 90-minute show, La Nouba, climaxes with a finale in which more than 70 performers execute an extraordinary trampoline routine. The ticket is quite pricey, but you're unlikely to be disappointed. ◈ Downtown Disney West Side • Map G2 • 407-939-7600 • Shows at 6 & 9pm Thu–Mon • Adm

Cirque du Soleil

For information on Disney sights and attractions, including up-to-date hours of operation, call 407-934-7639.

89

Walt Disney

Walter Elias Disney was just 26 years old when his most famous cartoon character, Mickey Mouse, was introduced in the film *Steamboat Willie* (1928). Despite escalating success in the film world as he embraced first sound then technicolor, Disney had his sights set on more than just animation. He was the man who created the theme park, which he envisaged as a kind of 3-D movie where each individual could spin his or her own story in a totally safe, controlled, and upbeat eviroment. His first, California's Disneyland Park, was the perfect vehicle for bringing Disney's clean-living family values and nostalgia for tradition to the masses. It was also the only one of his parks that came to fruition before his death in 1966 from lung cancer, 11 years after it opened.

DisneyQuest

This interactive, indoor theme park is divided into five floors and entertains adults as much as it does kids. Highlights of the Explore Zone include Pirates of the Caribbean®: Battle for Buccaneer Gold, and Aladdin's Magic Carpet Ride. The former puts you on the deck of a two-master schooner to play cat-and-mouse with foul-playing pirates and foul-smelling sea monsters. Aladdin's Magic Carpet involves wearing a virtual reality helmet and taking a ride through the 3-D Cave of Wonders in search of the genie. In the Score Zone, it's all about testing your game-playing skills. Don't miss Buzz Lightyear's Astroblasters, where you get to fly a space ship and blast gigantic robots, or the Mighty Ducks Pinball Slam, a life-size, sure-fire hit for pinball fans. The Create Zone unleashes the designer within:

build your own roller coaster (and then ride it in a simulator), or take a short course in cartooning at the Animation Academy. The Replay Zone is filled with games where for an extra charge, you can win tickets that can be redeemed for prizes you can live without. Crowds are worse after lunch. ◎ *Downtown Disney West Side • Map G2 • 407-828-4600 • Open 11:30am–10pm Sun–Thu, till 11pm Fri, Sat • Adm*

Richard Petty Driving Experience

Ever wanted to drive one of those souped-up, 600-horsepower NASCAR race cars, or even just be a co-pilot? Well, here's your chance to try for your dream – and a new land-speed record. The two-page waiver form that riders need to sign may shake your nerve, but there's nothing virtual about this attraction. There are two options: ride or drive. For the first, take the passenger seat while a professional drives off around the track at 145 mph (233 kmph); minimum age for this option is 16. Alternatively, spend a few hours or (if you have lots of cash to spare) days learning how to drive, and then race others for up to 30 laps (minimum age is 18 years). ◎ *Walt Disney World Speedway • Map F1 • 800-237-3889 • www.drive petty.com • Opening times vary • Adm*

Fantasia Gardens & Winter Summerland Miniature Golf

Orlando in general and Walt Disney World® Resort in particular have some great golf courses *(see pp54–5)*, but not everyone likes to take the game so seriously, or has the makings of a pro. These two miniature golf courses offer a total of 72 holes of putting fun. Inspired by the classic Disney cartoon, *Fantasia*, Fantasia Gardens'

Fantasia Gardens & Winter Summerland Miniature Golf

18 holes have an animal theme. Located near Disney Hollywood Studios®, it's the more forgiving of the two courses, and so the best choice for young kids or beginners. Winter Summerland is a scale model of a large course, complete with bunkers, water hazards, frustrating putting greens, and holes that are up to 75 ft (23 m) long. Choose between the winter and summer themed courses. ◈ *Fantasia Gardens • Map G2 • 407-560-4582 • Open 10am–11pm daily • Adm* ◈ *Winter Summerland • Map G1 • 407-560-3000 • Open 10am–11pm daily • Adm*

⑩ ESPN Wide World of Sports®

Disney's sports complex is the spring training home of Major League baseball's Atlanta Braves (Feb–Mar) and minor league baseball's Orlando Rays, a farm team for the Tampa Bay Devil Rays (Apr–Sep). It's also a winter home for basketball's Harlem Globetrotters. Other facilities in the 220-acre (90-ha) complex, which is used for all kinds of amateur sports and athletics, include: a fitness center; basketball, volleyball, and tennis courts; softball, soccer, and lacrosse fields; a martial-arts venue; and a golf-driving range. ESPN Wide World of Sports® is also the home of the NFL Experience *(see p56)*. There is an extreme sports area catering for skateboarders, in-line skaters, and cyclists, which is now open for special events. ◈ *Map G2 • 407-939-1500 • Opening times vary • Adm*

Hidden Mickeys

Hidden Mickeys started many years ago as a joke among park designers. Today they're a Disney tradition. They're images of the world's most famous mouse: silhouettes of Mickey's ears, his head and ears or his whole body, semi-hidden throughout the parks and resorts. They can be anywhere: in the landscaping, in the murals you pass while waiting in ride lines, and even overhead, for example on the Earffel Tower in Disney Hollywood Studios®. See how many you can spot (www.hiddenmickeys.org).

Mitsukoshi Department Store

TOP 10 Best Shops

1 House of Good Fortune

Here's an excellent source for all things Asian, from jade figurines to silk robes, and inlaid mother-of-pearl furnishings to wind chimes. ◈ *China Pavilion, World Showcase, Epcot®* • *Map G2* • *Adm*

2 Berber Oasis

Hand-tied Berber rugs, camel-bone boxes, and more are on offer in this square, which has the bustle but not the hustle of the real thing. ◈ *Morocco Pavilion, World Showcase, Epcot®* • *Map G2* • *Adm*

3 LEGO® Imagination Center

Kids love the play area, which has enough LEGO® pieces to build almost anything. Inside, the cash registers sing as parents buy the latest Lego gadgets. ◈ *Downtown Disney Marketplace* • *Map G2*

4 Mitsukoshi Department Store

An amazing selection of kimonos, samurai swords, bonsais, Japanese Disneyana, and kites is sold here. ◈ *Japan Pavilion, World Showcase, Epcot®* • *Map G2* • *Adm*

5 Harley-Davidson

Motorcycle lovers can buy everything from baby clothes to personalized leather vests with the iconic Harley logo, or hop on a real "hog" for a photo op. ◈ *Downtown Disney West Side* • *Map G2*

6 French Marketplace

Pick up fine soaps, wine, designer fragrances, kitchen gadgets, and even a dashing black beret. ◈ *France Pavilion, World Showcase, Epcot®.* • *Map G2* • *Adm*

7 Art of Disney

This large gallery is one of a kind in Florida. You'll find Disney sculptures, animation cels, and other collectibles. ◈ *Downtown Disney Marketplace* • *Map G2*

8 Hoypoloi Gallery

This small but sensory gallery sells sculptures, ceramics, and other imaginative oddities made of metal, stone, clay, and wood. ◈ *Downtown Disney West Side* • *Map G2*

9 Mickey's Mart

Everything in this shop located between Disney Tails and Disney at Home is $10 or less. Every week there is a featured sale item. ◈ *Downtown Disney Marketplace* • *Map G2*

10 TrenD

The stylish side of Mickey Mouse, with edgy, trendy, one-of-a-kind clothes and accessories, including organic loungewear, embroidered hand-bags, jeweled sun-glasses, and exclusive creations by cutting-edge designers. ◈ *Downtown Disney Marketplace* • *Map G2*

Forget to buy something? Call 407-363-6200, give the item's description and where you saw it. You can probably order it by phone.

Downtown Disney®

TOP10 Nighttime Attractions

1 House of Blues®
One of Orlando's best venues for live music with a wide variety of musical acts. *See p74.* Ⓝ *Downtown Disney West Side • Map G2 • 407-934-2583 • Adm*

2 Disney's BoardWalk®
By night, this "seaside" boardwalk is thronged with guests enjoying the buzzing vibe and some great restaurants and clubs. *See p46.* Ⓝ *Map G2 • Free*

3 Downtown Disney®
Probably Disney's best spot for night owls, with lots of bars and clubs to choose from. *See p46.* Ⓝ *Map G2 • Free to walk around*

4 Cirque du Soleil
In a tent-like theater in Disney's West Side, this avant-garde circus troupe spotlights superhuman acrobats. *See p89.*

5 DisneyQuest
Heaven for video gamers, here kids can design their own roller coaster and ride it, or steer a ship in Pirates of the Caribbean. *See p90.*

6 Bongo's Cuban Café
This venue evokes images of Havana of the 1940s and '50s, and has live music at weekends. *See p75.* Ⓝ *Downtown Disney®, 1498 E. Buena Vista Dr • Map G2 • 407-828-0999 • Adm on Sat*

7 ESPN Club
Watch big games on a giant screen, play arcade games, and join the audience for live shows at this sports bar, which serves burgers and steaks. Ⓝ *2101 Epcot Resorts Blvd • Map G2 • 407-939-1177*

8 Hoop-Dee-Doo Musical Revue
This family show combines an all-you-can-eat dinner with country & western dancing, singing, and comedy. Unlimited draft beer, wine, and soft drinks are included. *See p80.* Ⓝ *Disney's Fort Wilderness Resort • Map F1 • 407-WDW- DINE • 5, 7:15 & 9:30pm nightly*

9 Atlantic Dance Hall
This glorious kitschy 1930s-style dance hall has been repositioned as a place to dance along to music videos and dueling DJs. *See p75.* Ⓝ *Disney's BoardWalk® • Map G2 • Closed Sun & Mon • Adm*

10 Chip 'n' Dale's Campfire Sing-A-Long
Enjoy songs and marshmallows around a campfire, followed by a different Disney movie every night. It is open to all – just park at the River Country entrance and take the bus to the party. Ⓝ *Meadow Trading Post, Fort Wilderness Campground • Map G2 • 407-824-2900 • Free • 8pm (summer), 7pm (rest of the year)*

Guests must be 21 or over to get into clubs and bars in Orlando, and need to have picture ID (driving license or passport) to prove it.

Sanaa

Resort Area Restaurants

1 Victoria & Albert's
This romantic gem has an international menu that is served by staff dressed as Queen Victoria and Prince Albert. *See p68.*
Disney's Grand Floridian Resort & Spa • Map F1 • 407-824-1089 • Pre-arrange vegetarian entrées • No kids' menu • $$$$$

2 California Grill
This vegetarian-friendly restaurant offers delicious California cuisine in a romantic 15th-floor space. *See p68.*
Disney's Contemporary Resort • Map F1 • 407-824-1576 • $$$$

3 Be Our Guest
Modeled along the film, *Beauty and the Beast*, this high-end restaurant serves casual lunches and sit down dinners. Reserve ahead to enjoy French cuisine and wine. *Magic Kingdom Dr • Map F1 • 407-934-5277 • $$$$$*

4 Jiko – The Cooking Place
Jiko features a show kitchen and an inventive menu: banana-leaf steamed sea bass is a typical dish. *Disney's Animal Kingdom Lodge • Map G1 • 407-938-3000 • $$$$*

5 Artist Point
Bison rib-eye steak and nut-and-herb crusted lamb chops are a few of the delicious options here. There's patio dining as well.
Disney's Wilderness Lodge • Map F1 • 407-824-3200 • $$$$

6 Emeril's Tchoup Chop
The Polynesian fare here has a New Orleans twist. Menu highlights include dumplings and pot stickers followed by fish cooked in clay pots, and Kona-glazed duck. *Royal Pacific Resort, 6300 Hollywood Way • Map T2 • 407-503-2467 • No kids' menu • $$$$*

7 Sanaa
The Indian-spiced African menu here is loaded with slow-cooked delights, grilled over a wood fire or roasted in a tandoor oven. *Disney's Animal Kingdom Lodge • Map G1 • 407-WDW-DINE • $$$$*

8 Columbia Restaurant Celebration
Come here for a taste of old Havana. Indulge in crab-stuffed pompano or dive into the exquisite calamari. *649 Front St • Map G2 • 407-566-1505 • $$$*

9 Wolfgang Puck's Café
Grilled pizza, spicy tuna rolls, and pumpkin risotto are some of the eclectic options made here by the acclaimed California chef.
Downtown Disney West Side • Map G2 • 407-938-9653 • $$$$

10 Portobello Yacht Club Restaurant
This classy eatery is sure to please with thin crust pizzas, pastas, and Italian food such as slow-roasted pork loin. *Downtown Disney • Map G2 • 407-934-8888 • $$$$$*

Unless stated, all restaurants advise reservations, are non-smoking, take credit cards, and have DA, kids' menus, A/C, and vegetarian dishes.

Price Categories

For a three-course meal for one, a glass of house wine, and all unavoidable extra charges including tax.

$	under $20
$$	$20–$30
$$$	$30–$45
$$$$	$45–$60
$$$$$	over $60

Coral Reef

🔟 Theme Park Restaurants

1 Via Napoli
Authentic pizzas are made with ingredients from Italy in giant wood-burning ovens at this wonderful family-style restaurant. ✪ *Italy Pavilion, Epcot®* • Map G2 • 407-939-3463 • $$$$

2 Rainforest Café®
American cuisine inspired by Mexican, Carribean, and Asian flavors is served in an indoor rainforest setting. If you don't like volume and kids, this isn't for you. ✪ *Disney's Animal Kingdom* • Map G1 • 407-939-3463 • Park adm not required • $$$$

3 Coral Reef
Classical music and aquarium visuals are the setting here. Try the roasted snapper with veggies. ✪ *Living Seas Pavilion, Epcot* • Map G2 • 407-939-3463 • $$$$

4 Cinderella's Royal Table
This restaurant in a castle has a great menu, with tasty prime-rib pastry-pie leading the way. ✪ *Fantasyland, Magic Kingdom* • Map F1 • 407-939-3463 • Pre-arrange vegetarian entrées • No alcohol • $$$$

5 Akershus
Hunker down for traditional Norweigian dishes (herring, potato salad, gravlax in mustard sauce, venison stew, and more) in a medieval castle setting. ✪ *Norway Pavilion, Epcot* • Map G2 • 407-939-3463 • $$$

6 Hollywood Brown Derby
Polish off SoCal dishes such as skillet-seared tuna and grapefruit cake with cream-cheese icing. ✪ *Disney Hollywood Studios* • Map G2 • 407-939-3463 • Reserve ahead; pre-arrange vegetarian entrées • $$$$

7 San Angel Inn
Try *mole poblano* (chicken with spices and chocolate) or beef with black beans and fried plantain at this massive south-of-the-border eatery. ✪ *Mexico Pavilion, Epcot* • Map G2 • 407-939-3463 • $$$

8 Rose & Crown Pub & Dining Room
A pub-grub joint offering British staples such as bangers and mash, rib with Yorkshire pudding, and Cornish pasties. ✪ *UK Pavilion, Epcot* • Map G2 • 407-939-3463 • Pre-arrange vegetarian entrées • $$$

9 Chefs de France
Meet Remy from *Ratatouille* at this brasserie-style restaurant full of Gallic flare and flavor. ✪ *France Pavilion, Epcot* • Map G2 • 407-939-3463 • Pre-arrange vegetarian entrées • $$$$

10 Liberty Tree Tavern
Buffet-style American fare, such as roasted turkey, flank steak, and ham, is served in a colonial setting. ✪ *Liberty Sq, Magic Kingdom* • Map F1 • 407-939-3463 • Pre-arrange vegetarian entrées • No alcohol • $$$

For information on Priority Seating in Walt Disney World Resort **See p134**

Left **Wet 'n Wild®** Right **Universal Studios®**

International Drive Area

CONSIDERED THE TOURIST CENTER OF *Orlando, International Drive is a brash 10-mile (16-km) strip boasting five theme parks, countless attractions* open day and night, including Universal's CityWalk® entertainment complex, and the USA's second-largest convention center. Added to the mix are hundreds of hotels and resorts catering to all budgets, shopping malls and outlet stores, and themed and fast-food restaurants. As a package, the result is a frenetic zone, which, despite its wall-to-wall neon signs and visual overload, has become a serious competitor of Disney World, appealing to visitors who prefer to stay away from the clutches of Mickey but want to be in the thick of the action.

CityWalk®, Universal Orlando®

🔟 Sights & Attractions

1. Islands of Adventure®
2. Universal Studios Florida®
3. Wet 'n Wild®
4. SeaWorld® Orlando
5. Discovery Cove®
6. Fun Spot Action Park
7. Ripley's Believe It or Not®! Odditorium
8. The Holy Land Experience
9. WonderWorks
10. Titanic – The Experience

Islands of Adventure®

Islands of Adventure®
The addition of the Wizarding World of Harry Potter™ to the rides here makes this a popular destination. *See pp20–23.*

Universal Studios Florida®
Part studio and part attraction, the movie-themed rides and shows here really let visitors step inside the movies. *See pp24–7.*

Wet 'n Wild®
It's hard to out-do Disney and SeaWorld®, but Wet 'n Wild® is among Orlando's best sun-and-swim water park attractions, with plenty of slides and rides to amuse. *See pp34–5.*

SeaWorld® Orlando
Orcas, dolphins, and other animal attractions offer a refreshing change of pace from fast rides and cartoon characters. *See pp28–31.*

Discovery Cove®
You might be in land-locked Orlando, but you can still fulfill those tropical island fantasies of swimming with dolphins and snorkeling over coral reefs if you check in to Discovery Cove®. The dolphin swim is the biggest draw (each session lasts about one hour), but the white-sand beaches, snorkeling opportunities in fresh and

salt-water lagoons, and soothing beach-resort vibe elicits just as much praise. Admission is not cheap (largely because there are never more than 1,000 visitors daily), but you get almost everything you need for the day thrown in, including sun block, lunch, and snorkel gear, as well as a seven-day pass to SeaWorld®. Kids might miss the lack of thrill rides, but they will not be short of things to do. Redevelopment work on the park during 2012 and 2013 may affect some attractions. *See p48.* ✆ 6000 Discovery Cove Way • Map T6 • 407-370-1280 • Open 9am–5:30pm daily • Adm

Discovery Cove®

Fun Spot America
This arcade/amusement-park has something for everyone who has a little bit of the child in them. The park has four go-kart tracks, two giant roller coasters, as well as the world's biggest SkyCoaster. In addition, there are bumper boats and cars, a 100-ft (30-m) Ferris wheel, 100 arcade games, and a kid zone that has swings, a train, spinning tea cups, and flying bears. *See p44.* ✆ 5551 Del Verde Way, Orlando • Map U2 • 407-363-3867 • noon–11pm Mon–Fri, 10am–11pm Sat–Sun • Free (but ride and game prices vary) • Min age for solo go-karting is 10 yrs

Fun Spot America

Ripley's Believe It or Not!® Odditorium

7 Ripley's Believe It or Not!® Odditorium

If you're a fan of the bizarre, you'll love Ripley's. This worldwide chain of attractions displays the unbelievable finds of Robert Ripley's 40 years of adventures, the reports of which were published in more than 300 newspapers and read by more than 80 million people. The Orlando branch has a full-scale model of a 1907 Silver Ghost Rolls Royce (with moving engine parts) built out of 1,016,711 match sticks and 63 pints (36 l) of glue; a flute made of human bones; a mosaic of the Mona Lisa made of toast; shrunken heads; a five-legged cow; and a portrait of Van Gogh made from 3,000 postcards. You'll also see a holographic 1,069-lb-(485-kg) man, plus films of strange feats such as people swallowing coat-hangers. *See p44.* ◈ *8201 International Dr • Map T3 • 407-363-4418 • Open 9am–midnight daily • Adm*

The Peabody Ducks

Their existence came about because of a practical joke, but now these five mallards, which reside in the Peabody Hotel *(see p143)*, are among the best known and most unusual celebrities in I-Drive. As befits VIPs (Very Important Poultry), they spend much of each day in their $100,000 glass-enclosed home, called the 'Duck Palace'. But what draws the crowds is their twice daily procession (at 11am and 5pm), when they waddle through the hotel lobby, led by their own red-coated duck master, on the way to and from the lobby fountain.

8 The Holy Land Experience

Marvin J. Rosenthal, a Christian convert and Baptist minister, created quite a stir when he opened this religious theme park. Set in a half-scale reconstruction of the Temple of the Great King, which stood in Jerusalem in the 1st century AD, the park aims to take visitors 7,000 miles (11,200 km) away and 3,000 years back to the ancient Jerusalem of biblical times (BC 1450 to AD 66 to be exact). The attraction has models of the limestone caves where the Dead Sea Scrolls were discovered and of Jesus's tomb. It also has displays of rare antique Bibles and biblical manuscripts, an outdoor stage where actors portraying biblical personalities tell stories from the Old and New Testaments, and a café that serves Middle Eastern food. *See p44.* ◈ *4655 Vineland Rd • Map D4 • 407-872-2272 • Open 10am–6pm, sometimes later, closed Sun & Mon • Adm*

The Holy Land Experience

WonderWorks

You can't miss this attraction from the outside: it looks as though a classical building has landed upside down on top of a warehouse. Inside, there are 85 hands-on exhibits. Highlights include an earthquake simulator; a Bridge of Fire, where you can

WonderWorks

literally experience the hair-raising effects of 250,000 watts of static electricity; and Virtual Hoops, which uses some of the latest cinema technology to put you on TV to play basketball against one of the NBA's top players. You can also try Virtual Hang Gliding, which sends you soaring like a bird through the Grand Canyon, and WonderCoaster, which challenges your roller coaster-designing skills and then your nerve to ride your creation in a simulator. WonderWorks also runs a laser-tag venue and a twice-nightly magic show, both of which cost extra. *See p45.*

⊛ Pointe Orlando, 9067 International Dr • Map T4 • 407-351-8800 • Open 9am–midnight daily • Adm

Titanic – The Experience

This exhibit's 200 artifacts include a real life jacket and an old deck chair, which were both recovered from the wreckage of the fateful liner, as well as the Titanic's second-class passenger list. The attraction also has full-scale re-creations of some of the ship's rooms, including its grand

Titanic – The Experience

staircase, as well as memorabilia from three major Titanic movies – including one of the costumes worn by Leonardo DiCaprio. Actors in period garb play out events that occured on the fateful journey, telling the story of the White Star Line's supposedly unsinkable ship. Most of the artifacts came out of private collections from both the United Kingdom and the USA. *See p44.*

⊛ 8267 International Dr • Map T3 • 407-248-1166 • Timings vary • Adm

---

I-Ride Trolley

One of the best things about I-Drive itself is the tourist-oriented I-Ride Trolley, which offers an easy way to ogle some of the area's oddities and its high-density visual overload. It is also an excellent and extremely cheap way to get around this part of town while avoiding the need to get involved in fighting I-Drive's frustratingly heavy traffic, or walking any distance in the heat. There are 78 stops on the circuit, serving all the local major attractions, shopping malls, hotels, and restaurants. *See p127.*

Left **Ice Bar** Center **Ripleys Believe It or Not®! Odditorium** Right **WonderWorks**

🔟 Eye-Openers on I-Drive

1 Four Points by Sheraton Orlando Studio City
This distinctive 21-story circular hotel has a huge globe sitting on top of it. ✆ *5905 International Dr • Map T2*

2 Titanic – The Experience
Relive the tragedy, share in the inspirational personal stories of those aboard, and marvel at the splendor of this luxurious liner that has been impressively re-created. *See p99.*

3 Pirate's Cove Adventure Golf
The view of pirate ships and waterfalls at this mega-mini-golf spot, not to mention the sound of cannon fire, is unexpected on I-Drive. ✆ *8501 International Dr • Map T3 • 407-352-7378*

4 Bargain World
The doorway to this shop is straddled by a large flying saucer. Alighting from a nearby rocketship is a giant green Martian wearing casual clothes and holding a stick. ✆ *8520 International Dr • Map T2 • 407-352-7100*

5 King's Bowl
There are 22 bowling lanes over several levels on offer here, along with two full bars, a full service restaurant, and 60 giant TVs. ✆ *8255 S. International Dr • Map E3 • 407-363-0200 •11–2am daily*

6 Ice Bar
There's always something cool happening at this frozen cocktail bar, from karaoke and swing dance lessons to DJs. Be sure to grab your coat before you visit! ✆ *8967 International Dr • Map T2*

7 Ripley's Believe It or Not®! Odditorium
This place is built to look as if one of Florida's sinkholes opened up and nearly swallowed the building. *See p98.*

8 iFLY
Take a close look at this blue and purple building and you might see people floating in front of you – look closer and you will see they are actually flying. *See p45.*

9 WonderWorks
As the marketing story goes, a tornado picked up this four-story building and sent it crashing upside down on top of a 1930s-era brick warehouse. Silly perhaps, but it stops traffic. *See p99.*

10 Air Florida Helicopters
With flights starting at just $20 (plus $4 for fuel) per person, there's no reason not to enjoy a panoramic birds-eye view over the city. ✆ *8990 International Dr • Map T4 • 407-354-1400 • 9:30am–8pm daily*

For tips on shopping in Orlando See p132

Left **Edwin Watts Golf National Clearance Center** Right **Stores on I-Drive**

10 I-Drive Stores & Outlet Centers

1 Nike Factory Store
A gigantic collection of things adorned with the famous "swoosh," at discount prices. ✪ *Orlando Premium Outlets International, 5201 W. Oak Ridge Rd • Map U1 • 407-351-9400*

2 Kenneth Cole
Choose from recent lines of Cole shoes; bags and clothes also vie for attention with about 25 percent discount. ✪ *Orlando Premium Outlets International, 5247 International Dr • Map U1 • 407-903-1191*

3 Orlando Premium Outlets International
With more than 170 stores bursting with bargains, there's something for everyone. ✪ *5401 W. Oakridge Rd • Map U1 • 407-352-9611*

4 Bass Pro Shops Outdoor World
Overflowing with fishing, golf, camping, and hunting supplies and apparel, this is a vast shrine to the great outdoors. ✪ *5156 International Dr • Map U1 • 407-563-5200*

5 Coach Factory Store
Leather rules at this spacious store, and deals abound on current and last season's handbags, jackets, and luggage. ✪ *Orlando Premium Outlets International, 5269 International Drive • Map U1 • 407-352-6772*

6 Edwin Watts Golf National Clearance Center
Like cars, golf clubs also have model years. This store offers last season's hot drivers and putters at deep savings. ✪ *7024 International Dr • Map T3 • 407-352-2535*

7 Brooks Brothers Outlet
Slim pickings for suits, but there's a great range of casual sportswear for men and women, discounted by at least 40 percent. ✪ *Orlando Premium Outlets International, 5247 International Dr • Map G3 • 407-363-5918*

8 Off 5th
Like Sak's Fifth Avenue's regular stores, this outlet is heavy on high fashion brand names and has a rapid turnover. ✪ *Orlando Premium Outlets International, 5253 International Dr • Map U1 • 407-354-5757*

9 Oshkosh B'Gosh
This American company has sturdy kids' clothes, including its trademark overalls. ✪ *Orlando Premium Outlets International, 5401 International Dr • Map U1 • 407-352-6414*

10 Divers Direct Outlet
This deep discount outlet carries everything needed for underwater adventures. ✪ *5368 International Dr • Map U1 • 407-363-2883*

Most stores on I-Drive are open 10am–10pm Mon–Sat and noon–6pm Sun.

Left **Bob Marley – A Tribute To Freedom** Center **Red Coconut Club** Right **Hard Rock Live**

Bars, Clubs, & Entertainment

Hard Rock Live
One of the best spots in to see live music (national/local rock and R&B acts), with a top-notch sound system. *See p74.* ❧ *City-Walk • Map T1 • 407-351-5483 • Adm*

The Groove
This powerhouse dance club has slamming DJs, as well as several quiet chill-out lounges. *See p77.* ❧ *CityWalk • Map T1 • 407-224-3663 • Over 21 yrs • Adm*

Jimmy Buffet's Margaritaville
A mecca for Parrot Heads or anyone who wants to have a good time in the ultimate tropical setting. Great drinks, food, and live entertainment most evenings. ❧ *Universal CityWalk • Map T1 • 407-224-2155*

Howl at the Moon
Rock 'n' roll dueling pianos and signature drinks make this high-energy nightclub a fun adult getaway. ❧ *8815 International Dr • 407-354-5999 • Map T4 • Adm varies*

Lucky Leprechaun
Karaoke every night at this lively and popular Irish-themed bar – great selection of Irish beers. ❧ *7032 International Dr • Map T4 • 407-352-7031*

Latin Quarter
Expect anything Latin – from food to dance lessons – at this energetic venue. A 13-piece Latin band is on most nights. ❧ *CityWalk • Map T1 • 407-224-2800 • Adm after 10pm Thu–Sat*

Adobe Gilas
Crowds of 20-somethings swarm this restaurant/bar (with 65 varieties of tequila) and dance the night away. *See p75.* ❧ *Pointe Orlando, 9101 International Dr • Map T4 • 407-903-1477 • Free • DA*

Bob Marley – A Tribute To Freedom
Live outdoor reggae music is the big draw here, and the bands are often excellent. ❧ *CityWalk • Map T1 • 407-224-2690 • Over 21 yrs only after 10pm • Occasional evening adm*

Cricketers Arms Pub
A little piece of England, with European soccer on the TVs, darts, and nearly 20 ales, lagers, bitters, and stouts on tap. ❧ *Mercado, 8445 International Dr • Map T3 • 407-354-0686 • Free*

Red Coconut Club
A hip 50s retro lounge with three bars on two levels, plus live music and DJs. ❧ *CityWalk • Map T1 • 407-224-3363 • Occasional adm*

Age restrictions (18 or 21 years) for shows and clubs vary. Bring your photo ID to make sure you are not turned away at the door.

Price Categories

For a three-course meal for one, a glass of house wine and all unavoidable extra charges including tax.

$	under $20
$$	$20–$30
$$$	$30–$45
$$$$	$45–$60
$$$$$	over $60

Cuba Libre

🔟 Places to Eat

1 Café Tu Tu Tango
Local artists' work adorns the walls of this vaguely Latin-style eatery. Dishes include black bean soup, shrimp fritters, and quesadillas. ✎ 8625 International Dr • Map T3 • 407-248-2222 • $$

2 Fiorella's Cucina Toscana
Choose from high-end, hand-crafted Italian specialties in this hotel restaurant inside The Westin Imagine Orlando. *See p69.* ✎ 9501 Universal Blvd • Map T4 • 407-233-2950 • $$$

3 Roy's
On the menu here are Hawaiian fusion dishes such as sesame-oil-seared mahi-mahi with red Thai curry sauce. ✎ 7760 W. Sand Lake Rd • S3 • 407-352-4844 • $$$$

4 Everglades
A casual, intimate hotel restaurant with an imaginative chef and superb steaks and seafood. ✎ 9840 International Dr • Map T3 • 407-996-2385 • $$$

5 Seasons 52
The seasonally inspired menu includes grilled vegetables, crab-stuffed mushrooms, and rosemary and parmesan cheese flatbreads. All dishes have a low calorie content. ✎ 7700 W. Sandlake Road • 407-354-5212 • No kids' menu • $$$

6 Cuba Libre
Located in a Cuban hacienda courtyard, Cuba Libre serves Cuban cuisine and has choreographed floor shows on Saturday nights. ✎ Pointe Orlando, 9101 International Dr • Map T4 • 407-226-1600 • $$$$

7 NBA City
This is the place where you can cheer for your favorite team on TV while you eat. Enjoy the NBA memorabilia on the walls during the ad breaks. ✎ Universal CityWalk • Map T1 • 407-363-5919 • $$

8 Bahama Breeze
Trust the Caribbean menu and spirits to create some fun, but expect to wait up to two hours for a table. ✎ 8849 International Dr • Map T4 • 407-248-2499 • No reservations • $$$

9 Chili's Grill & Bar
One of the better chains offering Tex-Mex food including fajitas, sandwiches, and grills, with low-fat options. ✎ 7021 International Dr • T2 • 407-352-7618 • $$$

10 The Palm
Think high-end steaks, often belly-busters (up to a 36-oz [1.2-kg] strip for two) but don't overlook the lobster option. ✎ Hard Rock Hotel, 5800 Universal Blvd • Map T1 • 407-503-7256 • $$$$$

Unless stated, all restaurants advise reservations, are non-smoking, take credit cards, and have DA, kids' menus, A/C, and vegetarian dishes.

Left **Osceola County Historical Museum & Pioneer Center** Right **Gatorland**

Kissimmee

WHAT USED TO BE A COW TOWN *has in the past few decades evolved into an inexpensive hotel enclave for Disney World tourists. But there's more to Kissimmee than cheap places to sleep. Though U.S. 192 (also called the Irlo Bronson Memorial Highway) is dense with strip malls and hotels – and looks like a grim vision of tourist hell – downtown Kissimmee (centered on Broadway and Emmet streets) was built in the early 1890s and boasts attractive low-slung buildings, which house several antique and gift shops. The land surrounding U.S. 192 is relatively undeveloped, providing Kissimmee visitors with easy access to Florida's rich, natural beauty. A terrific variety of outdoor pursuits is available to the visitor who is willing to spend time away from the theme parks.*

Downtown Kissimmee

🔟 Sights & Attractions

1. Gatorland
2. Celebration
3. Zip Orlando
4. Osceola County Pioneer Village & Museum
5. Green Meadows Petting Farm
6. Lakefront Park
7. Old Town
8. Reptile World Serpentarium
9. Forever Florida – Florida Eco-Safaris
10. Silver Spurs Rodeo

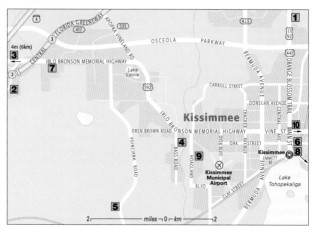

Celebration

Gatorland

Gatorland, Orlando's original theme park, opened more than 50 years ago as a swampy roadside stand, and is now home to well over 1,000 alligators, crocodiles, and snakes. Its appeal? A chance to gaze, just steps away from these mysterious creatures, who remain curiously similar to their prehistoric relatives. Visitors can stroll along a boardwalk over lakes full of cranky gators and buy hot dogs to throw into their mouths. A bizarre and unique attraction. *See p44.* ✆ *14501 S. Orange Blossom Trail • Map G4 • 800-393-5297 • Open 9am–sunset daily • Adm*

Celebration

When Walt Disney conceived of Epcot® *(see pp12–15),* he imagined it as a residential community happily engaged in road-testing futuristic technologies. After his death, that dream went out the window only to resurface years later here. However, instead of looking to the future, Celebration salutes the past in a cliché of small town USA (think *The Truman Show).* The houses are pretty, the downtown has some good restaurants and a cinema, and everything is upscale. This is not an attraction, but it is quite a sight. ✆ *Located E. of I-4 at Exit 25. Turn right at Celebration Ave and follow the signs • Map G2*

Zip Orlando

Zip on a 950-ft (290-m) long line over deer, raccoons, and alligators. Choose from a wide range of night or day activities including night-time tours and guided ATV tours. Moonlit zipline excursions are available for a headlamp-lit experience. *See p45.* ✆ *4509 S. Orange Blossom Trail • Map H3 • 407-808-4947 • Open 9am–6pm Mon–Sat, 12:30–6pm Sun • Adm*

Osceola County Pioneer Village & Museum

This homespun outdoor museum gives a glimpse of Kissimmee life before Disney. The focal point is a pair of late 1800s "Cracker-style" cypress wood buildings, complete with "possum trot" breezeway – an early form of air-conditioning. One showcases a simple home, while the other is reconfigured as a general store, selling local history books, crafts, and guides for the nature preserve located across the street. ✆ *750 N. Bass Rd • Map H3 • 407-396-8644 • Open Thu–Sun 10am–4pm • Adm*

Green Meadows Petting Farm

This educational spot is perfect for anyone who might enjoy milking a cow, riding a pony, or learning about over 300 friendly farm animals. A two-hour guided tour is included and picnic facilities are available. ✆ *1368 S. Poinciana Blvd • Map H3 • 407-846-0770 • Open 9:30am–4pm daily • Adm*

Green Meadows Petting Farm

6 Lakefront Park

This park offers a range of amenities, such as pavilions, picnic areas, and playgrounds, and hosts many community events and concerts. There are several miles of pathways for walkers, joggers, skaters, and bicycles, including a sidewalk by Lake Tohopekaliga that is popular with birdwatchers. It also has a superb white sand beach, a fishing pier, and impressive marina. The park has easy access to Kissimmee's historic district, and is close to Chisholm Park and Peghorn Nature Park. *See p48.*
⊗ *1104 Lakefront Blvd, St. Cloud • Map H6*

Lakefront Park

7 Old Town

Essentially, this is a tourist-oriented shopping mall filled with around 75 stores covering the usual array of gifts, novelty items, and souvenirs – kitsch or otherwise. What sets Old Town apart from other gift-shop strips are the numerous entertainment options: a cheerful 18-ride amusement park, Laser Tag, a Haunted House, carousel, live music performances, and a vintage car show every Friday and Saturday night. It's very much about family fun, and there's no charge for admission, although the carnival rides are priced separately. On a warm Florida night, the feeling is one of strolling the bustling midway of a state fair. ⊗ *5770 W. Irlo Bronson Hwy • Map G2 • Open 10am–11pm daily • Free*

8 Reptile World Serpentarium

This is a unique and educational attraction providing all the right ingredients to make your skin crawl. Visitors can watch a snake handler extracting poisonous venom from cobras, rattlesnakes, and other deadly serpents. The indoor exhibits house more than 60 species of reptiles, and it's the largest of its kind in central Florida. *See p45.* ⊗ *5705 E. Irlo Bronson Memorial Hwy (3.5 miles east of St. Cloud) • Map H6 • 407-892-6905 • Open 9am–5:30pm Tue–Sun • Adm*

9 Forever Florida – Florida Eco-Safaris

Go back in time to Old Florida on this working cattle ranch and nature preserve. The Forever Florida experience is based on the heritage of the Florida Cracker Cowboy. Take a tour on horseback or ride aboard an elevated cracker coach, then in the evening enjoy a

Forever Florida – Florida Eco-Safaris

Vintage cars, Old Town

meal at the Cypress Restaurant.
⊗ 4755 N. Kenansville Road, St. Cloud
• 407-957-9794 • Eco-Safaris on Safari
Coaches at 10am and 1pm daily
• www.foreverflorida.com

Silver Spurs Rodeo
The largest rodeo held east of the Mississippi, attracts all the top professional cowboys and is held several times a year. The Silver Spurs Rodeo dates back to 1944 and was from 1950 held in a specially constructed open-air arena, until that was replaced by the state-of-the-art, climate-controlled Silver Spurs Arena in 2002. The arena is also used for many other events, such as concerts and sports, but will always be chiefly associated with the excitement of bronc riding, steer wrestling, and bull riding.
⊗ Osceola Heritage Park, 1875 Silver Spur Lane • Map H5 • 407-67-RODEO
• www.silverspursrodeo.com

Silver Spurs Rodeo

A Day in Kissimmee

Morning

There are countless breakfast buffets in the area, all offering mounds of food, from fresh fruit to omelets. Find the one closest to you and start the day there. As mornings tend to be cooler and a bit less insect-ridden than afternoons, follow your meal with a self-guided tour of swamp life at **Airboat Rentals You Drive** (see p110). Head as far away as possible from the road, cut the engine, and enjoy the silence. Most of Florida used to be like this. For lunch, head to Kissimmee's historic Downtown and pop in to Azteca's (809 N. Main St), a tiny and original Tex-Mex restaurant. Be careful ordering anything "very hot"; the cook takes this as a personal challenge and will likely spice the dish so your head explodes.

Afternoon

From Downtown, it's a short drive north to **Gatorland**. The massive gators prowling the front lakes are the big attraction. But smart guests will take the Swamp Walk, check out the crocodile pens, and survey the alligator breeding marsh from the observation tower. There are four live animal shows but if time is tight, Gator Jump-A-Roo and Gator Wrestling are the essentials.

Evening

For dinner, the slightly camp **Pacino's Italian Ristorante** (see p111) is popular for its home-style Italian favorites and delicious pizza. Afterwards, take another short drive to **Old Town** where kids can play on the rides while adults watch from a bench enjoying an ice cream.

Left **Airboat ride, Boggy Creek** Center **Fishing, Kissimmee** Right **Warbird Adventures**

Leisure Pursuits & Activities

East Lake Fish Camp
This lakeside facility provides everything from fishing poles to boats, bait, and bunks. Large mouth bass and sometimes game fish hit the lines. ◈ *3705 Big Bass Rd* • *Off map* • *407-348-2040* • *Adm* • *No DA*

Extreme Jet Ski
Rent a Jetski or three, and race the family on Lake Cecile. ◈ *4914 W. Irlo Bronson Memorial Hwy* • *Map G3* • *407-390-9200* • *Adm* • *No DA*

Warbird Adventures
Have a flight in a vintage North American T-6 Texan or a Bell 47 helicopter. You'll even get the chance to take the controls and have the whole experience recorded on dvd. ◈ *233 N. Hoagland Blvd* • *Map H3* • *407-870-7366*

Thompson Aire
Hover high over Disney, and the wilds of Kissimmee in a hot-air balloon. Daily flights at sunrise. ◈ *13825 Avalon Rd* • *Map G1* • *407-421-9322* • *Adm* • *No DA*

Osceola Center For The Arts
Here, culture mavens will find anything from theater to music events, and exhibitions. ◈ *2411 E. Irlo Bronson Memorial Hwy* • *Map H5* • *407-846-6257* • *Adm*

Boggy Creek Airboat Rides
These 18-passenger flat-bottomed skiffs powered by giant fans make regular daylight wildlife tours and special one-hour night tours. ◈ *3702 Big Bass Rd* • *Off map* • *407-344-9550* • *Adm*

The Ice Factory
Get out of the Florida sun and do a few laps on this ice rink, which also has a kids' play area. ◈ *2221 Partin Settlement Rd* • *Map H5* • *407-933-4259* • *Adm* • *No DA*

Falcon's Fire Golf Club
This immaculately groomed public golf course is said to be one of the best in Florida. ◈ *3200 Seralago Blvd* • *Map G3* • *407-239-5445* • *Adm* • *No DA* • *www.falconsfire.com*

Central Florida Guide Service
This professional guide service takes clients fishing in some of the best big bass waters in Florida. ◈ *1326 Sweetwood Blvd* • *Map H4* • *407-908-4600* • *Adm* • *www.floridabassfishing.com*

Horse World Riding Stables
Enjoy horse riding on 750 acres (300 ha) of peaceful sandy trails. There are pony and hay rides, as well as friendly farm animals. ◈ *3705 S. Poinciana Blvd* • *Off map* • *407-847-4343* • *Adm*

For more sports & activities See pp56–7

Price Categories

For a three-course meal for one with a glass of house wine, and all unavoidable extra charges including tax.

$	under $20
$$	$20–$30
$$$	$30–$45
$$$$	$45–$60
$$$$$	over $60

Tarantino's Italian Restaurant

🔟 Places to Eat

1 Charley's Steak House
Charley's uses an Indian cooking method, yielding steaks that are charred outside, juicy inside.
⌘ *2901 Parkway Blvd • Map G2 • 407-239-1270 • Closed lunch • $$$$*

2 Azteca's Mexican
Authentic Mexican and Tex-Mex is served in an extravagantly decorated room. ⌘ *809 N. Main St • Map H4 • 407-933-8155 • $$ • No DA*

3 Tarantino's Italian Restaurant
This delightful Italian venue wins praise for charming ambience and well-prepared Italian classics. ⌘ *4150 W. Vine St • Map H3 • 407-870-2622 • Closed lunch • $$$*

4 Chef John's Place
John Walker's casual retreat serves fresh local fish which highlights the menu of grouper, catfish, smoked ribs and pork, and grilled steak. ⌘ *3753 Pleasant Hill Rd • off map • 407-343-4227 • Open daily • $$$$*

5 Pacino's Italian Ristorante
Sicilian specialties here include hand-cut steaks, veal chops, and great pizza and pasta. ⌘ *5795 W. Irlo Bronson Memorial Hwy • Map G2 • 407-396-8022 • $$$$*

6 Puerto Rico Café
It's a bit of a dive, but don't let that put you off trying the delicious *mojo*-enhanced steaks and seafood. ⌘ *507 W. Vine St • Map H4 • 407-847-6399 • Open daily • $$$ • No DA*

7 Celebration Town Tavern
A quiet local neighborhood gathering spot, which serves great seafood and burgers. Family-friendly yet grown-up happy hours are on offer, and football games are shown on the big-screen TV.
⌘ *721 Front St • Map G2 • 407-566-2526 • $$*

8 Black Angus Restaurant
Melt-in-your-mouth steaks are the focus of this award-winning, family eatery, but ribs and fried chicken are also popular. There's a great breakfast buffet, too.
⌘ *7516 W. Irlo Bronson Memorial Hwy • Map G1 • 407-390-4548 • $$$$*

9 Logan's Roadhouse
With its neon signs and country jukebox, the vibe here is 1940s, honky-tonk, roadside grill. Try the mesquite-grilled steaks or honey sweet rolls.
⌘ *5925 W. Irlo Bronson Memorial Hwy • Map G2 • 407-390-0500 • $$$*

10 Taste of Punjab
A perfect place for an authentic and reasonably priced Indian buffet, offering both meat and vegetarian dishes for lunch and dinner.
⌘ *4980 W. Irlo Bronson Memorial Hwy • Map G3 • 407-507-3900 • $$*

Unless stated, all restaurants advise reservations, are non-smoking, take credit cards, have DA, kids' menus, A/C, and vegetarian dishes.

111

Left **Downtown Skyline** Right **Orange County Regional History Center**

Downtown Orlando

ORLANDO IS NOT JUST about Walt Disney and amusement parks. Long a hub of the banking and citrus-growing industries, Downtown Orlando is also a historic district, and a cultural and natural retreat. It contains several of the city's leading museums, as well as its best-known park, a lovely green

oasis that surrounds Lake Eola, which boasts dramatic skyline vistas and hosts festivals and seasonal celebrations. By day Downtown is a relaxed southern enclave, but by night it transforms into a throbbing club scene – despite the decline of the famous entertainment, dining, and shopping zone, Church Street Station. Orange Avenue is the main street and most evenings, herds of party people, both gay and straight, migrate from club to club in search of cheap drinks and hot DJs – and there are plenty of both.

Orlando Science Center

🔟 Sights

1. Orlando Science Center
2. Orlando Museum of Art
3. Orange County Regional History Center
4. Harry P. Leu Gardens
5. Mennello Museum of American Folk Art
6. The Vietnamese District
7. Lake Eola Park
8. American Ghost Adventures
9. Church Street
10. Colonial Lanes

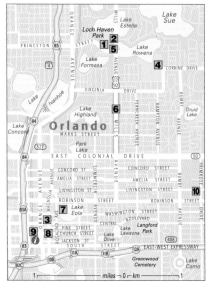

Orlando Science Center

The workings of the natural world, from the infinitesimal to the overwhelming, are on display here. Big interactive fun awaits at the Body Zone, where a huge mouth introduces an exhibit about the digestive system. The vast Cinedome shows movies about topics such as Egyptian treasures and ocean life, and on weekend evenings, stargazers can pick out the planets through a telescope. ◈ *777 E. Princeton St • Map M3 • 407-514-2000 • Open 10am–5pm Sun–Tue & Thu–Sat • Adm • www.osc.org*

Orlando Museum of Art (OMA)

The focus of exhibitions in this big, bright museum is American art from the 19th century onward, art from the ancient Americas and Africa, and blockbuster traveling shows. On the first Thursday evening of every month, you can enjoy music, food, and the work of local artists for an inventively themed get-together. ◈ *2416 N. Mills Ave • Map M3 • 407-896-4231 • 10am–4pm Tue–Fri, noon–4pm Sat–Sun • Adm • www.omart.org*

Orange County Regional History Center

From the informative to the kitsch, the History Center highlights the formative periods and industries of Central Florida. Dioramas show scenes of early Native Americans, and a re-created Florida Cracker house can be inspected. There's also a display called The Day We Changed, which chronicles the impact of the arrival of the Disney theme parks. Some exhibits fall a little flat, but many elements, such as the stuffed alligators and pink flamingos, betray a sense of fun. ◈ *65 E. Central Blvd • Map P3 • 407-836-8500 • 10am–5pm Mon–Sat, noon–5pm Sun • Adm • www.thehistorycenter.org*

Fountain, Lake Eola Park

Harry P. Leu Gardens

Well-tended pathways weave through this elegant 50-acre (20-ha) park. Earthy scents waft from an herb garden, while another contains plants that attract butterflies. Depending on the season, visitors might catch roses in bloom (in Florida's largest rose garden) or the grace of camellias. Guides conduct tours of the early 20th-century Leu House. ◈ *1920 N. Forest Ave • Map M4 • 407-246-2620 • Open 9am–5pm daily • Adm • www.leugardens.org*

Mennello Museum of American Folk Art

Half of the Mennello is devoted to the work of Florida folk artist Earl Cunningham (1893–1977), who created vibrant, whimsical pastoral paintings glowing with orange skies and yellow rivers. The other half houses traveling exhibits of folk art. The lakeside grounds contain wonderfully quirky sculptures scattered here and there. ◈ *900 E. Princeton St • Map M3 • 407-246-4278 • 10:30am–4:30pm Tue–Sat, noon–4:30pm Sun • Adm • www.mennellomuseum.com*

Mennello Museum of American Folk Art

6 The Vietnamese District

This area, also known as the ViMi district (for the crossroads at Virginia and Mills avenues), is a less obvious ethnic enclave than, say, New York's Chinatown. Nevertheless, it is still clustered with Vietnamese restaurants and shops, as well as delights from other Asian countries. The thickest concentration is south of Virginia, at Colonial Drive. ⚲ *Mills Ave bet Virginia Ave & Colonial Dr • Map N3*

7 Lake Eola Park

A pedestrian-only path encircles Lake Eola, offering a pleasing view of Downtown's skyline. Those willing to exert their leg muscles can rent swan-shaped paddle boats *(see p47)*. Real swans drift along in the lake's shallow water and will venture onto dry land if offered a handful of the food that can be bought for small change. Concerts are performed at the Walt Disney Amphitheater, a bandshell with surprisingly decent acoustics. The landmark illuminated fountain in the middle of the lake is computerized and produces on a light show of changing colors. ⚲ *Map P3*

Signs, Vietnamese Disctrict

8 American Ghost Adventures

A guide leads walking tours through Downtown Orlando, telling tales of the city's scandals, unsolved mysteries, and hauntings dating back to 1886. The two-hour walk circles back around to its starting point, the Orange County Regional History Center, where participants can carry out their own amateur ghost hunt with the help of handheld "ghost detectors". ⚲ *Depart from Orange County Regional History Center • Map P3 • 407-256-6225 • 8pm nightly • Adm*

9 Church Street

The Amway Center Arena has brought life and activity back to Church Street. The influx of new restaurants, the renowned drama company Mad Cow Theatre, and the upcoming SunRail station have made it even more popular. The Amway Center attracts big-name touring acts, and the stretch of Church Street that lies between Orange Avenue and I-4 once again has enough retail stores, restaurants, and bars to keep visitors interested. The area's original anchor is Church Street Station, a three-level complex constructed around the attractive historic building that was the city's original train station.The complex holds a variety of bars, restaurants, and shops, and it is easy to zigzag between watering holes. ⚲ *Church St bet. Orange Ave & I-4 • Map P3*

Lake Eola Fountain, Lake Eola Park

Church Street

10 Colonial Lanes

For more than 50 years, the venerable Colonial Lanes has offered patrons the sociable and quintessential blue-collar pastime of bowling. This 32-lane facility is a friendly and noisy place to knock over a few pins, so rent some shoes, pick out a ball, and let the computer keep score – but bear in mind that league bowling takes over the place between 6pm and 9pm every night, so

Bowling balls, Colonial Lanes

avoid those times, unless you're happy to watch. After the game, the place to go is the Colonial Lanes Bar & Restaurant, parts of which resemble a giant sunken living room (with bartenders standing on a lower floor than customers). Drinks are cheap, and the concept of rounding off prices never caught on here, so don't be surprised if your tab is a quirky $4.38. ◈ *400 N. Primrose Dr • Map P4 • 407-894-0361 • Timings vary • Free, but pay to play*

A Day Downtown

Morning

🕐 Begin with a big healthy breakfast at JP's Everyday Gourmet (63 E. Pine St) before visiting the **Orange County Regional History Center**, a homespun place that reveals the pre-Disney history of the region. For lunch, wander over to **Café Annie** *(see p117)*. This authentic café has Greek and Lebanese food, including mixed platters. This kind of food usually has lots of vegetarian options.

Afternoon

After lunch, jump in the car or grab a cab to Loch Haven Park, where the **Orlando Museum of Art**, the **Orlando Science Center,** and the **Mennello Museum of American Folk Art** *(for all see p113)* reside within easy walking distance of each other. The Science Center, with its four floors of interactive fun, is the best bet for kids. Art lovers can easily hit the Mennello and the OMA in the same afternoon but if time is short, the OMA deserves priority. Make a dinner stop in the Vietnamese district where Ha Long Restaurant (1231 E. Colonial Dr) serves up a top-notch bowl of comforting *pho*, a traditional, and delicious noodle soup.

Evening

The downtown club scene starts late, so kick off with an early cocktail at **The Bösendorfer Lounge** *(see p116)*. Fans of live music should head to **The Social** *(see p116)*, where shows start around 10pm. Die-hard clubbers should try **Firestone Live** *(see p76)*, where the DJs play well into the early hours.

Left **The Social** Right **Cowboys Orlando**

🔟 Nightspots

1 The Social

Orlando's best club for live music, bar none. The stage hosts an incredible variety of performers, from jazz to electronica. *See p74.* ◈ *54 N. Orange Ave • Map P3 • 407-246-1419*

2 The Beacham

This historic building in Downtown Orlando houses a state-of-the-art nightclub and live music venue showcasing a variety of musical styles. ◈ *46 N. Orange Ave • Map P3 • 407-246-1419*

3 Cowboys Orlando

This gigantic country music hot spot has four huge bars and nightly dance contests. ◈ *1108 S. Orange Blossom Trail • Map P2 • 407-422-7115 • Closed Sun–Wed*

4 The Bösendorfer Lounge

With upscale elegance, this lounge is perfect for sipping cocktails in stylish surroundings. Lounge singers and pianists play around the $250,000 Bösendorfer piano (Tue–Sat). *See p74.* ◈ *Westin Grand Bohemian Hotel, 325 S. Orange Ave • Map P3 • 866-663-0024*

5 Howl at the Moon

Dueling pianos, nightly sing-alongs and a full bar make this a pleasant nightspot. ◈ *8815 International Dr • Map E3 • Open till 2am • 407-354-5999 • Adm*

6 Sky 60

South Beach-style hip bar with a DJ every night. Great rooftop terrace with mood lighting. ◈ *64 N. Orange Ave • Map P3 • 407-246-1599*

7 Church Street

A two-block strip of bars, restaurants, and clubs that draws party people wanting to steer clear of the trendiness of other downtown clubs. ◈ *Church St, bet Orange Ave & I-4 • Map P3*

8 Firestone Live

This club offers lively techno, rave, and house dance beats. The best time to go is on the weekends, especially Saturday nights when there is a big crowd and occasional live acts. ◈ *578 N. Orange Ave • Map N3 • 407-872-0066*

9 NV Lounge

A small basement venue with dark decor and atmospheric lighting. A good place to hang out, and sample the terrific boutique beer and wine. ◈ *27 E. Pine St • Map P3 • 407-649-0000*

10 180 Grey Goose Lounge

Located in the Amway Arena, this is a before-, during-, and after-game hotspot for drinks and casual conversations on the balcony. ◈ *400 W. Church St • Map D4 • 407-913-0180 • Open on event nights till 2:30am*

Around Town – Downtown Orlando

Unless indicated Downtown's nightspots are open seven nights a week.

Price Categories

For a three-course meal for one with a glass of house wine, and all unavoidable extra charges including tax.	
$	under $20
$$	$20–$30
$$$	$30–$45
$$$$	$45–$60
$$$$$	over $60

The Boheme

🔟 Restaurants & Cafés

K Restaurant and Wine Bar
Downtown's best dining experience mixes bistro warmth with an adventurous menu of Asian, French, and Italian influences. ◈ 1710 Edgewater Dr • Map M2 • 407-872-2332 • Closed Sun • $$$$

The Boheme
This outstanding restaurant, with its sensual paintings and dark woods, serves game, steaks, and seafood to an upscale clientele. See p69. ◈ 325 S. Orange Ave • Map P3 • 407-581-4700 • $$$$$

Napasorn Thai Restaurant
This family-owned restaurant serves traditional Thai dishes and interesting pan-Asian variations. ◈ 56 E. Pine St • Map P2 • 407-245-8088 • $$$

Graffiti Junction American Burger Bar
The graffiti-covered exterior belies a great, high-energy burger joint within. Order the huge "Lone Star" for a messy delight. There is karaoke on Sunday afternoons. ◈ 900 E. Washington St • Map P2 • 407-426-9502 • $$

Café Annie
Head here for authentic Greek and Lebanese food, especially Zorba's platter, the chicken and beef kebabs, couscous and falafel. ◈ 131 N. Orange Ave • Map P3 • 407-420-4041 • Closed Sun • $$$

Dexter's of Thornton Park
A favorite after-work hangout, Dexter's offers exotic sandwiches, hearty salads, and entrées such as seared tuna and steak. ◈ 808 E. Washington St • Map P3 • 407-648-2777 • $$$

Ceviche Tapas Bar & Restaurant
Huge, noisy, and loads of fun, this restaurant offers an enormous menu, a tapas bar, and a large lounge with live flamenco music. ◈ 125 W. Church St • Map P2 • 321-281-8140 • Closed lunch • $$$

Little Saigon
This venue stands out in the city's thriving Vietnamese area for its huge bowls of *pho*, fragrant soup brimming with meat, seafood, noodles, and spices. ◈ 1106 E. Colonial Dr • Map N3 • 407-423-8539 • $$

White Wolf Café
This café serves great salads and Middle-Eastern-inspired fare in a former antiques store. It also sells most of its vintage furnishings. ◈ 1829 N. Orange Ave • Map N3 • 407-895-5590 • $$$

Pine 22
Choose your own combination of organic, grass-fed beef and dozens of locally sourced toppings at this relaxed, upscale burger joint. ◈ 22 E. Pine St • Map P2 • 407-574-2160 • $

Unless stated, all restaurants advise reservations, are non-smoking, take credit cards, have DA, kids' menus, A/C, and vegetarian dishes.

Left **Winter Park street scene** Right **Cornell Fine Arts Museum**

Winter Park, Maitland, & Eatonville

TRUE TO ITS NAME, *Winter Park was chartered in 1887 as a winter resort for wealthy – and cold – Northerners. Now nearly surrounded by metropolitan Orlando, it still retains the charm and character of a wealthy, small town, with excellent shops, bars, and restaurants, and a sprinkling of interesting museums. The towns of Maitland and Eatonville, to the north and east, are more residential, but also have some worthwhile attractions, which make a pleasant change from south Orlando's mass-market theme parks.*

Winter Park Scenic Boat Tour

Top 10 Sights & Attractions

1. Park Avenue
2. Charles Hosmer Morse Museum of American Art
3. Cornell Fine Arts Museum
4. Winter Park Scenic Boat Tour
5. Albin Polasek Museum & Sculpture Gardens
6. Waterhouse Residence & Carpentry Museum
7. Birds of Prey Center
8. Zora Neale Hurston National Museum of Fine Arts
9. Winter Park Farmers' Market
10. Enzian Theater

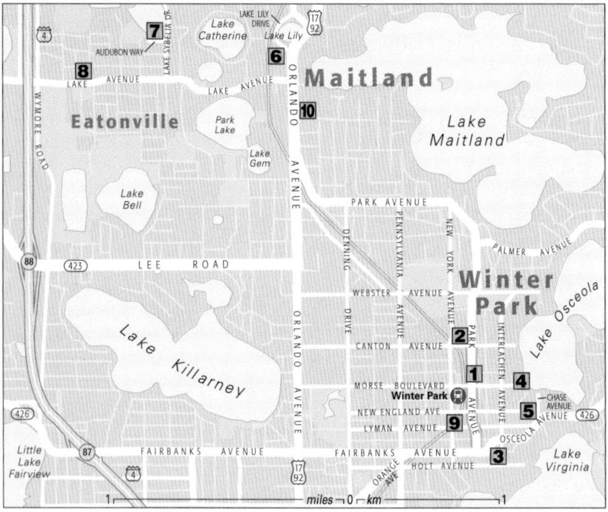

1 Park Avenue

The stretch of Park Avenue between Fairbanks and Webster avenues is a thriving and delectable slice of urban living. This is the kind of manageable, old-style downtown, which is usually erased in the rush to suburbanize the Sunshine State. There's bucolic Central Park; buildings are rarely over three stories and contain fashionable shops or eateries at ground level; and all around, the sidewalks are full of people enjoying the day. ◈ Map L4

Park Avenue

art – from the Renaissance to the 20th century – is impeccably presented and of an unusually high quality for a small college art museum. ◈ 1000 Holt Ave • Map L4 • 407-646-2526 • Open 10am–4pm Tue–Fri, noon–5pm Sat–Sun • Adm • www.rollins.edu/cfam

2 Charles Hosmer Morse Museum of American Art

This museum contains the world's largest collection of beautiful glass windows and objects by American artist Louis Comfort Tiffany. Other highlights include American ceramics and representative collections of late-19th- and early-20th-century paintings, graphics, and decorative arts. ◈ 445 N. Park Ave • Map L4 • 407-645-5311 • Open 9:30am–4pm Tue–Sat (to 8pm Fri Nov–Apr), 1–4pm Sun • Adm • www.morsemuseum.org

Albin Polasek Museum & Sculpture Gardens

4 Winter Park Scenic Boat Tour

The wealthiest sections of Winter Park were built around a series of lakes and along small, winding canals. This boat tour has been running since 1938, and is part nature trip and part local history lesson. It cruises lazily past Winter Park landmarks and lakeside mansions encountering wildlife, while the skipper tells stories about the area's legendary society crowd. See p45. ◈ Morse Blvd at Lake Osceola • Map L4 • 407-644-4056 • Tours depart on the hour 10am–4pm daily • Adm

3 Cornell Fine Arts Museum

The art collection at this museum, located on the scenic Rollins College Campus, is one of the oldest in the state. The range of European and American

Charles Hosmer Morse Museum of American Art

5 Albin Polasek Museum & Sculpture Gardens

Sculptor Albin Polasek moved here to retire, but in fact he kept producing his figurative works until his death in 1965. Now listed on the National Register of Historic Places, the museum and its sculpture gardens contain works spanning Polasek's entire career. ◈ 633 Osceola Ave • Map L4 • 407-647-6294 • Open 10am–4pm Tue–Sat, 1–4pm Sun • Adm • www.polasek.org

Waterhouse Residence & Carpentry Museum

6 Historic Waterhouse Residence & Carpentry Shop Museum

William H. Waterhouse was a carpenter who came to Central Florida in the early 1880s and built this lovely home overlooking Lake Lily. Pristinely restored and maintained by the Maitland Historical Society, the home, Waterhouse's carpentry shop, and the property's remarkable collection of handcrafted furniture offer a glimpse into Maitland's past. Woodworking buffs will be wowed by Waterhouse's extensive use of heart of pine, a wood rarely seen today. Tours lasting about 40 minutes are offered. The Waterhouse facilities complement the Maitland Historical Museum, Maitland Art Center, and Telephone Museum (see p61), all just a few blocks away and also run by the Maitland Historical Society. Ⓢ 820 Lake Lilly Dr • Map K3 • 407-644-2451 • Open noon–4pm Thu–Sun • Adm • artandhistory. org/waterhouse-museum

7 Audubon National Center for Birds of Prey

Think of this place as a halfway house for some of Florida's most impressive birds. It was created by the Florida Audubon Society to rescue, rehabilitate, and release wounded raptors (birds of prey). Those that wouldn't survive being released into the wild are kept here, living a pampered existence in a lovely lakeside location, while helping to educate visitors about wildlife issues and conservation. Guests aren't allowed to observe the rehabilitation process, but permanent residents on view usually include vultures, bald eagles, screech owls, hawks, ospreys, and more. Ⓢ 1101 Audubon Way • Map K3 • 407 644-0190 • Open 10am–4pm Tue–Sun • Adm • www.audubon offlorida.org

8 Zora Neale Hurston National Museum of Fine Arts

Zora Neale Hurston earned fame as one of the brightest stars of Harlem's literary heyday in the 1920 and 1930s. Many of her most famous writings (including the 1937 novel, Their Eyes Were Watching God) reflected life in Eatonville, the first incorporated African-American municipality in the USA. The front porches and stores of Eatonville, where Zora's characters lived and spun their tales, have long since disappeared, but she is not forgotten. This museum keeps the writer's memory alive, and plays a big part in the annual cultural Zora! Festival held in January. The museum also exhibits work by contemporary African-American artists. Ⓢ 227 E. Kennedy Blvd • Map K3 • 407-647-3307 • Open 9am–4pm Mon–Fri, 11am–1pm Sat • Free • www.zoranealehurston museum.com

Birds of Prey Center

Winter Park Farmers' Market

Some farmers' markets are serious business, packed with old trucks and farmers selling mountains of vegetables just pulled from the earth. The Winter Park Farmers' Market is altogether a different affair. More of a social gathering on the village green, Winter Park's yuppies come here to mingle, buy potted flowers, preserves, and herbs, and indulge in fresh croissants, muffins, and breads. Yes, the required vegetables are here, too, but this is more of a coffee and brunch gathering. ® 721 W. New England Ave • Map L4 • 407-599-3397 • Open 7am–1pm Sat • Free

Exhibit, Zora Neale Hurston National Museum of Fine Arts

Enzian Theater

The art of film tastes different at the Enzian. This not-for-profit 250-seat theater doesn't just show American independent and foreign films, but also offers a full menu with beer, wine, and table service. Relax with dinner or snacks and enjoy films with all the comforts of your own living room (if that living room has a 33-ft (10-m) wide screen). The Enzian also produces the 10-day Florida Film Festival (see p65) and smaller niche festivals throughout the year. ® 1300 S. Orlando Ave • Map K3 • 407-629-1088 • Open evenings daily & weekend afternoons • Adm • www.enzian.org

A Day in Winter Park

Morning

Begin with a hearty breakfast at the **Briarpatch Restaurant** (see p123). You'll probably have to wait a bit, especially on weekends, so grab a newspaper. Then take time to wander the north end of **Park Avenue** (see p119), where a multitude of charming one-off boutiques cater to upscale shopping tastes. At Canton Avenue pop in to the **Charles Hosmer Morse Museum** (see p119); its outstanding collection of Tiffany glass is a must-see. Follow this with a relaxing trip on the **Winter Park Scenic Boat Tour** (see p119), which departs from a dock on Morse Street, just a 15-minute walk away. On your return, lunch options are plentiful, but if the weather is good, grab one of the sidewalk tables at the **Park Plaza Gardens** (see p122) for some good food and people-watching.

Afternoon

After lunch, continue south on Park Avenue to Rollins College, home of the excellent **Cornell Fine Arts Museum** (see p119) and spend the rest of the afternoon enjoying this small but excellent collection.

Evening

Then, it's a 10-minute car ride north to Maitland's **Enzian Theater** where you can settle in to enjoy the latest in US and foreign independent films with a bottle of wine and a cheese plate. End the day at the bustling **Brio Tuscan Grille** (see p123) just a few minutes south by car, savoring a pink cosmopolitan or a gorgonzola-encrusted steak.

Around Town – Winter Park, Maitland, & Eatonville

Left **Hillstone** Right **Fiddler's Green**

🔟 Bars & Nightspots

Brio Tuscan Grille
The trendy grill at Brio is wildly popular, but a lot of people come just to hang out at the bar here. Cocktails flow fast and furious for a crowd of well-heeled locals. *See p123.*

Dexter's of Winter Park
Home to a serious collection of wines, this branch of Dexter's is more upscale than Downtown's, except on Thursdays when there's a band playing classic rock. ◈ *558 W. New England Ave • Map L4 • 407-629-1150*

Fiddler's Green
This energetic Irish pub has darts, music, and a full selection of draft beers and stouts. It stays open until 2am most nights, making it popular for a last round. The food is good, too. *See p123.*

Park Plaza Gardens
With tables spilling out onto Park Avenue, this café bar is the bar of choice for those seeking live bands. Popular with the university crowd. *See p123.*

Hannibal's on the Square
Part café, part casual upscale bar, Hannibal's shares space with a tremendous French restaurant, Chez Vincent. ◈ *511 W. New England Ave • Map L4 • 407-629-4865*

Copper Rocket Pub
With a small stage that hosts jazz jams to psycho rock, Copper Rocket is the only true music bar in the area. Microbrews and import beers fuel the young audience. ◈ *106 Lake Ave • Map K3 • 407-645-0069*

Eola Wine Co.
An extensive menu of 70 wines by the glass is on offer at this wine shop and bar. Drinks are complemented by a wide range of snacks and desserts. ◈ *136 Park Ave • Map L4 • 407-647-9103*

Hillstone
At one of Winter Park's top spots in which to be seen, the draw may be the generous glasses of wine, or the fact that the entire restaurant menu is available at the bar. *See p123.*

Shipyard Emporium
A microbrewery and café in one, which brews its own Shipyard beers in big copper stills. Wooden beams and white-washed walls give a nod to the brewery's New England roots. ◈ *200 W. Fairbanks Ave • Map L3 • 321-274-4045*

Mellow Mushroom Beer Bar
This friendly bar offers an extraordinary selection of beers. It serves very good pizza as well. ◈ *2015 Aloma Ave • Map L5 • 407-657-7755*

Winter Park's nightspots are usually open seven days a week.

Price Categories

For a three-course meal for one with a glass of house wine, and all unavoidable extra charges including tax.

$	under $20
$$	$20–$30
$$$	$30–$45
$$$$	$45–$60
$$$$$	over $60

Brio Tuscan Grille

🔟 Cafés & Restaurants

1 Cask & Larder
Local, organic, and Southern food made by James Beard-nominated chefs is served alongside a wide choice of drinks at this brewery and kitchen. ◈ *565 W. Fairbanks Ave • Map L4 • 321-280-4200 • $$$$$*

2 Panullo's Italian Restaurant
From the crispy calamari to the lobster ravioli, this reasonably priced neighborhood eatery is a great place to bring the whole family. ◈ *216 S. Park Ave • Map L4 • 407-629-7270 • $$*

3 Park Plaza Gardens
The menu at this garden restaurant is regional Americana with a focus on seafood, such as blue crab cakes with mustard sauce. *See p69.* ◈ *319 S. Park Ave • Map L4 • 407-645-2475 • $$$$*

4 Fiddler's Green
A wooden bar imported from Ireland, weekly folk bands, and authentic Gaelic dishes contribute to Fiddler's real Irish atmosphere. ◈ *544 W. Fairbanks Ave • Map L3 • 407-645-2050 • $$*

5 4Rivers Smokehouse
Widely acclaimed as the best BBQ in town, this bustling place is always crowded, and worth the wait. ◈ *W. Fairbanks Ave • Map L3 • 407-474-8377 • No vegetarian dishes • $$*

6 Briarpatch Restaurant
Winter Park's homey breakfast landmark is known for big omelets and fresh fruit platters, but the creative, healthy American menu will make you consider returning for lunch. ◈ *252 N. Park Ave • Map L4 • 407-628-8651 • $$*

7 Hillstone
Here, various cuts of meat are chopped thick and cooked on a wood-burning grill. Portions are huge, particularly the salads and desserts. There are also seafood options. ◈ *215 S. Orlando Ave • Map L3 • 407-740-4005 • $$$$*

8 Brio Tuscan Grille
This local favorite has a huge dining room that buzzes with chatter and the sizzle of grilling in the open kitchen. ◈ *480 N. Orlando Ave • Map L3 • 407-622-5611 • $$$*

9 Luma on Park
Superlative cuisine, a head-spinning wine list, and an ultra-hip environment can be found at Luma on Park, which throbs with beautiful people. ◈ *290 S. Park Ave • Map L4 • 407-599-4111 • No kids' menu • Dinner only • $$$$*

🔟 Café de France
Despite the name, this eatery has an international menu served in an upbeat setting. ◈ *526 S. Park Ave • Map L4 • 407-647-1869 • No kids' menu • No vegetarian dishes • $$$$*

 Unless stated, all restaurants advise reservations, are non-smoking, take credit cards, have DA, kids' menus, A/C, and vegetarian dishes.

123

STREETSMART

ORLANDO'S TOP 10

Left **Monorail, Orlando International Airport** Right **Summer theme park crowds**

Things to Know Before You Go

1 Orlando International Airport

Serving more than 100 cities worldwide, and handling 35 million passengers a year, Orlando International is the city's busiest airport. Forty scheduled airlines use it: the major domestic carriers include Delta, American, Spirit, US Airways, JetBlue, Frontier, and Southwest. British Airways, Virgin Atlantic, Air Canada, and Lufthansa are some of its international carriers. Check the website *(see p130)* for information and maps to make sure you don't spend more time there than you need to. The airport is located about a 30-minute drive from Walt Disney World® – if traffic is good.

2 Orlando Sanford International

Orlando's second airport, used primarily by international flights, is around an hour's drive from the Disney resorts. It is far smaller (used by just 1.2 million passengers per year) and promises a less crowded, less hectic start to a vacation.

3 Orlando Executive Airport

Situated just 3 miles (5 km) from the city's business center, Orlando's original airport is today used by private charters for both business and pleasure travelers.

4 US Entry Requirements for Canadian Visitors

Canadians need a passport to travel to the US.

5 US Entry Requirements for Overseas Visitors

International visitors must register with the Electronic System for Travel Authorization (ESTA) well in advance of travel; this can be done online (http://esta.cbp.dhs.gov) or at a travel agents. Citizens from the UK, South Africa, Australia, New Zealand, and many European countries may visit for up to 90 days without a visa if they have a valid passport. Other nationals should apply for a visa from their local US consulate or embassy well before they travel. Visit www.state.gov for the latest information.

6 Arriving by Train & Bus

Two Greyhound bus terminals and four Amtrak rail stations (including Sanford's Auto train terminal) serve the Orlando area. Bus lines such as Red Coach transports visitors within Florida.

7 Consolidators & Packagers

Consolidators buy bulk airline seats (and sometimes rooms) to sell at cheaper prices. Try 800-FLY-CHEAP (800-359-2432; www.1800 flycheap.com). Packagers sell full or partial packages

that can include flight, room, rental car, and theme park tickets. Some parks have their own; or try www.vacation packager. com. ◎ *Disney packages • 407-828-8101 • www. disneyworld.com* ◎ *Sea-World packages • 407-351-3600 • www.seaworld parks.com/seaworld-orlando/ vacations* ◎ *Universal packages • 407-224-7000 • www.universalorlando.com*

8 Beat the Crowds

Theme park crowds are thinnest from the second week in September to the third week in November, the first two weeks of December, mid-January to mid-March, and late April through the third week of May. Weekends are always busy.

9 Weather Wise

Heat and humidity can be oppressive in summer, when temperatures easily hit 90°F (32°C) and lightning is another summer threat. High pollen counts in spring can make life hell for allergy sufferers and hurricane season is from August to November.

10 Online Planning

USA Tourist (www. usatourist.com) has multilingual information on attractions, hotels, restaurants, and more. Search engines are also useful for planning a trip, while Map Quest (www.mapquest.com) can help you plan a route once you've arrived.

Left **I-Ride Trolly** Center **Lynx Bus Stop** Right **Taxi**

🔟 Tips on Getting Around Orlando

1 Renting a Car
Most major car rental companies have offices at or near both major airports, as well as in town. Many also have shuttles serving the Amtrak and Greyhound stations. Most agencies offer special deals via their websites *(see p130)* or packagers. Local maps are provided, and staff can help plan the route to your hotel.

2 Navigating Orlando
The city's major north–south artery is Interstate Highway 4 (Hwy I-4), which connects the main tourist areas. The Beachline Expressway (Hwy 528) is an east–west tollway useful for reaching the Kennedy Space Center *(see pp38–41)*. Most main roads suffer gridlock during rush hour (7–9am and 4–6pm daily).

3 Shuttle Options
Mears shuttle buses travel from Orlando International Airport to hotels (the price varies according to distance), and around the tourist areas, including the Kennedy Space Center. Quick Transportation offers the same service, and can carry up to six people but offers personalized pickup and takes you straight to your destination. ✆ *Mears • 407-423-5566 • www. mearstransportation.com* ✆ *Quick Transportation • 407-354-2456 • www. quicktransportation.com*

4 Hotel Shuttles
Some hotels offer an airport shuttle service, and many offer transport to and from theme parks and other attractions several times per day. The service is usually free of charge to the parks nearest them, or available for a small charge to get to the others. Inquire about services when booking or planning your vacation.

5 Taking a Taxi
Taxis can be an economical way to get around for groups of four or five people. The fares from Orlando International and Orlando Sanford International airports to Walt Disney World® are around $60 and $150 (plus tip) respectively. Extra charges apply at nights, weekends, and on public holidays. Cabs are easily found at airports and major hotels – otherwise call *(see p131)*, as they are not that easy to flag down in the street.

6 The Disney Transportation System
Disney's free transportation system (monorail, buses, water taxis, and ferries) means you can save money by not renting a car and paying for gas and parking. It's best for guests who will spend most of their time with Mickey. But the circuits are set in stone and it can sometimes take an hour to reach some destinations in the resort.

7 The I-Ride Trolley
This service is a convenient and cheap way to get from A to B along the Universal, Sea-World®, and International Drive corridor. Trolleys run every 20–30 minutes, 8am–10:30pm daily, and make 42 stops. Exact change is required. ✆ *407-248-9590 • www.iridetrolley.com*

8 Lynx Buses
Other than walking or cycling, Orlando's public bus system is the least popular way for most visitors to get around: buses can be frustratingly slow. Bus stops are marked with a paw print. Exact change is required. ✆ *Lynx Downtown Bus Terminal • 78 W. Central Blvd • 407-841-8240 • www.golynx.com*

9 Hiring a Limo
The least economical but most luxurious way to get around is by limousine – an option for travelers who want to be pampered and who have deeper pockets. ✆ *Advantage Limousine Service • 407-438-8888 • www.advantagelimo.com*

10 Walking
This is one of the USA's most dangerous cities for pedestrians: apart from wide highways with fast-moving traffic, there's a shortage of sidewalks, crosswalks, and street lights.

Left **Newspaper vending machines** Right **Kissimmee Convention & Visitors Bureau**

Sources of Information

1 Orlando/Orange Co. Convention & Visitors Bureau

Billed as "the official destination marketing organization for Orlando", this group provides an impressively comprehensive service. Their website is outstanding, offering up-to-date information and on-line booking, while the office can provide maps, directions, and answer questions. ® *8723 International Dr • 407-363-5872 • www.visitorlando.com*

2 Kissimmee/St. Cloud Convention & Visitors Bureau

Focusing on the south of Orlando, this organization offers an excellent website and an office stocked with brochures from area attractions. ® *215 Celebration Pl • 407-742-8200 • www.visitkissimmee.com*

3 Orlando Sentinel

The sole major daily newspaper in town is conservative in political matters, but the Friday edition carries an excellent arts and events section called the Calendar. There's an on-line version too (www.orlandosentinel.com).

4 Orlando Weekly

O-Town's primary "alternative" paper is this free weekly, which carries excellent and extremely detailed club and arts listings. The columnists –

all good, some hilarious – know the local scene intimately. The paper's website (www.orlandoweekly.com) offers all the articles as well as terrific search capabilities for movie and music listings. The paper is available in restaurants, shops, clubs, convenience stores, and street boxes all over town.

5 Watermark

This free bi-weekly newspaper is the voice of Orlando's extensive gay and lesbian community. Not particularly radical, it offers splendid coverage of arts and events and is the best resource for clubs, shows, and more for the community. Available at gay-friendly businesses and in street boxes. There's also an on-line version: www.watermarkonline.com.

6 Lesbian, Gay, Bisexual & Transgender Community Services of Central Florida

This LGBT community center is the city's clearinghouse for gay community information, ranging from art openings to health alerts. The organization regularly sponsors a variety of cultural events around town. ® *407-228-8272 • www.thecenterorlando.com*

7 News Channel 13

This is Orlando's own version of CNN – a 24-hour cable news channel

devoted to O-Town. It is probably most useful to visitors for the weather update that runs every ten minutes (1:01, 1:11, 1:21, etc). ® *Only available on TVs subscribed to Time Warner Cable*

8 WTKS 104.1-FM

The weekday schedule of this radio station is filled with local talk radio personalities hosting shows including "Monsters in the Morning," "SBK Live," and "The Phillips Phile." All offer an interesting window into Orlando's current state of mind. On weekends, the format switches to classic rock.

9 WMFE 90.7-FM

This station is the area's outlet for all-day programming from National Public Radio, including intelligent hourly news. It's a respite from the fanatical talk shows and light pop music broadcast by many of the other local radio stations.

10 Brochure Racks

Virtually every hotel, restaurant, and attraction offers a huge lobby display packed with brochures and tourist guides covering almost all the hotels, restaurants, and smaller attractions in the area. Besides the maps and general information, discount coupons are common in these publications, so they're worth picking up *(see p133)*.

SeaWorld® Adventure Camp

Behind-the-Scenes Tours

1 Backstage Magic

Disney's most complete but expensive tour is ideal for guests who have to know how things tick. The seven-hour visit explores the inner workings of Epcot® technology, the Tower of Terror at Disney Hollywood Studios®, and the Magic Kingdom®'s underground operations hub. ✆ 407-939-8687 • Max 20 people, 16 yrs & over • 9am Mon–Fri

2 Keys to the Kingdom

A useful, 4–5 hour Magic Kingdom® taster tour for guests who'd like to see what's on offer before they really get started. It gives a basic park orientation as well as a glimpse of some of the usually hidden high-tech magic. ✆ 407-939-8687 • Min age 16 yrs • Cost does not include park adm • 8:30am, 9am & 9:30am daily

3 Around the World at Epcot®

This 2-hour Segway tour offers a closer view than most park guests get of Epcot®'s multi-cultural treasures. ✆ 407-939-8687 • Max 10 people, min age 16 yrs • Cost does not include park adm • 7:45am, 8:30am, 9am, 9:30am

4 Family Magic Tour

Kids love this two-hour scavenger hunt in Disney World's most child-friendly park, the Magic Kingdom®. Characters also meet guests at the end of the tour. ✆ 407-939-8687 • Cost does not include park adm • 10am daily.

5 VIP Tours

Both Disney and Universal offer VIP tours – at a price. Disney's lets guests create their own itinerary, which could take in one or more parks, meals, golf, spa treatments, and more. The tour includes reserved show seating and expedited access to rides. Universal's five-hour fixed tour offers line-cutting privileges at up to eight rides and shows. ✆ Disney • 407-560-4033 • Up to 10 people per tour, 5-hour min ✆ Universal • 407-363-8000 • 10am & noon daily

6 Scenic/Eco Lake Tours

See the real Florida and its wildlife during a fascinating one-hour narrated tour in a 24-ft (7-m) pontoon boat. Fishing and private charters, as well as island and gator tours, are also available. ✆ 101 Lakeshore Blvd, Kissimmee • 800-244-9105, 407-908-5688 • www.fishingchartersinc.com

7 Yuletide Fantasy

It's hard to beat Disney's Christmas celebration. This 3-hour tour gives guests a front-row look at how the four theme parks and resorts are transformed into a winter wonderland. Highlights include a candlelight procession and Epcot®'s massed choir. This tour is guaranteed to get visitors into the holiday spirit. ✆ 407-939-8687 • Park adm not required • 9am Mon–Sat Nov 30–Dec 24

8 SeaWorld® Adventure Camp

During the summer, Sea-World® offers several day programs to suit all budgets. The camps are divided by age from preschool through 8th grade (13 yrs) and are designed to help kids better understand the marine animal world. There are family sleep-over programs, too. ✆ 407-370-1380 • Jun–Aug

9 Up-Close Tours

Get a close-up look at SeaWorld®'s penguin, dolphin, and sea lion habitats, with opportunities to feed or touch the animals, in 45–60-min walking tours. ✆ 407-351-3600 • Cost does not include park adm • Times vary

10 Family Fun Tour

A 4-hour tour behind the scenes at SeaWorld®, including reserved seats at the One Ocean show, front-of-the-line access to some family rides, and a light meal at Happy Harbor. Kids will enjoy visiting Shamu the killer whale. ✆ 407-351-3600 • Cost does not include park adm • Times vary

Useful Addresses

Tourist Information

Orlando/Orange County Convention & Visitors' Bureau
6700 Forum Dr, Ste 100 (I-D)
• 407-363-5872 • www.
visitorlando.com

Tourist Information Center
8723 International Dr (I-D)
• 407-363-5872

Websites

Orlando's Weekly Calendar
http://calendar.
orlandoweekly.com

Citysearch
orlando.citysearch.com

The Daily City
www.the dailycity.com

Inside Central Florida
www.wftv.com/icflorida

Theme Park Insider
www.themeparkinsider.com

Visit Orlando
www.visitorlando.com

Airports

Orlando Executive Airport (ORL)
501 Herndon Ave • 407-894-9831 • www.orlando
airports.net/orl

Orlando International Airport (MCO)
1 Airport Blvd • 407-825-2001
• www.orlando airports.net

Orlando Sanford Airport (SFB)
2 Red Cleveland Blvd, Sanford
• 407-322-7771 • www.
orlandosanfordairport.com

American Automobile Association (AAA)

783 S. Orlando Ave • 407-647-1033 • www.aaa.com

Amtrak Train Stations

1400 Sligh Blvd (DO)
• 407-843-7611
• www.amtrak.com

150 W. Morse Blvd (WP)
• 407-645-5055
• www.amtrak.com

600 S. Persimmon Ave
(Sanford) • 407-330-9770
• www.amtrak.com

111 E. Dakin St (K)
• 407-933-1170
• www.amtrak.com

Greyhound Bus Terminals

103 E. Dakin Ave (K) • 888-332-6363; 407-847-3911
• www.greyhound.com

555 N. John Young Pkwy
(DO) • 888-332-6363; 407-292-3424 • www.grey
hound.com

Car Rental

Alamo
8200 McCoy Rd
• 800-462-5266
• www.alamo.com

Avis
8600 Hangar Blvd
• 800-230-4898
• www.avis.com

Budget
1 Airport Blvd
• 800-527-7000
• www.budget.com

Dollar
9201 Airport Blvd
• 800-800-4000
• www.dollarcar.com

Enterprise
9400 Airport Blvd
• 800-325-8007
• www.enterprise.com

Hertz
1 Airport Blvd
• 800-654-3131
• www.hertz.com

National
5398 Bear Rd • 800-227-7368 • www.national
car.com

Thrifty
9302 Airport Rd • 800-847-4389 • www.thrifty.com

Taxis & Private Cars

Mears
324 W. Gore St
•407-422-2222 •www.
mearstransportation.com

Airport Orlando Shuttle
•407-797-0717
•airportorlandoshuttle.com

Orlando Airport Van
•866-204-4000 • www.
orlandoairportvan.us

Banks

Bank of America
390 N. Orange Ave (DO)
• 407-244-7041

Chase
7674 Dr. Phillips Blvd
(WDW) • 407-352-5832

Regions Bank
111 N. Orange Ave (DO)
• 800-734-4667

517 Morse Blvd (WP)
• 800-734-4667

SunTrust
1675 E. Buena Vista Dr
(WDW) • 407-828-6103

1000 N. Main St (K)
• 407-870-0022

400 S. Park Ave (WP)
• 800-786-8787

Wells Fargo
7950 Orange Blossom Tr
(I-D) • 407-649-5158

Credit Cards

American Express
800-528-4800
• www.american
express.com

Key: DO: Downtown; I-D: International Drive; K: Kissimmee; WDW:
Walt Disney World & Lake Buena Vista; WP: Winter Park & Maitland

Diners Club
800-234-6377 • www.dinersclub.com

Discover
800-347-2683 • www.discovercard.com

MasterCard
800-826-2181 • www.mastercard.com

Visa
800-336-8472 • www.visa.com

Hospitals

Celebration Health
400 Celebration Pl (WDW)
• 407-303-4000

Dr. P. Phillips Hospital
9400 Turkey Lake Rd (I-D)
• 407-351-8550

Florida Hospital
601 E. Rollins St
(DO) • 407-303-5600

Orlando Health
1414 Kuhl Ave (DO)
• 321-841-5415

Winter Park Memorial Hospital
200 N. Lakemont Ave (WP)
• 407-646-7000

Walk-In Clinics

Centra Care Walk-In Clinic
12500 S. Apopka Vineland Rd (WDW)
• 407-934-2273

4320 W. Vine St (K)
• 407-390-1888

ExpressCare
2700 Old Winter Garden Rd (DO) • 407-656-2055

Nightlight Pediatrics
7556 W. Sandlake Rd (ID)
• 407-506-0002

WinterPark Family Practice
2950 Aloma Ave (WP)
• 407-679-9222

24-hour Pharmacy

CVS Pharmacy
1205 W. Vine St (K)
• 407-847-5174

7599 W. Sandlake Rd (ID)
• 407-352-1177

Walgreens
2420 E. Colonial Dr (DO)
• 407-894-6781

6201 International Dr (I-D) • 407-345-8402

13502 Apopka Vineland Rd (WDW) • 407-348-2323

Dentists

Advanced Dental Care
12131 S. Apopka Vineland Rd (WDW) • 407-477-5004

Coast Dental
2200 E. Irlo Bronson Memorial Hwy (K) • 407-935-1772

2907 Vineland Rd (K)
• 407-396-1288

Greenburg Dental Associates
4780 S. Kirkman Rd (I-D)
• 407-292-7373

3727 N. Goldenrod Rd (WP)
• 407-671-0001

Help Lines

Central Florida Helpline
407-333-9028

Society for Accessible Travel & Hospitality
212-447-7284

Help Now of Osceola
407-847-8562

Internet Access

Orlando Public Library
101 E. Central Blvd (DO)
• 407-835-7323

South Orange Library
7255 Della Dr
• 407-835-7323

Post Offices

51 E. Jefferson St (DO)
• 407-425-6464

10450 Turkey Lake Rd (I-D)
• 407-351-2492

2600 Michigan Ave (K)
• 407-846-0999

8546 Palm Parkway (WDW)
• 800-275-8777

300 N. New York Ave (WP)
• 407-647-6807

Police

City of Kissimmee Police
8 N. Stewart Ave (K) • 407-847-0176 • Emergency: 911

City of Orlando Police
100 S. Hughey Ave (I-D)
• 407-246-2470
• Emergency: 911

Orange County Sheriff
2500 W. Colonial Dr (DO)
• 407-254-7000
• Emergency: 911

Osceola County Sheriff
2601 E. Irlo Bronson Memorial Hwy (K) • 407-348-1100
• Emergency: 911

Winter Park Police
500 N. Virginia Ave (WP)
• 407-644-1313
• Emergency: 911

Consulates

Germany
100 N. Biscayne Blvd, Ste 2200, Miami • 305-358-0290

Canada
200 S. Biscayne Blvd, Ste 1600, Miami • 305-579-1600

Japan
80 S.W. 8th St, Miami
• 305-530-9090

United Kingdom
200 S. Orange Ave, Ste 2110, Orlando • 407-254-3300

For more on tourist information See p128

Left **Fastpass ticket outlet** Center **Souvenirs from SeaWorld®** Right **Disney memorabilia**

Tips on Shopping & Tickets

1 Shopping Hours
Shops in theme parks keep the same hours as the parks. Malls and outlets are usually open from 9 or 10am until 9pm Monday to Saturday and at least noon to 6pm on Sunday. Shops outside the main tourist areas tend to open from 9am to 5pm Monday through Saturday.

2 Sales Tax
With the exception of groceries and some medications, all purchases in Orlando are subject to a 6.5 percent state and local sales tax.

3 Sales
Look for winter-wear bargains from March through April, and summer bargains from August to October as the seasonal stock changes. In August, with the approach of the new school year, there are good buys on kids' clothes. The day after Thanksgiving is the biggest shopping day of the year, with huge pre-Christmas sales attracting hordes of shoppers.

4 Outlets
Outlet stores sell last season's fashions at discounted prices. Shoppers who know the suggested retail prices of the goods they seek will be able to tell what is – and what isn't – a bargain. Some stores promise as much as 75 per cent discount and some actually deliver. Others don't. The big

player is Orlando Premium Outlets, with two giant locations *(see p66)*.

5 Gifts & Souvenirs
Apart from cheap T-shirts, stuffed animals, and baseball caps, Orlando does have some more original souvenirs. These include Florida oranges, alligator meat and leather products, and manatee memorabilia.

6 Shipping Home
If you have bought more souvenirs than you can carry home, why not ship them? Disney and Universal parks, resorts, and shops can make the arrangements, usually via United Parcel Service (UPS). Do-it-yourselfers must take their packages to UPS (call 1-800-742-5877 for the nearest center) or the US Postal Service (1-800-275-8777).

7 Buy Theme Park Tickets Online
Disney (www.disneyworld.com) allows guests to buy tickets online, saving on time waiting in line, but they must be picked up in person. Universal (www.universalorlando.com) allows visitors to print out tickets or pick them from the will-call gate for an additional $2.50 per ticket. SeaWorld®'s online service (www.seaworld.com) lets buyers print out their tickets and, when they arrive at the park, go straight to the turnstiles, where they are verified.

8 Multi-Day & Multi-Park Passes
Disney's Park Hopper and Park Hopper Plus tickets are valid for four to seven days. Both include unlimited entry to the four parks; the Park Hopper Plus tickets also include entry to other Disney attractions. The discounts aren't great, but you save time waiting in line. Universal Studios Florida®, Universal's Islands of Adventure®, Wet'n Wild®, Sea World® Orlando, Aquatica® Water Park, and Busch Gardens® Tampa Bay have joined up to offer the unlimited access, 14-day FlexTicket.

9 Cutting in Line
Disney (FastPass) and Universal and SeaWorld® (Express Access) offer a system that cuts out the long wait for the most popular rides and shows. Just slide your ticket through the turnstile to get an allocated time for your visit. When it's time, simply go to the particular attraction's designated entrance to take your place.

10 Concierge Desks
Most upscale and some moderately priced hotels have concierge desks in the lobby. They're great places to make restaurant reservations or buy tickets for theme parks and other attractions. They don't give discounts, but most do offer the convenience of waiting in a short line as opposed to a long one in the parks.

Left **Hotel shuttle bus** Right **Leaflets in a hotel lobby**

🔟 Tips for the Budget Conscious

1 The Magicard
The Orlando/Orange County CVB's *(see p128)* Magicard offers $500 worth of discounts on accommodation, car rentals, attractions, meals, shopping, and more. It also offers deals that combine rooms with attraction and theme park tickets. Each card is valid for up to six people, and it's free. Allow four weeks for delivery.
🕿 407-363-5872
• www.visitorlando.com

2 Hotel Handouts
Many hotels and motels offer freebies such as continental breakfasts, evening hors d'oeuvres, and newspapers. Their coupon racks are stuffed with two-for-one and other special deals on meals and attractions. For those without a car, most hotels have free or low-fee shuttle services to the parks.

3 Newspaper Coupons
The Sunday travel sections in many major US newspapers lure people to Orlando with offers of coupons, cheap fares, and package deals. Once here, read the Orlando Sentinel (especially Friday's Calendar section), as well as the free papers available on street corners and in hotel lobbies, all of which feature lots of discounts and offers. See p128.

4 Rooms with Cooking Facilities
Travelers can save big by booking a room with a kitchen, kitchenette, or even just a microwave and refrigerator. Apart from Walt Disney World properties, most accommodation is close to supermarkets or delicatessens, some of which deliver for a small fee.

5 Pack a Snack & Water
Theme-park prices for refreshments are 30–50 percent higher than what people pay outside the parks. The parks prohibit coolers (containers for keeping food and drink cool), but guests can bring their own bottled water and snacks. Some parks have fountains, but the water in Central Florida does not taste particularly sweet.

6 Eat Big Early & Late
It's often unnecessary to eat three big meals a day, particularly in the hottest months of the year. If you want to skip, or go light on, lunch, you can eat well – and cheaply – before and after your theme-park visit by having a low-priced, all-you-can-eat, buffet breakfast and an early-bird dinner *(see p134)*.

7 Fast Food & Family Restaurants
Orlando is chock-full of fast-food outlets. The city also has an abundance of very well-priced family restaurants *(see pp70–71)*. Most have kids' menus, which can be even cheaper at lunchtime.

8 Red Chair Project
The cultural crowd isn't left out of the discount mix. The city's CVB *(see p128)* regularly has half-price tickets, including those for opera, ballet, music, and theater. The tickets are for same-day performances, and while information is available by phone, the tickets must be picked up in person. 🕿 407-872-2382

9 Staying at Disney on the Cheap
People who really want to stay at Disney World, but can't afford the prices, can find the cheapest rates at the All-Star resorts *(see p142)*. Rack rates (those anyone can get without a discount) are extraordinarily reasonable and kids also stay free. But be warned: rooms at these "value" resorts are very cramped.

10 Gas for Renters
Never buy gas for a rental car from the car hire company itself. Some of their offers sound enticing, especially those offering cheaper gas if you buy up front rather than when the car is returned. Most of the time, fuel prices are cheaper – sometimes much cheaper – around town.

Buffet breakfast

Tips on Eating & Drinking

1 Disney Restaurant Reservations

Some Disney restaurants use Priority Seating; kind of a FastPass for food. The more upscale ones ask for reservations, sometimes as much as 180 days in advance. Be aware that diners who do not show up are charged anyway. Note that all restaurants inside Disney parks, except Animal Kingdom's Rainforest Café, require park admission.

2 Reservations

Whenever restaurants accept reservations, make them – especially in the main tourist areas of I-Drive, Lake Buena Vista, and along Irlo Bronson Memorial Highway in Kissimmee. Not having a reservation can mean waiting two hours for a table during prime dining time, usually 6–8:30pm. Some restaurants refuse to seat diners who have not reserved in advance and upscale eateries may be unable to accommodate you unless you reserve far ahead.

3 Gratuities

Wait staff expect a tip of at least 15 percent. Those who are particularly helpful may deserve 20 percent; you may want to give just 10 per cent to those who aren't. Some restaurants now add tips to the bill, so check before paying.

4 Smoking

After the laws were passed most hotels and all restaurants are now non-smoking establishments. If you want to smoke while you drink, you have to find a bar where eating is only incidental to drinking. If you aren't sure, just smoke outside.

5 Buffet Breakfast Bargains

There are several modestly priced, all-you-can-eat breakfast buffets around town (especially on I-Drive and in Kissimmee). For a handful of dollars, you can fill your stomach and save money by eating a light lunch or skipping it altogether.

6 Early Birds

Some value restaurants offer cut-rate meals when business is slow, which is usually between 4pm and 6pm, Monday–Friday. These early-bird deals are usually advertised outside and are offered in the free coupon books found in hotel lobbies and tourist attractions. Many of these restaurants also offer 2-for-1 drink specials during these times.

7 Lunch Menus vs Dinner Menus

Many upscale restaurants are not only hard to get in to at dinnertime, but the menus are very expensive. The lunch menu might have fewer options, and portions tend to be a little less generous, but the prices are lower. To save money – and your digestive system – consider eating your main meal at mid-day and eating lighter at night.

8 Special Diets

Some restaurants that don't normally offer meat- and seafood-free options are happy to prepare vegetarian dishes, with some prior warning. Disney restaurants go one step further and provide for a variety of other dietary needs, including kosher, fat- or sugar-free, plus lactose intolerance and allergies. Give 24 hours' notice.
🕾 407-824-2222
(407-939-3463 if staying on Disney property).

9 Happy Hours

Many bars (and restaurants) have happy hours, usually from 4–7pm, when drinks are often two for the price of one. They sometimes serve special hors d'oeuvres as well.

10 Hotel Mini Bars

Put bluntly, these are rip-offs. Years ago, inventive guests drank the good stuff and refilled the bottles with cheap brands. So now the mini bars have a sensor: remove the bottle for 10 seconds and you get charged – a lot – for it.

Left **Sun protection** Right **24-hour pharmacy**

🔟 Health Tips

1 Heat, Sun & Insects

Heat and humidity during the summer season (June to mid-September) can cause dehydration, so be sure to drink at least two quarts (two liters) of fluids (preferably water) each day, and wear a wide-brimmed hat and airy clothes. Not only does too much sun result in nasty burns, but it can also cause sun poisoning. Use a sunscreen with a high protection factor. And as much as Disney and Universal want to erase blood-sucking flies and mosquitoes, they can't, so remember to use insect repellent in summer.

2 911

This is the number to call for emergency health matters and for immediate police or fire assistance.

3 Hospitals & First Aid

Ask at your hotel or resort reception for the nearest hospital. Make sure you have some kind of insurance, otherwise hospital costs can be crippling. All of the major parks have first-aid clinics for minor ailments.

4 Ask-A-Pharmacist

Most pharmacists are happy to give you first aid advice, as well as advice regarding how to take medicines. Most pharmacies are not open 24 hours, but pharmacists will usually give advice over the phone so call a Walgreens or a CVS Pharmacy, which are usually open 24 hours. See p131.

5 In-Room Medical Care

House calls are a thing of the past in most US cities, but the tourist areas in Orlando have two services that make house and hotel-room calls. Doctors on Call Service and Centra Care In-Room Services cover most of the areas from Downtown south to Disney and Kissimmee.
Ⓢ *Doctors on Call Service • 407-399-3627* Ⓢ *Centra Care In-Room Services • 407-238-2000*

6 Centra Care Walk-In Clinics

Centra Care (affiliated with the Florida Hospital) has walk-in clinics scattered throughout Orange, Seminole, and Osceola counties *(see p131)*. These clinics can handle minor emergencies (broken limbs, cuts requiring stitches, and fevers), but not life-threatening situations, for which you should call 911.

7 24-Hour Pharmacies

Several drug stores sell over-the-counter and prescription drugs around the clock *(see p131)*. Additional pharmacies, with regular hours, are listed in the Yellow Pages.

8 Dental Referral Service

This nationwide, toll-free service helps people to find the nearest suitable dentist. The telephones are answered 8am–8pm Monday–Friday; the automated answering service informs callers of the website then puts them on hold to speak to an operator. Those who prefer to choose for themselves, or anyone needing 24-hour aid, should use the Yellow Pages *(or see p131)*. Ⓢ *888-343-3440 800-511-8663 • www.dentalreferral.com*

9 Poison Control

This 24-hour hotline can and has saved lives. Operators can help deal with a problem, summon rescuers, and answer questions. But, don't overlook 911 for any emergency situation.
Ⓢ *800-222-1222.*

10 Visit Florida

While it shouldn't be used for emergencies, Florida's official tourism marketing corporation can provide basic information about medical services and assistance throughout the state. It also has a range of other services, including assistance with lost credit cards and documents, help with accidents, directions, and more. Operators can help in more than 150 languages. Ⓢ *850-488-5607 • www.visitflorida.org*

Left **ATM machine** Right **Quarters (25¢) & pennies (1¢)**

Communications & Money Tips

1 Making Phone Calls

Orlando's numbers have 10 digits – the area code (Central Florida's are 407 and 321), plus the seven-digit number. If calling a number with a different area (or toll-free) code, dial 1 before the code and phone number. To make calls overseas, consider buying a phone card.

2 Internet Access

Many coffee shops, restaurants, and office copy stores *(see p131)* offer free Wi-Fi access. Public libraries and the airport provide free access to the Internet.

3 Languages

Disney, Universal, and larger hotels have multilingual staff who speak Spanish, French, German, and, in some cases, Dutch, Japanese, and other languages. They also have information printed in these languages. The Orlando/ Orange County Convention & Visitors Bureau and USA Tourist have multilingual websites.
- www.visitorlando.com
- www.usatourist.com

4 Post Offices

The United States Postal Service (USPS) *(see p131)* has 11 post offices in the Orlando area. Opening hours vary, but they are usually 9am to 5pm weekdays, although some open Saturday mornings as

well. Drugstores and hotels often sell stamps, but they are slightly more expensive than those sold at post offices. Mailboxes, which are blue, are on most main streets and in hotels. Most major hotels also have daily collection services.

5 Credit Cards & Traveler's Checks

Most hotels, restaurants, attractions, and shops accept American Express, Discover, MasterCard, and Visa credit cards. Some also take Diners Club, Carte Blanche, and JCB cards. US dollar denominations of American Express, Thomas Cook, and Visa traveler's checks are widely accepted with ID.

6 Currency & Exchanges

Dollar notes come in $1, $5, $10, $20, $50, and $100 bills. Coins in circulation are of 1 cent, 5 cents (a nickel), 10 cents (a dime), and 25 cents (a quarter) value. One-dollar and 50 cent coins exist but are very rare. Currency exchanges are based at all the airports, major branches of banks, and near guest services or guest relations in all major theme parks.

7 ATMs

Automatic Teller Machines (ATMs) are located at almost all bank branches, in all major theme parks, major

shopping malls, some hotels, and at airports. Most also accept withdrawals on American Express, MasterCard, and Visa credit cards. There is a $1.50 to $3 advance charge for cards not affiliated to that particular bank. It's often cheaper to use a debit card, but not all debit systems are supported by US banks; check the symbols on the ATM to see if yours is one that is accepted.

8 Bank Opening Hours

Most Central Florida banks are open 9am to 4pm weekdays (to 6pm on Friday). A few branches also open Saturday mornings. Most have ATMs with 24-hour access.

9 Western Union

International money transfers can be sent to more than 101,000 Western Union agents and offices in 187 countries. They can also arrange international telegrams.
- 1-800-325-6000

10 Taxes

The USA doesn't have a national sales tax. Instead, individual states and counties set the rate of sales tax. Florida levies a 6 percent sales tax (6.5 percent in Orlando) on everything except groceries and certain medicines. Hotels also add an extra 3 to 5 percent bed tax *(see p141)*.

For useful addresses **See pp130–31**

Left **Valuables** Center **Orange County Sheriff's car** Right **Residential speed limit**

SPEED
LIMIT
35

🔟 Safety Tips

On the Coast
Florida's beaches are usually well supervised by lifeguards, but still keep a close eye on young children and stick to areas where you can see the lifeguards. The same goes for rivers and pools.

Non-Emergency Numbers
Outside city limits, county sheriff's offices *(see p131)* are the primary police agencies: in Central Florida they are in Orange County, Osceola County, and Seminole County. For traffic and highway-related matters, call the Florida Fish and Wildlife Commision. For coastal issues, see the Florida Marine Patrol. ◎ *Florida Highway Patrol • 407-897-5959* ◎ *Fish and Wildlife Commission • 352-732-1225*

Hurricanes
The coast is usually hit hard by hurricanes, but Central Florida is also affected. Hurricane season is from August to November. If caught in one, stay inside, away from windows, and have water, canned food, and a flashlight to hand. For more tips and up-to-date forecasts, see the National Hurricane Center. ◎ *www.nhc.noaa.gov*

General Safety
Always keep car and hotel-room doors locked. Before leaving, ask the rental-car company, your hotel's front-desk staff, or Visit Florida, the Florida tourism marketing corporation *(see p135)* for the safest and most direct route to your destination. Don't let strangers change your currency, and when paying for anything, check you've been given the correct change before leaving the premises.

Valuables
Smart travelers leave valuables at home. If you do bring watches, jewelry, or other items of value, keep them in a hotel safe. The safes in hotel rooms should only be used for less valuable items. It's also advisable to carry credit cards or traveler's checks rather than large amounts of cash.

Stay in Populated, Well-Lit Areas
Orlando doesn't have the same crime rate as many cities, but it has its share of thieves who prey on the unsuspecting. At night, avoid badly lit areas (especially Downtown's westside, south of Colonial Drive), and at all times be wary of pickpockets.

Lost Children
Nothing frightens a parent or guardian more than turning away for a moment only to find their child gone. It happens every day in Orlando's theme parks. To help staff reunite familes, children under seven should wear tags with their name, hotel, and a contact number on it. When any member of your group gets lost, find a park employee for assistance.

Seat Belts
Florida law requires seat belts to be worn by the driver and all passengers. Children five years and under need a federally approved child restraint: for those under three years the restraint must be a child seat; children four through five years can use a child seat or a seat belt. A fine of at least $50 will be made for non-compliance.

Drinking & Driving
In a word: Don't. Florida strictly enforces this law. Violators risk time in jail if convicted of a drink-driving offense. Have a designated driver in the group, skip alcohol for the night, use public transport, or take taxis. Police are known to survey bars to see who is drinking, then wait outside until drinkers get in a car to drive off, when they are tested.

Speed Limits
Speed limits on interstates, toll roads, and major highways range from 55 to 70 mph (88–112 kmph). On smaller highways, the limit is 45 mph (72 kmph), and in residential areas, it's 25 to 35 mph (40–56 kmph). Fines begin at $160, doubling if it's in a school or construction zone.

Left **Mobility products** Center **Disabled parking facility** Right **Mature travelers**

Tips for Seniors & Disabled People

Orlando for Mature Travelers
VisitOrlando.com has plenty of suggestions for older travelers who prefer to balance theme park fun with more relaxing cultural pursuits.
⊗ 407-363-5872 • www.visitorlando.com

AARP
The AARP (American Association of Retired Persons) is America's most vocal group for seniors, but it doesn't forget there's room for fun. The website's travel articles are available to the public, but only members find out about AARP's travel deals and discounts. Membership costs are minimal but require a US address.
⊗ 1-202-434-2277 • www.aarp.org

Road Scholar
This educational travel organization sends people 55 and over on courses (usually for a week) all over the world. The choice of courses in Orlando is astounding, from travel photography to politics and philosophy. Stay at retreats, hotels, or campsites. ⊗ 1-800-454-5768
• www.roadscholar.org

Disney Grandkids & You Getaway
Knowing that a lot of seniors come to Orlando with their grandkids, Disney occasionally offers discounted packages. Most include three nights in a Disney hotel, multiple-day tickets to the parks, and a range of goodies for the kids, such as dolls and autograph books. ⊗ 407-934-7639
• www.disneyworld.com

Accessible Mini Van Rentals
This service offers accessible van rentals by the day, week, or month. Vehicles include rear- and side-entry vans, and minivans with ramps or electric lifts. ⊗ 6307 Hansel Ave, Orlando • 407-438-8010
• www.accessibleminivanrentals.com

Walker Medical & Mobility Products
The local franchise for Walker Medical & Mobility Products rents wheelchairs and three-wheel rechargeable electric scooters, including ones for people weighing more than 375 lbs (170 kg). They all fit into Disney's transport vehicles and can be taken apart to fit into cars. The company delivers to local hotels and houses. ⊗ 888-726-6837
• www.walkermobility.com

Disney for Disabled Guests
The free *Guidebook for Guests with Disabilities* details special needs services, including: accessibility in parks; Braille directory locations; special-needs parking; wheelchair and electric-cart rentals; audio tours; and translator units for the deaf. They are available at Guest Services in all the theme parks or at Disney hotels' front desks. ⊗ 407-824-4321
• www.disneyworld.com

Universal for Disabled Guests
Universal's parks and hotels have the following services: audio guides; wheelchair and scooter rentals; and telecommunications devices for the deaf. A free booklet is available from Guest Relations at park entrances and resort front desks. Call to have the brochure sent to you in advance, or check it out online.
⊗ 407-363-8000 • www.universalorlando.com

SeaWorld® for Disabled Guests
SeaWorld® provides a Braille guide, plus a written synopsis of its shows and telecommunications devices for the hearing impaired. Most of its rides and shows are accessible. It rents wheelchairs and scooters. A small guidebook is available at Guest Relations. ⊗ 407-351-3600
• www.seaworld.com

Society for Accessible Travel & Hospitality
Members pay an annual subscription for access to a range of services, but non-members can get information on travel for the disabled (including specific hotels and attractions) for a small fee. ⊗ 1-212-447-7284
• www.sath.org

Left **Getting wet** Center **Kids' menu** Right **SeaWorld® stroller rental**

TOP 10 Tips for Families

1 Name Tags & Reunion Places
It's very easy to get lost in crowded theme parks. If that happens, find a park employee (they're usually in uniform) and ask for help. Kids seven and under should wear tags bearing their name, hotel, and a contact number. Older kids and adults should pick a place inside the park to meet if they become separated.

2 Parent-Swaps
Height restrictions *(see below)* mean that some younger children may not be able to go on certain rides. The theme parks usually have a program that lets one parent ride while the other tends to the kids in a special waiting area. Then the second parent can go on the ride: it might not be so much fun riding by yourself but at least you don't have to wait in line again.

3 Stroller Rental & Baby Care
All the major theme parks offer stroller rental. There are also excellent nursing facilities, often with free formula provided. Diaper changing tables can be found in women's and some men's restrooms. Orlando is very family-friendly so finding facilities is not a problem.

4 Breaks
Theme parks are tiring at any time of year, but excessively so in summer, when even standing in line can be exhausting. Plan regular breaks at air-conditioned venues (best visited around midday, when it's hottest outside), or "splash areas" *(see below)*.

5 Refreshments
Bring snacks for energy and don't forget water. The parks have a few drinking fountains, but bottled water is very expensive.

6 Getting Wet & Not Getting Wet
Take a change of clothes to the theme parks, if not for yourself then for the children. Apart from water rides where you might expect to get wet, kids enjoy running through "splash areas" to cool off, and drying off naturally might not be possible. A rain poncho is smart year round, since Florida has rainy spells in both summer and winter.

7 Theme Park Ride Restrictions
Disney parks tend to have few health and height restrictions, although Disney Hollywood Studios® is a little limiting. Universal's parks can be more restrictive for younger kids, especially Islands of Adventure® (with warnings on most of the major rides), but like Universal Studios, it has a dedicated kids' area. SeaWorld® has height restrictions on a couple of rides, while at Discovery Cove®, you must be at least six years old to swim with the dolphins. Non-swimmers can still join in, but obviously can't enjoy the full experience.

8 Children's Menus
Most of the more expensive and dressy restaurants discourage young diners either by failing to provide children's menus or with outright bans on anyone under 17 years of age. However, most restaurants have some kind of kids' menu, usually in the $4 to $6 range. Some also provide distractions such as crayons and coloring-in placemats.

9 Character Meals
Disney lures families with children to a dozen of their restaurants to charge exorbitant prices for eating breakfast, lunch, or dinner with humans dressed in Disney character costumes. Universal also has one "character" restaurant, and there are some similar set-ups outside of theme parks. See p71.

10 Kids Stay Free
Orlando is Kidsville. The little ones don't pay, but they're the reason adults do. Smart hoteliers let kids stay free. Most rooms have beds for four, so even if there are only two in the party, the extra beds are part of the deal.

Left **Rush hour on I-4** Right **Merritt Island National Wildlife Refuge**

🔟 Things to Avoid

1 Park Visits When School's Out
All the parks are packed during school breaks (late Jun–late Aug; late Dec–early Jan; mid-Feb, and Easter), since that's when families hit the parks with their kids. Summer is the worst, since not only is it crowded, but it's also brutally hot. The least crowded months are November plus early and late February.

2 Theme Park Isolation
Don't spend every waking minute in Orlando's theme parks, because burn-out is inevitable. Make sure you take time to see Central Florida's natural attractions (see pp82–5), smaller attractions (see pp44–5), and museums (see pp60–61).

3 Early Arrivals
It might seem smart to hit the theme parks as soon as they open, but it is not always the best plan. Kids who arrive early tend to collapse by 2pm and are a mess the rest of the day. Instead, take it easy in the morning and head for the parks in late afternoons and evenings. Temperatures are cooler and the parks take on a magical glow under the lights.

4 Inflexibility
Relax. It's a vacation. There are no prizes for those who joylessly cram every single ride at their chosen theme park into one day. Make plans, but be flexible. Don't attempt to do everything on your list, and maybe save a few things for the next visit.

5 Big Meals In-Park
In general, theme-park food is bland and overpriced, so don't waste your main meal of the day on it. Instead, at Universal, check out the eateries on CityWalk® (see p105); while at Disney, visit one of the excellent resort dining options, where you'll find that high-end restaurants offer great value. Parks allow same-day reentry on single tickets – every ticket-holder gets a fingerprint scan for reentry.

6 Free and Discount Tickets
There are a lot of offers floating around Orlando that sound too good to be true. If someone promises free or heavily discounted tickets, ask "What's the catch?", especially if they're promising a Disney ticket. Most are timeshare salespeople trying to get you to "buy" a week's holiday for the next 20 years. In some cases they have legitimate tickets, but most of the time you have to endure hours of sales pitches. Usually, such properties are overpriced.

7 Wearing Skimpy Bathing Suits at Water Parks
Women should consider one-piece suits at water parks since most of the best rides can quickly rip off a bikini top. Bare feet are not a good idea, since the ground can get very hot – take a pair of flip-flops or water shoes.

8 Public Transport
Lynx buses might appear to be everywhere, but don't set your schedule by them, especially for longer trips. They stop frequently and are notoriously slow, but they do offer inexpensive transportation to and from the airport.

9 Downtown's Westside
The area of Downtown south of Colonial Drive and west of I-4 is not a particularly safe place to wander around. Avoid it. But if you are going to a destination here, including the Greyhound Bus station, call a cab.

10 Rush Hour on I-4
Sometimes called "Orlando's Parking Lot", I-4 can get very congested, particularly during evening rush hour (3–6:30pm), as attraction employees head home. Disney-generated traffic on I-4, between Lake Buena Vista and US Hwy 192, has a life of its own. Traffic jams there can occur around the clock.

Left **Family-friendly motel** Right **View from hotel room**

🔟 Accommodation Tips

Bed & Sales Taxes
Hotels have an assortment of hidden add-ons that can come as a surprise when you get the bill. Charges for the mini-bar and pay-per-view movies are always inflated. But the sales tax (see p132) and bed tax can really add to the bill. Orange County, including the theme parks, I–Drive, and downtown Orlando, adds 6 percent bed tax; Osceola County, which includes Kissimmee, adds 6 percent; and Seminole County, which includes Sanford (see p85), adds a 5 percent tax. Don't forget to factor in these extras when determining your budget.

Rack Rates
These are the rates no one should agree to pay for a room! They're the walk-in-and-ask rates anyone can get without a coupon or package, and without asking for a discount or special deal. They're used in this book to provide a guide price, but don't settle for them. Insist on a better deal – it is almost always possible. Always ask if there is an additional resort charge to avoid a surprise charge at the checkout.

Rooms with a View
Many properties charge more for a room that has a view of anything other than the parking lot or the building next door. Before you pay, consider how much time you will want to spend in your room.

The Pros of Staying with Mickey
The main benefits are proximity to the parks, access to the free Disney transportation system (see p127), preferred tee times at Disney golf courses (see pp54–5), extra hours in the parks, and an easy way to break up the day by returning to base for a midday nap or swim.

The Cons of Staying with Mickey
The main drawback is the cost. Rates at Disney World® Resorts are about 30 per cent more than comparable accommodation on the outside.

Types of Accommodation
Orlando has more than 117,000 hotel rooms. Most tend to be functional budget options, but there are plenty of upscale choices, too, from lavish resorts to one-off B&Bs and boutique hotels.

Booking Services
In addition to making independent reservations or dealing directly with Disney or Universal resorts, vacationers can use reservations networks to book rooms. Central Reservation Service (CRS), Orlando. com, and Kayak.com are three of the more popular ones. Ⓢ Walt Disney World • 407-828-8101 • www.disneyworld.com Ⓢ Universal • 407-224-7000 • www.universal orlando.com Ⓢ CRS • 407-740-6442 • www.crshotels.com Ⓢ Orlando.com • 800-675-2636 • www. orlando.com Ⓢ Kayak • www.kayak.com

Land-Sea Options
A different approach is to take a seven-day land-sea package that includes a stay at any one or more Disney resorts plus a Caribbean cruise. Ⓢ Disney Cruise Line • 800-951-3532 • www.disneycruise.com

Family-Friendly Motels
Most Orlando properties go the extra mile to make sure kids are treated like royalty. In fact, most let kids under 17 stay free with accompanying adults. Nickelodeon Suites Resort (see p145) and Holiday Inn Resort (see p145) offer more than the usual child-friendly amenities.

In-Room Calls
Don't use the in-room phone without knowing the billing policy. Some hotels offer free local calls; others charge steep rates. Some impose a $1-plus service charge whenever the phone is used (including for toll-free numbers), in addition to long-distance rates.

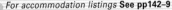 *For accommodation listings* **See pp142–9**

Portofino Bay Hotel, a replica of a real village in Italy

Disney & Universal Resorts

1 Disney's Grand Floridian Resort & Spa

Disney's top hotel is an opulent, early 20th-century New England-style resort. Expect a ragtime mood and intimate rooms that promise romance and great views. The resort also has a full spa, health club, and tennis courts. ✆ 4401 Floridian Way • Map F1 • 407-824-3000 • www.disneyworld.com • $$$$

2 Disney's Board-Walk Inn & Villas

This re-created 1940s seaside village is Disney's smallest deluxe hotel. The rooms are delightfully quaint; if you want more space, villas are available too. It is ideally located for all the facilities and buzz of the BoardWalk. ✆ 2101 N. Epcot Resorts Blvd • Map G2 • 407-939-5100; www.disneyworld.com • $$$$

3 Portofino Bay Hotel

This Universal resort is a replica of Italy's Portofino village, right down to the boats and "fishermen" in the harbor. The rooms are spacious and feature luxe bed linen. The gelati (ice cream) machines by the pool are another nice touch. Guests get to skip the line for rides and shows at Universal's parks. ✆ 5601 Universal Blvd • Map T1 • 407-503-1000 • www.universalorlando.com • $$$$

4 Walt Disney World Dolphin

This resort is on Disney property and offers some Disney perks, such as use of the free transportation system (see p127). The 27-floor pyramid contains oversize sculptures, a waterfall, and more than 1,500 suites and rooms. ✆ 1500 Epcot Resorts Blvd • Map G2 • 407-934-4000 • www.swandolphin.com • $$$

5 Walt Disney World Swan

With two 46-ft (14-m) swans gracing its roof, this hotel is hard to miss. The beach-themed rooms are a little smaller than at its sister hotel, the Dolphin, but Swan guests share some of the facilities and perks of the Dolphin, including a spa. ✆ 1200 Epcot Resorts Blvd • Map G2 • 407-934-3000 • www.swandolphin.com • $$$

6 Disney's Yacht Club Resort

The theme here is New England yacht club. Some of the 630 nautical-style rooms have views over a lake. Guests can walk to Epcot® in about 10 minutes. ✆ 1700 Epcot Resorts Blvd • Map G2 • 407-934-7000 • www.disneyworld.com • $$$$

7 Disney's Wilderness Lodge

Live oaks and tall pines surround this lovely wooded resort, modeled on the Yosemite Lodge at Yosemite National Park. Some rooms overlook woodlands; the villas are roomy and come with kitchens. ✆ 901 W. Timberline Dr • Map F1 • 407-824-3200 • www.disneyworld.com • $$$$

8 Disney's Port Orleans Resort

You can opt to stay in the French Quarter's colonial houses with iron balconies or in the Riverside's southern-style mansions. Gardeners love the landscaping, and shoppers like the location. ✆ 2201 Orleans Dr • Map F2 • 407-934-5000 • www.disneyworld.com • $$$

9 Hard Rock Hotel

This Universal resort boasts Mission-style architecture and a rock 'n' roll theme. Rooms are attractive and comfortable; the best views are from those facing the lake. Guests get to skip the lines for rides and shows at Universal's parks. ✆ 5000 Universal Blvd • Map T1 • 407-503-7625 • www.universalorlando.com • $$$$

10 Disney's Value Resorts

The All-Star Movies, All-Star Music, and All-Star Sports resorts have relatively small rooms, but rates here are the cheapest in Walt Disney World Resort. ✆ 407-934-7639 • Map G1 • www.disneyworld.com • $$

Unless indicated, all hotels have DA, A/C, pool, parking, and kids' accommodations, and accept credit cards

Price Categories

For a standard, double room per night (with breakfast if included), taxes and extra charges.

$	under $90
$$	$90–180
$$$	$180–250
$$$$	over $250

Villas of Grand Cypress

🔟 Luxury Hotels

1 Hyatt Regency Grand Cypress

This vast resort is one of Orlando's most amazing places to stay. The 18-story atrium has inner and outer glass elevators with great views, some rooms have whirlpool baths, and the resort boasts a golf course, tennis courts *(see p56)*, a beach, and plenty of nature, including a lake and waterfalls. ✪ 1 Grand Cypress Blvd • Map F2 • 407-239-1234 • www.grandcypress.hyatt.com • $$$$

2 Buena Vista Palace Hotel and Spa

The classy rooms at this, the largest Lake Buena Vista hotel, have either balconies with lake views or patios. Hypo-allergenic evergreen rooms have air and water filter systems. This spacious and luxurious hotel has rooms, which offer great views of the nightly Epcot® fireworks from the private balconies. ✪ 1900 Buena Vista Dr • Map F2 • 407-827-2727 • www.buenavistapalace.com • $$$

3 Villas of Grand Cypress

The Hyatt's sister property offers condos and town houses, plus some suites. Some accommodations have Roman tubs and patios. Amenities include a golf course, tennis courts, bike trails, and fishing. ✪ 1 N. Jacaranda • Map F2 • 800-835-7377 • www.grandcypress.com • $$$$

4 Gaylord Palms Resort

Located on acres of beautiful gardens, this resort hosts five restaurants, two pools, two bars and three separate Florida-style residences. There's a full-service spa and childcare center, and it's well located for theme parks. ✪ 6000 W. Osceola Pkwy • Map G2 • 407-586-2000 • www.gaylordhotels.com • $$$

5 Renaissance Orlando at SeaWorld®

Both the amenity-filled rooms and their marble bathrooms in this snazzy hotel are massive. Even the atrium, filled with aquariums, waterfalls, and palm trees, is 10 stories high. ✪ 6677 Sea Harbor Dr • Map T5 • 407-351-5555 • www.renaissancehotels.com • $$$$

6 Peabody Orlando

This hotel boasts an elegant feel, friendly staff, and a great location for I-Drive attractions. Home of the Peabody Ducks *(see p46)*, it has a rooftop tennis court, as well as a health center. ✪ 9801 International Dr • Map T4 • 407-352-4000 • www.peabody-orlando.com • $$$$

7 Marriott's Orlando World Center

The 2,000 rooms at this 28-story tower tend to be a bit smaller than others in this price category, but they come with plenty of in-room features. The resort boasts a wide array of facilities including a spa and the biggest pool in town. ✪ 8701 World Center Dr • Map G2 • 407-239-4200 • www.marriott-hotels.com • $$$

8 Grand Bohemian

Soft-as-clouds beds are one of this elegant downtown hotel's greatest selling points. Rooms are modern, and public areas display rare artworks. ✪ 325 S. Orange Ave • Map P3 • 407-313-9000 • www.grandbohemianhotel.com • $$$$

9 Waldorf Astoria

This elegant hotel sits among 482 acres (195 ha) of land and features elegantly furnished rooms, a championship golf course, and bars and restaurants that mirror the hotel's original New York establishments. ✪ 14200 Bonnet Creek Resort Lane • Map G2 • 407-597-5500 • www.waldorfastoriaorlando.com • $$$$

10 Disney's Animal Kingdom® Lodge

This Disney resort resembles a South African game lodge in a semi-circular *kraal* (compound). Rooms have an African theme and some have views of a wildlife-filled tropical savanna. ✪ 2901 Osceola Pkwy • Map G1 • 407-938-3000 • www.disneyworld.com • $$$$

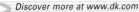

Left **Doubletree by Hilton Guest Suites** Right **Holiday Inn Walt Disney**

TOP 10 Mid-Price Hotels (A-G)

1 Best Western Lake Buena Vista Resort Hotel

All rooms have balconies at this official Disney hotel; some of them overlook beautiful gardens bordering the lake. There's free transportation to Disney's major parks, and it's within walking distance of Downtown Disney. ✆ *2000 Hotel Plaza Blvd • Map F2 • 407-828-2424 • www.lakebuenavista resorthotel.com • $$*

2 Caribbean Beach Resort

Disney's largest hotel (with 2,112 rooms) is split into five "villages": Aruba, Trinidad, Martinique, Barbados, and Jamaica, each with its own pool and sandy beach. The rooms are on the small side but are good value. ✆ *900 Cayman Way • Map G2 • 407-934-3400 • www. disneyworld.com • $$$*

3 Bohemian Hotel Celebration

The elegant lakefront rooms at this three-story, timber-framed resort offer a tranquil water-and-woodlands view. Facilities include an outdoor pool with Jacuzzi, a fitness center, and nature trails. There's an 18-hole golf course *(see p54)* too. ✆ *700 Bloom St • Map G2 • 407-566-6000 • www. celebrationhotel.com • $$$*

4 Courtyard at Lake Lucerne

Downtown's best B&B has four period buildings, from the Victorian Norment-Parry Inn to the Art Deco Wellborn Suites, which has apartments and a honeymoon suite. ✆ *211 N. Lucerne Circle E • Map P3 • 407-648-5188 • www. orlandohistoricinn.com • No pool • $$*

5 Courtyard by Marriott, Lake Buena Vista Centre

This mid-priced hotel has two outdoor heated swimming pools, a games room, and a Pizza Hut restaurant on site. It is well located for theme parks. ✆ *8501 Palm Pkwy • Map F3 • 407-239-6900 • www.courtyard.com • $$*

6 Extended Stay Deluxe Orlando Convention Center

Some of the 137 suites have wheelchair access, others are tailored to the hearing impaired. There's a heated pool, barbecues, and a Jacuzzi, and it's on the I-Ride Trolley circuit and provides a free shuttle to Disney. ✆ *8750 Universal Blvd • Map E3 • 407-903-1500 • www. extendedstay.com •$$*

7 The Holiday Inn Resort Orlando – The Castle

The towering spires of this themed hotel make it look like a fairytale castle – if castles came in pink and blue, that is. Its 216 rooms and seven suites come with bigscreen TVs and Sony Playstations. The resort has a roof terrace, a fitness center, and two restaurants. ✆ *8629 International Dr • Map T3 • 407-345-1511 • www.thecastle orlando.com • $$*

8 Doubletree by Hilton Guest Suites

After being welcomed with home-made cookies, head to your cozy one- or two-bedroomed suite at this official Disney hotel. With a landscaped pool and a spa, you can't fail to relax. ✆ *2305 Hotel Plaza Blvd • Map F2 • 407-934-1000 • www. doubletreeguestsuites.com • $$*

9 Doubletree by Hilton Universal Orlando

A $16 million renovation helped convert this former convention hotel into one that woos travelers who want to be near the Universal parks. The hotel's two towers house 742 modern rooms and suites; those on the west side overlook the parks and CityWalk. ✆ *5780 Major Blvd • Map U1 • 407-351-1000 • www.doubletreeorlando. com • $$*

10 Caribe Royale

This hotel has well-appointed one-bedroom suites on 53 acres (21 ha), with shuttles to Downtown Disney® and theme parks. ✆ *8101 World Center Dr • Map G3 • 407-238-8000 • www.thecaribe orlando.com • $$$*

Unless indicated, all hotels have DA, smoking rooms, A/C, pool, parking and kids' accommodation, and accept credit cards.

Price Categories

For a standard, double room per night (with breakfast if included), taxes and extra charges.

$	under $90
$$	$90–180
$$$	$180–250
$$$$	over $250

Nickelodeon Suites Resort

TOP 10 Mid-Price Hotels (H-Z)

1 Nickelodeon Suites Resort

Children rule in this resort, which has Kidsuites (sleeping up to seven) with big-screen TVs. Other types of suite include Cinemasuites, with even bigger TVs. Activities offered range from karaoke to ping-pong, and there are also two water parks. ✆ 14500 Continental Gateway • Map G3 • 407-387-5437 • www.nickhotel.com • $$$

2 Holiday Inn Lake Buena Vista Resort

If keeping the kids happy is top priority, this hotel is a good bet. Apart from the themed, two-roomed Kidsuites, there's a free activities program for 3–12-year- olds. Children can watch movies from the pool, and kids eat free. ✆ 13351 Apopka-Vineland Rd • Map G3 • 407-239-4500 • www.hiresortlbv.com • $$

3 Holiday Inn Walt Disney

This comfortable hotel makes for a good choice on the Hotel Plaza strip. The glass elevator scales the 14-story, plant-filled atrium and makes for a very exciting ride. The hotel provides a free Disney shuttle, free Wi-Fi and does not charge any resort fee. ✆ 1805 Hotel Plaza Blvd • Map F2 • 407-828-8888 • www.hiorlando.com • $$

4 Quality Suites Orlando

These modern luxury suites in neutral tones, with spacious living rooms and kitchens, can sleep up to six. Free coffee and tea is provided in the lobby apart from a free shuttle to the Disney parks. Rates include breakfast. ✆ 8200 Palm Pkwy • Map F2 • 407-465-8200 • www.qualitysuites-lvb.com • No DA • $$

5 Hotel Royal Plaza

Some of the spacious rooms at this hotel have whirlpools; pool-side ones have balconies or patios. The pool is heated, and there's a Jacuzzi, fitness center, and four lit tennis courts. ✆ 1905 Hotel Plaza Blvd • Map F2 • 407-828-2828 • www.royalplaza.com • $$$

6 World Gate Resort

Catering to business travelers and families, the rooms offer work stations, refrigerators, Internet access, and lush linens. Price, location, and service make it attractive. ✆ 3011 Maingate Lane • Map G2 • 407-396-1400 • www.worldgateresorts.com • $$

7 Heron Cay Lakeview B&B

This Victorian-style hotel situated within a large garden overlooks Lake Dora. The Queen Victoria suite, with its crimson furnishings and four-poster bed, is the most inviting of the six rooms. Gourmet breakfasts can include spinach strata and potato pancakes. ✆ 495 Old Hwy 441 • Off map • 352-383-4050 • www.heroncay.com • $$$

8 Springhill Suites

This pleasant suite hotel located in the Marriott Village is close to Disney. All the suites have a king-size or two double beds, plus separate living and cooking areas. ✆ 8601 Vineland Ave • Map G3 • 407-938-9001 • www.marriott.com • $–$$

9 Thurston House

Built in 1885, and set in woodland, just minutes north of Orlando, this charming B&B offers a quiet retreat, popular with adults. The four rooms, with queen-size beds, overlook Lake Eulalia. It's smoke-free and has no pool, but the home-away-from-home atmosphere is a winner. ✆ 851 Lake Ave • Map K3 • 407-539-1911 • www.thurstonhouse.com • No DA • $$

10 Liki Tiki Village

Just 7 miles (11 km) from the south gate of Disney, Liki Tiki is a luxurious complex offering furnished condos. With a vast water park on site, the kids may never leave for the parks. ✆ 17777 Bali Blvd, Winter Garden • Off map • 407-856-7190 • www.likitiki.com • $$

Left **Rosen Inn International** Right **Quality Inn sign**

TOP 10 Inexpensive Hotels (A-H)

1 Best Western Mount Vernon Inn

Located some 20 miles (32 km) north of Disney World, this is a cozy, colonial-style motel, with friendly staff. There's a city park nearby, and a charming Winter Park is minutes away. ❧ 110 S. Orlando Ave • Map L3 • 407-647-1166 • www.bestwestern.com • $

2 Clarion Inn Lake Buena Vista

Well located for the theme parks, this hotel offers a free shuttle service for Walt Disney World®, Universal Studios®, and Seaworld®. There are two swimming pools and a mini-market deli for buying snacks. Kids stay and eat for free at the on-site restaurant. ❧ 8442 Palm Pkwy • Map F3 • 407-996-7300 • www. clarionlbv.com • $

3 Howard Johnson Inn Maingate East

Rooms at this inn are sparse and small but comfortable and well-equipped . Ask for a room at the rear to escape the noise of traffic. One child eats free with each paying adult in the restaurant. Efficiencies (small serviced apartments) are available. ❧ 6051 W. Irlo Bronson Memorial Hwy • Map G2 • 407-396-1748 • www. hojomge.com • $

4 Rosen Inn

The Rosen Inn's 315 rooms, renovated in 2013, all have double or king beds, refrigerators, and microwaves. There is a pool as well as several restaurants on site. Guests can take the free shuttle service to Universal® Orlando or Sea-World® Orlando, or use the I-Drive Trolley stop in front of the hotel. ❧ 6327 International Dr • Map T3 • 800-999-6327 • www. roseninn6327.com • $

5 Drury Inn & Suites

Located conveniently near the theme parks, this hotel provides clean rooms at a bargain price. Facilities here include a fitness center, Wi-Fi, free breakfast and light supper. ❧ 7301 Sand Lake Rd • Map T3 • 407-354-1101 • www.drury hotels.com • No smoking rooms • $$

6 Days Inn Convention Center

This branch of the Days Inn chain boasts a fitness centre, a sundeck, and an outdoor pool. The hotel is surrounded by landscaped grounds and has a pancake restaurant and playground. Transport service is provided. ❧ 9990 International Dr • Map T5 • 407-352-8700 • www.days inn.com • $

7 Maingate Lakeside Resort

Located just 2 miles (1km) from Disneyworld, the hotel offers a free shuttle service to many theme parks. There are also three restaurants and three pools within its 24 landscaped acres. Rooms are bright and spacious, offering good value for money. ❧ 7769 W. Highway 192 • Map G2 • 407-396-2222 • www.maingatelakesideresort.com • $

8 Fairfield Inn & Suites Orlando Lake Buena Vista

Part of the landscaped Marriott Village, this is located near Disney. The facilities on offer include luxury bedding, a mini-fridge, free Wi-Fi, fitness center, and a pool. ❧ 8615 Vineland Ave • Map G3 • 407-938-9001 • www. marriott.com • No smoking rooms • $$

9 Galleria Palms Hotel & Suites

This hotel has a better feel than most establishments in this price bracket. Rooms are smallish but sleep up to four. There's a free Disney shuttle, and rates include breakfast, free internet access, and free local phone calls. ❧ 3000 Maingate Lane • Map G2 • 407-396-6300 • www.galleria kissimmeehotel.com • $$

10 Coco Key

If water parks delight you then this family-friendly, pool-centric resort is a great option. A canopy over the kids' pool, high-speed slides for the older ones, free Wi-Fi, and fitness center are among the highlights here. ❧ 7400 International Dr • Map T2 • 407-351-2626 • www. cocokeyorlando.com • No smoking rooms • $$

Unless indicated, all hotels have DA, smoking rooms, A/C, pool, parking and kids' accommodation, and accept credit cards.

Price Categories

For a standard, double room per night (with breakfast if included), taxes and extra charges.

$	under $90
$$	$90–180
$$$	$180–250
$$$$	over $250

Left **Best Western Mount Vernon Inn**

🔟 Inexpensive Hotels (I–Z)

1 Rosen Inn International

With its convenient location, quality service, and top-notch amenities, this hotel is a pretty good bargain. Kids can eat for free. ✪ *7600 International Dr • Map T3 • 407-996-1600 • http:// roseninn7600.com• No smoking rooms • $$*

2 Parc Corniche Suites

Conveniently located midway between Walt Disney World® and Universal Studios®, Parc Corniche is surrounded by golf course fairways and pines. It offers well-equipped suites at reasonable prices. ✪ *6300 Parc Corniche Dr • Map T6 • 407-239-7100 • www. parccorniche.com • No smoking rooms • $*

3 Comfort Suites Universal Studios

This hotel is just a few minutes from I-Drive, Wet 'n Wild®, and Universal Studios Florida®. Rooms have refrigerators, microwaves, and free Wi-Fi, and breakfast is included. ✪ *5617 Major Blvd • Map U1 • 407-363-1967 • www. comfortsuites.com • $*

4 Enclave Suites at Orlando

The Enclave Suites are close to the major theme parks. Family-friendly features include swimming pools, children's play areas, and several on-site dining options, including Pizza Hut. ✪ *6165 Carrier Dr • Map T2 • 800-457-0077 • www. enclavesuites.com • $$*

5 Ramada Convention Center I-Drive

The rooms are a step above most in this price category, and the majority are situated away from the noise of I-Drive traffic. The motel is located between SeaWorld® and the Universal parks, and it's on the I-Ride Trolley circuit *(see p127)*. Rates include breakfast. ✪ *8342 Jamaican Ct • Map T3 • 407-363-1944 • www. ramada.com • $*

6 Rosen Inn at Pointe Orlando

This is a good-value hotel given its location on I-Drive, just opposite Pointe Orlando. The standard rooms are really quite small, so if space is an issue, opt for a semi-suite. Three pools, two games rooms, and a 24-hour deli are among the on-site amenities. ✪ *9000 International Dr • Map T4 • 407-996-8585 • www. rosen inn9000.com • $*

7 La Quinta Inn & Suites UCF

This hotel, near the University of Central Florida, is for guests who want an east Orlando location. Rooms are comfortable, and rates include breakfast, local phone calls, Internet access, and weekday newspapers. ✪ *11805 Research Pkwy • Off map • 407-737-6075 • www.lq. com • $$*

8 Ramada Orlando International Drive Lakefront

Close to Universal and Wet 'n Wild®. Rooms have lake views, and there's free Wi-Fi and shuttles to Disney. Facilities include basketball and tennis courts. No resort fee. ✪ *6500 International Dr • Map T3 • 407-345-5340 • www.ramada. com • $$*

9 Palms Hotel & Villas

This condo-style hotel is well located for Walt Disney World® Resort and offers a free shuttle service to the Disney theme parks. There is a complimentary breakfast and free Wi-Fi. ✪ *3100 Parkway Blvd • Map G2 • 407-396-8484 • www. thepalmshoteland villas. com • $$*

10 Royal Celebration Inn

Situated on Lake Cecile, this motel is 5 miles (8 km) from Mickey's place. The rooms are a bit cramped, but they offer free continental breakfast and shuttles to Disney. The inn has a lakeside beach, with jet skis and water-skiing. ✪ *4944 W. Irlo Bronson Mem. Hwy • Map H3 • 407-396-4455 • www.royalcelebration orlando.com • $*

For ways to have fun on the cheap See **pp46–7**

Left **Sheraton's Vistana Resort** Right **Beach Tree Villas**

Condo & Timeshare Rentals

1 Disney Vacation Club

The same upscale Disney units that are sold as timeshares are also available for rental. Properties are located on land owned by Disney, including Old Key West Resort, Animal Kingdom Lodge, and Boardwalk Villas. ✆ 800-800-9100 • Map F2, G2 & F1 • www.dvcresorts.com • $$$$

2 Sheraton's Vistana Resort

This resort offers modern one- and two-bedroom villas and town houses, packed with home comforts, that can be rented by the week. The tennis facilities are excellent, with both clay and all-weather courts. ✆ 8800 Vistana Center Dr • Map G2 • 407-239-3100 • www.starwood.com/sheraton • $$$

3 Summer Bay Resort

Accommodation at Summer Bay ranges from one-bedroom condos to three-bedroom villas; all have washers and dryers. The property has a clubhouse and offers jet-skiing, waterskiing, and canoeing on several lakes. ✆ 17805 W. Irlo Bronson Memorial Hwy • Map G1 • 877-782-9387 • www.summerbayresort.com • $$

4 Liki Tiki Village

This lush Polynesian-themed resort has one- and two-bedroom condos with fully equipped kitchens, large TVs, whirlpool tubs, and washers and dryers. The resort itself offers poolside dining, a kids' water park, tennis, mini golf, and many other diversions. ✆ 17777 Bali Blvd, Kissimmee • Off map • 888-697-7152 • www.liki tiki.com • $$

5 Marriott Vacation Club International

Marriott's timeshare program covers five Orlando locations. The apartments and villas can also be rented by the week. Some of the villas have patios or porches, and facilities include activity programs, fitness centers, golf-course privileges, tennis courts, clubhouses, and saunas. ✆ 800-845-5279 • www.vacationclub.com • $$$

6 Holiday Villas

For generous living space, Holiday Villas offers two- and three-bedroom condos that can sleep up to eight, on eight different properties near Disney. Each comes with a washer and dryer. ✆ 4201 Vineland Rd • 800-344-3959 • www.holiday villas.com • $$

7 Blue Tree Resort

Blue Tree's elegant and spacious one- and two-bedroom villas are well-located for Disney attractions. The resort has four pools, two tennis courts, a volleyball court, and a playground. Rates are available with or without housekeeping services. ✆ 12007 Cypress Run Rd • Map F3 • 407-238-6000 • www.bluetree-orlando.com • $$

8 Orlando Breeze Resort

This resort, with its two and three-bedroom villas, is a real home-away-from-home for timeshare owners. It lacks the crowds and tourist frenzy of the mainstream areas. ✆ 121 Emerald Loop • Off map • 1-800-613-0310 • www.silverleafresorts.com • Smoke free • $$

9 Island One Resorts

There are four themed resorts to choose from, offering roomy one- to three-bedroom condos and villas. Facilities vary, but range from whirlpools to nature trails, and they sell discount attraction tickets. ✆ 8680 Commodity Circle • 407-859-8900 • www.islandone.com • $$

10 Beach Tree Villas

Great for families, the Beach Tree has two- to four-bedroom homes, the larger of which have private pools. There's an on-site recreation center, sauna, and a tennis court, but rates don't include an extra cleaning fee. Villas have a four-night minimum stay; houses have a five-night minimum. ✆ 2545 Chatham Circle • Map G3 • 407-396-7416 • www.beachtreevillas.com • Smoke free • $$

Unless indicated, all hotels have DA, smoking rooms, A/C, pool, parking and kids' accommodation, and accept credit cards.

Price Categories

For a standard, double room per night (with breakfast if included), taxes and extra charges.

$	under $90
$$	$90–180
$$$	$180–250
$$$$	over $250

Left **Orlando Southwest Fort Summit KOA**

🔟 Close to Nature

1 Fort Wilderness Resort & Campground

Vast tracts of cypress and pine trees, fish-filled lakes, and fresh air envelop this Disney resort. It has 783 camp sites plus 409 cabins, which sleep up to six and have kitchens (the newer ones also have sun decks). Canoeing and horseback riding are two of the many outdoor activities on offer. ◎ *4510 N. Fort Wilderness Trail • Map F1 • 407-824-2900 • www. disneyworld.com • $$$$*

2 Disney's Saratoga Springs Resort & Spa

Choose from onebedroom bungalows, twobedroom town houses, fairway villas next to Disney golf courses, or three-bedroom Treehouse Villas 10 ft (3 m) off the ground. Most include daily house-keeping and there are lots of recreation choices. ◎ *1960 Broadway • 407-827-1100 • www.disneyworld.com • $$$$*

3 Southport Park Campground & Marina

This relaxing park is in 25-acres (10 ha) of lakeside woods. While away time by fishing, wandering among the wildlife (such as deer and eagles), or taking an airboat trip. There are RV and tent sites with full hook-ups. ◎ *2001 E. Southport Rd • Off map • 407-933-5822 • www. southportpark.com • $*

4 Floridian RV Resort

This woodsy retreat near East Lake Tohopekaliga has full hook-ups for RVs, two clubhouses, a playground, tennis courts, and a volleyball court. There are plenty of leisure activities in the area, such as airboat rides and parasailing. ◎ *5150 Boggy Creek Rd • Off map • 407-892-5171 • www. florida-rv-parks.com • $*

5 Kissimmee/Orlando KOA

A great place to camp if you want to be close to Walt Disney World and SeaWorld®. There are RV sites, camp sites, and cabins. The RV sites can have cable TV and modem dataport connected for an extra charge. ◎ *2644 Happy Camper Pl • 407-396-2400 • www.koa.com • $*

6 Clerbrook Golf & RV Resort

This large site, popular with golfers, offers 1,250 RV hook-ups, nonsmoking villas, as well as amenities including a driving range, four whirlpools, a library, and a beauty salon. ◎ *20005 Hwy 27 • Off map • 352-394-5513 • www.florida-rv-parks.com • $*

7 Cypress Cove Nudist Resort

Unself-conscious couples and families with American Association for Nude Recreation or Cypress Cove resort membership, can stay in villas, rooms, and RV sites here. ◎ *4425 Pleasant Hill Rd • Off map • 407-933-5870 • www. cypresscoveresort.com • $$*

8 Orlando Southwest Fort Summit KOA

This resort offers full hook-ups for RVs, as well as small timber cabins and pitches for tents. There's a store, laundromats, and internet access. ◎ *2525 Frontage Rd • Off map • 863-424-1880 • www.fort summit.com • $*

9 Circle F. Dude Ranch Camp

This kids' summer camp is also a family retreat on selected weekends between November and May. Hay rides, horseback riding, lake swimming, and sailing are some of the activities on offer. Weekend rates include five meals. ◎ *Hwy 60 & Dude Ranch Rd • Off map • 863-676-4113 • www.circlefdude ranchcamp.com • smoke-free • No DA • $$*

10 Orlando Winter Garden RV Resort

Pines and ponds are all around this RV resort, about a 30-minute drive from Disney World. It boasts lots of facilities such as laundry, games room, dances, bingo, and barbecues. Popular with an older crowd. ◎ *13905 W. Colonial Dr • Map C1 • 407-656-1415 • www. wintergardenrv.com • $*

General Index

Acknowledgments

The Authors
Richard Grula lives in Orlando and specializes in writing about the downtown and cultural scenes. He's contributed to the *Orlando Weekly*, *Orlando Magazine*, *Sidewalk.com*, and *Time Out's Guide to Miami and Orlando*.

Jim and Cynthia Tunstall are Central Florida natives who have written five other Florida guides, including Frommer's *Walt Disney World & Orlando*.

Produced by Departure Lounge, London
Editorial Director Naomi Peck
Art Editor Lee Redmond
Editor Clare Tomlinson
Designer Lisa Kosky, Rachel Symons
DTP Designer Ingrid Vienings
Picture Researcher Monica Allende, Ellen Root
Research Assistance Amaia Allende, Ana Virginia Aranha, Diveen Henry, Faiyaz Kara
Proofreader Stephanie Driver
Indexer Hilary Bird
Fact Checkers Phyllis and Arvin Steinberg
Photographers Gregory Matthews, Magnus Rew
Additional Photography Dan Bannister, Demetrio Carrasco, Stephen Whitehorn, Linda Whitwham,
Illustrator Lee Redmond
Maps John Plumer

AT DORLING KINDERSLEY
Publishing Manager Kate Poole
Senior Art Editor Marisa Renzullo
Director of Publishing Gillian Allan
Publisher Douglas Amrine
Revisions Team Ashwin Adimari, Emma Anacootee, Claire Baranowski, Sherry Collins, Joseph Hayes, Christine Heilman, Laura Jones, Bharti Karakoti, Sumita Khatwani, Esther Labi, Kathryn Lane, Anwesha Madhukalya, Sonal Modha, Mary Ormandy, Rada Radojicic, Mani Ramaswamy, Beverly Smart, Susana Smith Ros Walford, Ajay Verma, Marian Virginia Warder
Cartography Co-ordinator Casper Morris
DTP Jason Little, Conrad van Dyk
Production Sarah Dodd

Picture Credits
Key: a-above; b-below/bottom; c-center; f-far; l-left; r-right; t-top.

This book makes reference to various Disney copyrighted characters, trademarks, marks and registered marks owned by The Walt Disney Company and Disney Enterprises, Inc.

The publishers would like to thank the following individuals, companies and picture libraries for permission to reproduce their photographs:

ALAMY IMAGES: Gerrit de Heus 27cl; Kelly Shannon Kelly 92tl; Ilene MacDonald 66tl; ARABIAN NIGHTS: 80b; BLUE MARTINI 74tl; BOGGY CREEK AIRBOAT RIDES: 110tl

CHOICE HOTELS INTERNATIONAL, INC.: 146tl; CHRIS CASLER: 77ca, 78b; 2000 CORNELL FINE ARTS MUSEUM: 118tr

CORBIS /Phelan Ebenhack/ZUMA Press 107tl; /Kevin Morris 64tr; /David Muench 36-7; /Michael T. Sedam 64tr; /Patrick Ward 109bl; COWBOYS ORLANDO: 116tr
DEPARTURE LOUNGE: 136tr, 137tl; DISCOVERY COVE: 48tc, 50–51, 97c;

© DISNEY 8–9, 10, 12–13, 14, 16–17, 18–19, 56cl, *La Nouba* by Cirque du Soleil, 89, 91, 93, 94, 95, DOUBLETREE GUEST SUITES: 144tl; FIRESTONE LIVE: 76tl, 78tl; FLORIDA ECO_ SAFARIS: 108bl, FLORIDA FILM FESTIVAL 64c, 65br; GAY DAYS: 65bl; GAYLORD PALMS RESORT & CONVENTION CENTER: 58c; GENESIS SPACE PHOTO LIBRARY: 40tc, 40c; GUESTCOUNTS HOSPITALITY: 105tl; HARD ROCK Orlando: 76cl; © HEIDI TARGEE: 46tl, 99c, 114b; HOLIDAY INN: 141tl; HOLIDAY INN WALT DISNEY: 144tr; ICEBAR Orlando: 100tl.

KENNEDY SPACE CENTER: 3br, 7b, 38–39c, 38c, 38b, 39t, 39c, 39b, 40tl; KISSIMMEE-ST CLOUD CONVENTION & VISITORS' BUREAU, 48c, 108tc, 110tr; Doug Dukane: 47, 56tl, 56tr, 57tr, 106tl, 109tl, 110tc

MAD COW THEATRE Tom Hurst 63ca; © MEDIEVAL TIMES: 80tl; MERRITT ISLAND NATIONAL WILDLIFE REFUGE: 7cr, 36c, 36, 37b

© NASA: 40tr, 41c, 41b; ORLANDO TOURISM BUREAU, London: 53, 57cl, 57cr, 60tl, 60tr

ORLANDO & ORANGE COUNTY CONVENTION & VISITORS' BUREAU, INC: 3tr, 44tl, 54b, 55, 62tl, 62tr, 62b, 67tl, 75tr, 76cl, 101tr, 106tr, 109tr, 109br, 112c, 115cr, 119t, 127tl; ORLANDO INTERNATIONAL FRINGE FESTIVAL: 64tl; PARK PLAZA GARDENS: 68tr; PARLIAMENT HOUSE: 79; RIVERSHIP ROMANCE: Jeff Drake 84cr; ROMANO'S MACARONI GRILL: 70cl; ROSEN INN INTERNATIONAL: 146tl

SEAWORLD PARKS AND ENTERTAINMENT All rights reserved: 3bl, 3tl, 7tr, 28–29c, 28t, 28c, 29t, 29clb; 30tl, 30tr, 30b, 31c, 31b, 32–33, 42–43b, 43t, 43c, 129, 139tl, Jason Collier 29clb; SKYVENTURE LLC, ORLANDO: 45tc; THE SOCIAL CLUB: 116tl; SPA AT THE WYNDHAM PALACE RESORT: 59; STARWOOD 148tl

© UNIVERSAL ORLANDO RESORT All rights reserved: 3tc, 4–5, 6tr, 6bl, 20–21c, 20t, 20c, 20b, 21t, 22tl, 22tc, 22tr, 22c, 23c, 23b, 24–25, 24t, 24c, 24b, 25t, 26t, 26tl, 42tl, 42tr, 42c, 43b, 46tr, 65cr, 68b, 86–87, 96tr, 97t, 104tl, 104tc, 126tr, 142; US FISH AND WILDLIFE SERVICE: Gary M. Stolz 37t; VILLAS OF GRAND CYPRESS: 56tl, 57br, 88tr, 143; WALT DISNEY WORLD DOLPHIN RESORT: 69tl; WET 'N WILD: 7cl, 34–35c, 34t, 34cl, 34b, 35t, 35cr, 35b, 48tl, 96tl; WONDERWORKS: 100tr

THE ZIMMERMAN AGENCY: The Kessler Collection: 72tl, 117tl; © ZORA NEALE HURSTON NATIONAL MUSEUM OF FINE ARTS *Festival Girl*, Jane Turner 121cl

Front Flap: SEAWORLD PHOTO/VIDEO SERVICES, FLORIDA: bcl

All other images are © Dorling Kindersley. For further information see www.dkimages.com.

Index of Main Streets

'You were a virgin,' Leo repeated. 'We will therefore be married as soon as I can arrange it. I am honour-bound to offer you this.'

'Stuff your honour.' Heaving in a deep breath, Natasha climbed off the other side from where he was sitting, trailing the sheet around her as she went. 'Having just escaped one sleazy marriage by the skin of my teeth, I am *not* going to fall into another one!'

'It will not be a sleazy marriage.'

'Everything about you and your terrible family is sleazy!' She turned on him savagely. 'You're all so obsessed with the value of money you've lost touch with what's really valuable in life! Well, I haven't.' She tossed her chin up, eyes like blue glass on fire with contempt. 'We made a deal in which I give you sex for six weeks until I can give you back your precious money. Show a bit of your so-called honour by keeping to that deal!'

Michelle Reid grew up on the southern edges of Manchester, the youngest in a family of five lively children. But now she lives in the beautiful county of Cheshire, with her busy executive husband and two grown-up daughters. She loves reading, the ballet, and playing tennis when she gets the chance. She hates cooking, cleaning, and despises ironing! Sleep she can do without, and produces some of her best written work during the early hours of the morning.

Recent titles by the same author:

THE DE SANTIS MARRIAGE
THE MARKONOS BRIDE

THE GREEK'S
FORCED BRIDE

BY
MICHELLE REID

MILLS & BOON®
Pure reading pleasure™

First published in Great Britain 2008
Paperback edition 2009
Harlequin Mills & Boon Limited,
Eton House, 18-24 Paradise Road, Richmond, Surrey TW9 1SR

© Michelle Reid 2008

ISBN: 978 0 263 86997 2

Set in Times Roman 10½ on 12¼ pt
01-0209-55413

Printed and bound in Spain
by Litografia Rosés, S.A., Barcelona

THE GREEK'S
FORCED BRIDE

CHAPTER ONE

LOUNGING in his chair at the head of the boardroom table, Leo Christakis, thirty-four-year old human dynamo and absolute head of the Christakis business empire, held the room in a state of near-rigid tension by the sheer power of his silence.

No one dared to move. All dossiers resting on the long polished table top remained firmly closed. Except for the folder flung open in front of Leo. And as five minutes edged with agonising slowness towards ten, even the act of breathing in and out became a difficult exercise and not one of those present had the nerve to utter so much as a sound.

For Leo's outwardly relaxed posture was dangerously deceptive, as was the gentle way he was tapping his neatly clipped fingernails on the polished surface as he continued to read. And anyone—anyone daring to think that the sensual shape of his mouth was relaxed in a smile needed a quick lesson in the difference between a smile and a sneer.

Leo knew the damn difference. He also knew that the nasty stuff was about to hit the fan. For someone around here had pulled a fast one with company money and what made him really angry was that the fiddle was so badly put together anyone with a rudimentary grasp of arithmetic could spot it a mile away. Leo did not employ incompetents. Therefore the list of employees who might just dare to believe they could get away with ripping him off like this could be shortlisted to one.

Rico, his vain and shallow, gut-selfish stepbrother, and the only person employed by this company to earn his place in it by favour alone.

Family, in other words.

Damn, Leo cursed within the depths of his own angry thinking. What the hell gave Rico the idea he could get away with this? It was well known throughout this global organisation that each branch was hit regularly by random internal audits for the specific purpose of deterring anyone from trying a stunt like this. It was the only way a multinational the size of this one could hope to maintain control!

The arrogant fool. Was it not enough that he was paid a handsome salary for doing almost nothing around here? Where did he get off believing he could dip his greedy fingers in the pot for more?

'Where is he?' Leo demanded, bringing half a dozen heads shooting up at the sudden sound of his voice.

'In his office,' Juno, his London based PA quickly responded. 'He was informed about this meeting, Leo,' the younger man added in case Leo was living with the mistaken belief that Rico had not been told to attend.

Leo did not doubt it, just as he did not doubt that everyone sitting around this table believed that Rico was about to receive his just desserts. His stepbrother was a freeloader. It went without saying that the people who worked hard for their living did not like freeloaders. And all it took was for him to lift his dark head with its hard, chiselled bone structure, which would have been stunningly perfect if it weren't for the bump in the middle of his slender nose—put there by a football boot when he was in his teens—and scan with his rich, dark velvet brown eyes half a dozen carefully guarded expressions to have that last thought confirmed.

Theos. There was little hope of him managing to pull off a cover-up with so many people in the know and silently baying for Rico's blood, he concluded as he hid his eyes again beneath the thick curl of his eyelashes.

Did he *want* to cover up for Rico? The question flicked at the muscle that lined his defined jawbone because Leo knew the answer was yes, he did prefer to affect a cover-up than to deal with the alternative.

A thief in the family.

Fresh anger surged. With it came a grim flick of one hand to shut the folder before he rose to his feet, long legs thrusting him up to his full and intimidating six feet four inches immaculately encased in a smooth dark pinstripe suit.

Juno also jumped up. 'I will go and—'

'No, you will not,' Leo said in tightly accented English. 'I will go and get him myself.'

Everyone else shifted tensely as Juno sank down in his seat again. If Leo had been in the mood to notice, he would have seen the wave of swift, telling glances that shifted around the table, but he was in no frame of mind to want to notice anything else as he stepped around his chair and strode out through the door without bothering to spare anyone another glance.

Just as he didn't bother to look sideways as he strode across the plush hushed executive foyer belonging to the Christakis London offices. If he had happened to glance to the side, then he would have seen the lift doors were about to open—but he didn't.

He was too busy cursing the sudden heart attack that took his beloved father from him two years ago, leaving him with the miserable task of babysitting the two most irritating people it had been his misfortune to know—his high-strung Italian stepmother, Angelina, and her precious son, Rico Giannetti.

Ah, someone save me from smooth, handsome playboys and hypersensitive stepmothers anxiously besotted with their beautiful sons, he thought heavily. Family loyalty was the pits, and the day that Rico's ever-looming marriage took place and he took his life and his gullible new wife back to his native Milan to live with Angelina, could not come soon enough for Leo.

If he could get Rico out of this mess without compromising his own reputation and standing in this company that was, or Rico would not be going anywhere but a prison cell.

A sigh hurt his chest as Leo chose to suppress it, the knowledge that he was already looking for a way out for Rico scraping the sides of his pride in contempt.

What was Natasha going to do if she found out she was about to marry a thief?

Though why the hell his stepbrother had chosen to marry Miss Cool and Prim Natasha Moyles was a mystery to Leo. She was not the nubile celebrity stick-like variety of female Rico usually turned on for. In fact, she lived inside a pretty much perfect long-legged and curvy hourglass shape she ruined by hiding it with her lousy dress sense. She was also cold and polite and irritatingly standoffish—around Leo anyway.

So why Natasha had fallen in love with a life-wasting playboy like Rico was just another puzzle Leo could not work out. The attraction of opposites? Did the cool and prim disguise fall apart around Rico?

Perhaps she became a bodice-ripping sex goddess in the bedroom, because she sure had the potential to be a raging sex goddess with her soft feminine features and her wide-spaced, too-blue eyes and that lush, sexy mouth she could not disguise, which just begged to be kissed out of its—

Theos, Leo cursed yet again as something familiarly hot gave a tug low down in his gut to remind how Natasha Moyles's mouth could affect him—while behind him the object of his thoughts walked out of the lift only to pull to a shuddering halt when she caught sight of his instantly recognisable, tall, dark suited shape striding into the corridor across the other side of the foyer.

Natasha's heart did a funny little squirm in her chest and for a moment she actually considered giving in to the sudden urge to leap back into the lift and come back to see Rico later when his stepbrother wasn't about.

She did not like Leo Christakis. He had an uncomfortable way of always making her feel tense and edgy with his hard-nosed, worldly arrogance and his soft, smooth sarcasms that always managed to make such accurate swipes at just about every insecurity she possessed.

Did he think she never noticed the sardonic little smile he always wore on his mouth whenever he was given an opportunity to run his eyes over her? Did he think it was great fun to make her freeze with agonising self-consciousness because she knew he was mocking the way she preferred to hide her curves rather than put them on show like the other women that circled his wonderful self?

Not that it mattered what Leo Christakis thought about her, Natasha then told herself quickly, while refusing to acknowledge the way her eyes continued to cling to him, or that one of her hands was nervously slotting a loose golden strand of hair back to her neatly pinned knot and the other hand clutched her little black purse to the front of her pale blue suit as if the purse acted like a piece of body armour meant to keep him at bay.

She wasn't here to see him. He was just the arrogant, self-important, overbearing stepbrother of the man she was supposed to be marrying in six weeks. And unless Rico had some very good answers to the accusations she was about to fire at him, then there wasn't going to be a wedding!

Natasha felt herself go pale as she recalled the scene some kind person had relayed to her mobile phone this morning. Why did some people take pleasure in sending another person images of their fiancé locked in the arms of another woman? Did they think that because she was attached to the pop-music industry she couldn't possibly have feelings to wound?

Well, look at me now, Natasha thought bleakly as she dragged her eyes away from Leo to stare at the way her trembling fingers were gripping her purse. *I'm not just wounded, I'm dying*! Or her love for Rico was dying, she revised bleakly. Because this was it, the final straw, the last time she was going to turn blind eyes and deaf ears to the rumours about his cheating on her.

It was time for a showdown.

Pale lips pressed together now, eyes fixed on the expanse of grey carpet spread out in front of her, Natasha set herself walking across the foyer and into the corridor that led the way to Rico's office in the now-forgotten wake of Leo Christakis.

The door was shut tight into its housing. Leo didn't bother to knock on it before he twisted the handles and threw it open wide, then took a long step forwards, ready to give Rico Giannetti hell—only to find himself freezing at the sight that met his flashing dark gaze.

For the next few numbing seconds Leo actually found himself wondering if he was dreaming what he was seeing. It was so difficult to believe that even Rico could be this crass! For standing there in front of his desk was his handsome stepbrother with his trousers pooled round his ankles and a pair of slender female legs wrapped around his waist. The very air in the room seethed with gasps as Rico's tight and tanned backside thrust forwards and backwards while soft groans emitted from the naked and not-so-prim female spread out on the top of the desk.

Clothes were scattered all over the place. The smell of sex was strong and thick. The very floor beneath Leo's feet vibrated to Rico's urgent gyrations.

'What the *hell*—?' Leo raked out in a blistering explosion of grinding disgust at the precise moment that an entirely separate sound hit him from behind and had him wheeling about.

He found himself staring into the shock-frozen face of Rico's fiancée. Confusion locked onto his hard golden features because he had believed the blonde ranging about on the desk must be her!

'Natasha?' he ground out in a surprise-driven rasp.

But Natasha didn't hear him. She was too busy seeing her worst nightmare confirmed by the two people who were beginning to realise they were no longer alone. As she watched as if from a strange place somewhere way off in the distance she saw Rico's handsome dark head lift up and turn. Sickness clawed at the walls of her stomach as his heavy-lidded, passion-glazed eyes connected with hers.

Then the woman moved, dragging Natasha's gaze sideways as a blonde head with a pair of blue eyes lifted up to peer around Rico's blocking frame. The two women looked at each other—that was all—just looked.

'*Who* the—?' Leo spun back the other way to discover that the two lovers were now aware of their presence.

The woman was trying to untangle herself, levering herself up on an elbow as she pushed at Rico's bared chest with a slender hand. Shifting his eyes to her, Leo felt true hell arrive as the full horror of what they were witnessing slammed like a truck into his face.

Cindy, Natasha's sister. Two blondes with blue eyes and an age gap that made Cindy seem still just a kid.

His stomach revolted. He swung back to Natasha, but Natasha was no longer standing behind him. Her tense long-legged curvy shape in its stiff pale blue suit was already half-way back down the corridor, making as fast as she could for the lift.

Anger on her behalf roaring up inside him, Leo twisted back to the two guilty lovers. The serious questions Rico should be answering suddenly flew right out of his head. 'You are finished with me, Rico,' he raked out at the younger man. 'Get your clothes on and get the hell out of my building before I have you thrown out—and take the slut with you!'

Then he walked out, pulling the door shut behind him before taking off after Natasha at a run and feeling an odd sense of disorientating empowerment now that Rico had given him just cause to kick him right out of his life.

The lift doors closed before he got there. Cursing through his clenched teeth, Leo turned and headed for the stairs. One flight down and the single lift up to the top floor became three lifts, which fed the whole building. Glancing up to note that Natasha was going down to the basement just before he strode inside another lift, he hit the button that would take him to the same place.

His insides were shaking. All of him was pumped up and pulsing because—*Theos*, sex did that to you. Even when what you'd seen sickened and disgusted, it still had a nasty way of playing its song in your blood.

Striding out of the lift, Leo paused to look around the base-ment car park. Natasha's Mini stood out like a shiny red stain in a murky world of fashionable silver and black. He saw her then. She was leaning heavily on the car and her shoulders were heaving. He thought she was weeping but as he ap-proached her he realised that she was being violently sick.

'It's OK…' he muttered for some stupid reason because

nothing could be less *OK*, and he placed his hands on her shoulders.

'Don't touch me!' She jerked away from him.

Offence hit Leo full on his chiselled chin. 'I am not Rico!' he raked back in sheer reaction. 'Just as you are not your slut of a sister—!'

She turned and slapped him hard on the face.

The stinging slap rang around the basement as Leo rocked back on his heels in surprise. Natasha was quivering all over, nothing going on inside her burning brain but the remains of that searing surge of violence that had made her turn and lash out. She had never done anything like it before, not in her entire life!

Then she was suddenly having to reel away and double up to retch again, while sobbing and shaking and clutching at the car's bodywork with fingernails that scraped the shiny red paint.

Rico with Cindy—how could he?

How could *she*?

A pair of long fingered hands dared to take hold of her shoulders again. She didn't pull away, but just sagged like a quivering sack into his grasp as the final dregs of her stomach contents landed only inches away from her low-heeled black shoes. By the time it was over she could barely stand upright.

Grim lips pressed together, Leo continued to hold her while she found a tissue in her jacket pocket and used it to wipe her mouth. Beneath the grip of his fingers he could feel her trembling. Her head was bowed, exposing the long, slender whiteness of her nape. That hot sensation flicked at his insides again and he looked away from her, flashing an angry look around the car park like a man being hunted by an invisible quarry and wondering what the hell he was going to do next.

She was not his problem, one part of his brain tried telling him. He had a meeting to chair and a serious financial discrepancy to deal with, plus a dozen or so other points of business to get through before he flew back to Athens this evening and…

A man suddenly appeared from the lurking shadows where the security offices were situated in a corner of the basement. It was Rasmus, his security chief, eyeing them curiously. Leo dismissed him with a frowning shake of his dark head that sent the other man melting back into the shadows again.

His next thought was to coax Natasha back into the lift and take her up to his own office suite to recover. But he could not guarantee that he could get her in there without someone—Rico or her sister—seeing them and starting up another ugly scene.

'OK now?' he dared to question once her trembling started to ease a little.

She managed a single nod. 'Yes. Thank you,' she whispered.

'This is not a moment for polite manners, Natasha,' he responded impatiently.

Natasha jerked away from him, hating him like poison for being here and witnessing her complete downfall like this. Receiving picture evidence that Rico was cheating on her was one thing, but to actually see him doing it with her own sister was absolutely something else.

Just thinking about it had fresh nausea trying to take a grip on her stomach. Working desperately to control it, Natasha fumbled in her bag for her car keys, then turned to unlock the Mini so she could reach inside it for the bottle of water she always kept in there. She wanted to dive into the car and just drive away from it all, but she knew she didn't have it in her yet to drive herself anywhere. She was still too shaken up, too sick and dizzy with horror and shock.

As she straightened up again she had to step around the mess she had ejected onto the ground. *He* didn't move a single inch so she brushed against him in an effort to gain herself some space. It was like brushing against barbed wire, she likened as a hot-rod prickle scraped down through her body and forced her to wilt backwards with a tremor of flayed senses against the side of the car.

Keeping her eyes lowered and away from Leo, she twisted the cap off the bottle of water and put it to her unsteady lips so she could take a couple of careful sips. Her heart was pounding in her head and her throat felt so thick it struggled to swallow. And he continued to stand there like some looming dark shadow, killing her ability to think and making her feel the insignificance of her own diminutive five feet six inches next to his overpowering height.

But that was the great and gloriously important Leo Christakis, she mused dismally—a big, tough, overpowering entity with a repertoire in sardonic looks and blunt comments that could shrivel a lesser person to pulp, and a brain that functioned for only one thing—making money. Even as she stood here refusing to look at him she could feel him fighting the urge to glance at his watch, because he must have more important things to do with his time than to stand here wasting it on her.

'I'll be all r-right in a minute,' she managed. 'You can go back to work now.'

She'd said that as if she believed work was the only thing he lived for, Leo picked up. His chiselled chin jutted. Natasha Moyles always had a unique way of antagonising him with her polite, withdrawn manner or her swift, cool glances that dismissed him as if he were nothing worthy of her regard. She'd been doing it to him from the first time they were introduced at his stepbrother's London apartment.

Leo thrust his clenched hands into his trouser pockets, pushing back the flaps of his dark pinstripe jacket to reveal the pristine white front to his handmade shirt. She shifted jerkily as if the action threatened her somehow and he was suddenly made acutely aware of his own long, muscled torso and taut, bronzed skin. Even the layer of hair that covered his chest prickled.

'Take some more sips at the water and stop trying to out-guess what I might be thinking,' he advised coolly, not liking these sensations that kept on attacking him.

'I wasn't trying to—'

'You were,' he interrupted, adding curtly, 'You might dislike me intensely, Natasha, but allow me a bit more sensitivity than to desert you here after what you have just witnessed.'

But he did not possess quite enough sensitivity to hold back from reminding her of it! Natasha noted as the whole sickening horror of what she had seen sucked her right back in. Her inner world began to sway dizzily, the groan she must have uttered bringing his fingers back up to clasp her arms. She wanted to shrug him off, but she found that she couldn't. She needed his support because she had a horrible feeling that without it she was going to sink into a great dark hole in the ground.

An eerie-sounding beep suddenly echoed through the car park. It was the executive lift being called back up the building to pick up new passengers. Leo bit out a curse at the same time that Natasha's head shot up to stare at him, her wide, blue eyes clashing full on with his dark brown eyes. For a long moment neither of them moved as they stood trapped by a strange kind of energy that shimmered its way through Natasha's body right down to her toes.

Theos, she's beautiful, Leo heard himself think.

She made a sudden dive towards her open car door. Moving like lightning, Leo managed to get there before her, one set of fingers closing around her slender wrist to hold her back while he closed the car door, then took the keys from her hand.

'W-what—?'

Her stammered half-question was cut short by a man used

to making snap decisions. Leo turned and all but frogmarched her across the basement to where his own low sleek black car was parked.

'I can drive myself!' she protested when she realised what he was doing.

'No, you cannot.'

'But—'

'That could be Rico about to walk out of the lift,' he turned on her forcefully. 'So make your mind up, Natasha, which one of us would you prefer to be with right now!'

So very brutal in its delivery. Natasha's mind flooded yet again with what she had witnessed upstairs and she turned into a block of ice.

Opening the car door, Leo propelled her inside. She went without protest, accidentally dropping the water bottle as she did. Jaw set like a vice now, Leo closed the door as, like a man born with special mental powers, Rasmus reappeared not far away. Leo tossed her keys at him and didn't need to issue instructions. His security chief just slunk away again, knowing exactly what was expected of him.

Ignoring the fallen water bottle, Leo strode around the car and got in behind the wheel. She was huddled in the passenger seat, staring down at her two hands where they knotted together on the top of her little black purse and she was shivering like crazy now as the classic reaction to shock well and truly set in.

Pinning his lips together, Leo switched on the engine and thrust it into gear, then sent the car flying towards the exit on an ear-shattering screech of tires. They hit daylight and the early afternoon traffic in a seething atmosphere of emotional stress. A minute later his in-car telephone system burst into life, the screen on his dashboard flashing up Rico's name. A choice phrase locked in the back of his throat and he flicked a switch on the steering wheel that shut the phone down.

Ten seconds later and Natasha's phone started to ring inside her bag.

'Ignore it,' he gritted.

'Do you think I am stupid?' she choked out.

Then they both sat there in thick, throbbing silence, listening to her phone ring until her voicemail took over the call. Her phone kept on ringing repeatedly as they travelled across London with the two of them sitting there like waxwork dummies waiting for her voicemail to keep doing its thing while anger pumped adrenalin into Leo's bloodstream making his fingers grip the steering wheel too tight.

Neither spoke a word to each other. He didn't know what to say if it did not include a string of obscenities that would probably make this woman blanch.

Natasha, on the other hand, had closed herself off inside a cold little world filled with reruns of what she had witnessed. She knew that her sister's behaviour was out of control, but she'd never thought Cindy would sink so low as to...

She had to swallow to stop the bile from rising again as she replayed the moment when Cindy had seen her standing in the door. She saw the look of triumph hit her sister's face followed by the oh-so-familiar pout of defiance that revealed the truth as to why she was doing that with Rico.

Cindy didn't really want him. She did not even like him that much, but she could not stand the thought that Natasha had anything she hadn't first tried out for herself.

Selfish to the last drop of blood, Natasha thought painfully. Spoiled by two parents who liked to believe their youngest daughter was the most gifted creature living on this earth. She was prettier than Natasha, more outward-going than Natasha. Funnier and livelier and so much more talented than Natasha ever could or wanted to be.

Blessed, their parents called it, because Cindy could sing

like a bird and she was the latest pop discovery promising to set the UK alight. After a short stint on a national TV singing competition, Cindy's was the face that everyone recognised while Natasha stood in the background like a shadow. The quiet one, the invisible one whose job it was to make sure everything ran smoothly in her talented sister's wonderful life.

Why had she allowed it to happen? she asked herself now when it all felt so ugly. Why had she agreed to put her own life on hold and be drawn into playing babysitter to a self-seeking, spoiled brat who'd always resented having an older sister to share anything with?

Because she'd known their ageing parents couldn't cope with Cindy. Because from the moment that Cindy's singing talents had been discovered she'd realised that someone had to attempt to keep her from going right off the egotistic rails.

And, face it, Natasha. At first you were excited about being part of Cindy's fabulous life.

Cindy, of course, resented her being there. *Riding on her coat-tails*, she'd called it. Natasha was unaware that she'd said it out loud until Leo flicked a gruff-toned, 'Did you say something?'

'No,' she mumbled—but it was exactly what she'd let herself become: a pathetic hanger-on riding on the coat-tails of her sister's glorious popularity.

Meeting Rico had been like rediscovering that she was a real person in her own right. She'd stupidly let herself believe he had actually fallen in love with her in her own right and not just because of whom she was attached to.

What a joke, she thought now. What a sick, rotten joke.

Rico with Cindy...

Hurt tears scalded the back of her throat.

Rico doing with Cindy what he had always held back from doing with her...

'Oh,' a thick whimper escaped.

'OK?' the man beside her shot out.

Of course I'm not OK! Natasha wanted to screech at him. *I've just witnessed my fiancé bonking the brains out of my sister*!

'Yes,' she breathed out.

Leo brought his teeth together with a steel-edged slice. He flashed her a quick glance to find that she was still sitting there with her head dipped and her slender white fingers knotted together on top of her bag.

Had Rico ever taken this woman across his desk the way he'd been having her sister?

As if she could hear what he was thinking, her chin lifted upwards in an oddly proud gesture, her blue eyes staring directly in front. She possessed the flawless profile of a chaste Madonna, Leo found himself thinking. But when he dropped his eyes to her mouth, he was reminded that it was no chaste Madonna's mouth. It was a soft, very lush, very sexy mouth with a short, vulnerable upper lip and a fuller lower lip that just begged to be—

That sudden burn grabbed hold of him right where it shouldn't—residue from what had happened to him as he'd travelled down in the lift, he stubbornly informed himself.

But it wasn't, and he knew it. He had been fighting a hot sexual curiosity about Natasha Moyles from the first time he'd met her at her and Rico's betrothal party. Her sister had been there, claiming centre stage and wowing everyone with her shimmering star quality, wearing a flimsy flesh-coloured dress exclusively designed for her to show off her stem-like figure and her big hairstyle that floated all around her exquisite face, accentuating her sparkling baby-blue eyes.

This sister had worn classic black. It had shocked him at the time because it was supposed to be Natasha's party yet she'd chosen to wear the colour of mourning. He remembered remarking on it to her at the time.

One of his shoulders gave a small shrug. Maybe he should not have made the comment. Maybe he should have kept his sardonic opinion to himself, because if he had done it to get a rise out of her, then he'd certainly got one—of buttoned-lipped, cold-eyed ice.

They'd exchanged barely a civil word since then.

So, she'd taken an instant dislike to him, Leo acknowledged with a grimace that wavered towards wry. Natasha didn't like tall, dark Greeks with a blunt, outspoken manner. He didn't like loud pop-chicks with stick figures and big hair.

He preferred his woman with more softness and shape.

Rico didn't.

Natasha had both.

Leo frowned as he drove them across the river. So what the hell *had* Rico been doing with Natasha, then? Had the stupid fool started out by playing a game with one sister to get him access to the other one, only to find he'd got himself embroiled too deep? Natasha wasn't the type you messed around with. She just would not understand. Had his bone-selfish step-brother discovered a conscience somewhere between hitting on Natasha and asking her to marry him within a few weeks?

If so, the bad conscience had not stretched far enough to make him leave the other sister alone, he mused grimly as he shot them through a set of lights on amber and spun the car into a screeching left turn.

'Where are you going?' Natasha burst out sharply.

'My place,' he answered.

'But I don't want—'

'You prefer it if I drop you off at your apartment?' Leo flicked at her. 'You prefer to sit nice and neat on a chair with the bag on your lap waiting for them to appear and beg you to forgive?'

His English was failing, Leo noticed—but not enough

to mask the sarcasm from his voice that managed to shock even him.

'No,' she quivered out.

'Because they will appear,' he persisted nonetheless. 'She needs you to keep her life running smoothly while she struts about playing the pop-chick with angst. And Rico needs you to keep his mama happy because Angelina likes you, and she sees you as her precious boy's saviour from a life of wild women and booze.'

Was that it? Had Rico been using her to appease his old-fashioned mother who'd taken a liking to her on sight? Natasha felt hot tears fill her eyes as she replayed the relieved smile Angelina had sent her when they'd happened to bump into her at a restaurant one night. 'Such a nice girl,' Angelina had said later.

Was that the moment when Rico decided that it might be a good idea to make her his wife? He'd asked her to marry him only a few days later. Like a fully paid-up idiot, she had jumped at the chance. They'd barely shared a proper kiss by then!

And no wonder. She wasn't Rico's type, she was *his mother's* type. Cindy was Rico's type.

Her heart hurt as she stared out of the car window. Beside her, Leo felt the truth hit him hard in the gut.

He had his answer as to what had made Rico want to marry this sister while lusting after the other one. He was keeping his mother happy because Angelina had been making stern warning noises about his lifestyle and Rico saw his loving mama as his main artery source to the Christakis coffers—next to Leo himself, of course.

Which made Natasha Rico's love stooge as much as Leo was his family stooge. From the day eight years ago when his father had brought Angelina home as his new bride with her eighteen-year-old son in tow, Leo's life had become round after round of making Rico feel part of the family because Angelina was so hypersensitive to the differences between the two sons. And his father would do anything to keep Angelina happy and content. When Lukas died so suddenly, Leo continued to keep Angelina, via Rico, happy because she'd been so clearly in love with his father and naturally devastated by his death.

Well, not any longer, he vowed heavily. It was time for both Angelina and Rico to take control of their own lives. He was sick and tired of sorting out their problems.

And that included the money Rico had stolen from him, Leo determined, a black frown bringing his eyebrows together across the top of his nose because he'd allowed himself to forget the reason he'd gone into Rico's office in the first place.

Natasha was yet another of Rico's problems, he recognised, winging another swift, frowning glance her way. She was sitting there with her face turned the colour of parchment, looking as if she might be going to throw up in his car.

What, *this* woman? he then cruelly mocked. This ultra-composed creature would rather choke on her own bile than to allow herself to do anything so crass as to throw up on his Moroccan tan leather.

Which then brought back the question—what had such a dignified thing seen in a shallow piece of manhood like Rico?

Fresh anger tried to rip a hole in his chest.

'Think about it,' he gritted, wishing he could keep his mouth shut, but finding out he could not. 'They are more suited to each other than you and Rico. He famously likes them like your sister—surely you must have known that, heard some of his history with women? He's been playing the high-rolling playboy right across fashionable Europe for long enough. Did you never stop to ask yourself what it was he actually saw in you that made you stand out from the flock?'

The hurt tears gathered all the stronger at his ruthless barrage. Feeling as if she'd just been knocked over by a bus then kicked for daring to let it happen, 'I thought he loved me,' Natasha managed to push out.

'Which is why he was enjoying your sister over his desk when he should have been attending my board meeting, defending himself.'

'Defending?' she picked up.

Leo didn't answer. Clamping his lips together, he climbed out of the car, annoyed with himself for wanting to beat her up for Rico's sins. Rounding the car bonnet, he opened her door, then reached in to take hold of one of her wrists so he could tug her out, even though he knew she didn't want to get out. Her phone started ringing again, distracting her long enough for him to get her into his house.

He pulled her into the living room and pushed her down into a chair then strode off to the drinks cabinet to pour her a stiff drink.

His hands were trembling, he noticed, and frowned as he splashed neat brandy into a glass. When he walked back to Natasha, he saw that she was sitting on the edge of the chair, all neat and prim with the bag on her lap as he'd predicted she would do.

Fresh anger ripped at him. 'Here.' He handed her the glass. 'Drink that, it might help to loosen you up a bit.'

What happened next came without any warning at all that he was about to receive his just desserts when Natasha shot to her feet and launched the full contents of the glass at his face.

'W-who do you think you are, Mr Christakis, to *dare* to think you can be this horrid to me?' she fired up. 'Listening to you, anyone would be f-forgiven for thinking that it had been *you* who'd been betrayed back there! Or is that it?' she then shot out. 'Are you being this downright nasty to me because you wished it *had* been you doing *that* with my sister instead of Rico—is that what your foul temper is about?'

Standing there with brandy dripping down his hard golden cheekbones, Leo Christakis, the dynamic and cut-throat head of one of the biggest companies in the world, heard himself utter...

'No. I wished it had been you with me.'

CHAPTER TWO

IN THE thick, thrumming silence that followed that mind-numbing declaration, Natasha stared up at Leo's liquor-drenched face—and wished that the brandy were still in the glass so she could toss it at him again!

'H-how dare you?' she shook out in tremulous indignation, eyes like sparkling blue diamonds darkening to sultry sapphires as the tears filled them up. 'Don't you think I've been h-humiliated enough without you poking fun at me as if it's all been just a jolly good joke?'

'No joke,' Leo heard himself utter, then grimaced at the full, raw truth in his answer. There was definitely no joke to find anywhere in the way he had been quietly lusting after Natasha for weeks.

No, the real joke here was in hearing himself actually admit to it.

Turning his back on her, Leo dug a hand into his jacket pocket to retrieve the never-used handkerchief his various housekeepers always insisted on placing in his suits. Wiping the brandy from his face, he flicked a glance at the way Natasha was standing there in her neat blue suit and her sensible heeled shoes but with her very expressive eyes now blackened by shock.

'You have a strange idea about men, Natasha, if you believe that the scraped-back hair and the buttoned-up clothes stop them from being curious about what it is you are attempting to hide.'

She blinked at him.

Leo laughed—oddly.

'We don't all go for anorexic pop-stars barely out of the schoolroom,' he explained helpfully. 'Some men even like a challenge in a woman instead of seeing it all hanging out and handed to us on a plate.'

His gaze dropped to the rounded shape of her breasts where they heaved up and down inside her jacket. It was pure self-defence that made her pull in her chest. His eyes darkened as he flicked them back to her face and Natasha knew then what it was he was talking about.

'You want to unwrap yourself and fulfil my curiosity?' he invited. 'I didn't think so.' He smiled at her drop-jaw gasp.

'Why are you doing this—s-saying these things to me?' she whispered in genuine bafflement. 'Do you think that because you witnessed what I witnessed it gives you the right to speak to me as if I am a slut?'

'You would not know how to play the slut if your life depended on it,' Leo grimly mocked. 'It is a major part of your fascination to me that with a sister like yours, you are like you are.'

Natasha just continued to stare at him, trying to work out what it was she must have done to deserve any of this. 'Well, you are being loathsome,' she murmured finally. 'And there is nothing in the least bit fascinating about being that, Mr Christakis.'

Her bag had fallen to the floor when she'd jumped to her feet. Natasha bent to recover it, then with as much dignity as she could muster, she turned to leave.

'You're right,' he responded.

'I know I am.' She nodded, taking a shaky step towards the door, and heard him suck in his breath.

'All right,' he growled. 'I'm sorry. OK?'

For mocking her situation just to get the clever quips in?

Straightening her trembling shoulders, 'I didn't ask you to bring me here,' Natasha pushed out in a thick voice. 'I have never asked you to do anything for me. So my sister is a slut. Your stepbrother is a slut. Other than that you and I have nothing in common or to say to each other.'

With that she took another couple of steps towards the door, just wanting to get out of here as quickly as she could do now and willing her legs to continue to hold her up while she made her escape.

Her mobile phone started ringing.

It was like chaos arriving to further agitate havoc because yet another telephone started ringing somewhere else in the house and Natasha's feet pulled her to a confused standstill, the sound of those two phones ringing shrilly in her head.

Behind her *he* wasn't moving a muscle. Was he—was Leo Christakis really as attracted to her as he'd just made out? Her jangling brain flipped out.

Then a knock sounded on the door and the handle was turning. Like a switch that kept on flicking her brain from one thing to another, Natasha envisaged Rico about to walk in the room and her feet were taking a stumbling step back. Maybe she swayed, she didn't know, but a pair of hands arrived to clasp her upper arms and the next thing she knew she was being turned around and pressed against Leo Christakis's shirt front.

'Steady,' his low voice murmured.

Natasha felt the sound resonate across the tips of her breasts and she quivered.

'Oh, I'm sorry, Mr Christakis,' a female voice exclaimed in surprise. 'I heard you come in and assumed you were alone.'

'As you see, Agnes, I am not,' Leo responded.

Blunt as always. His half-Greek housekeeper was used to it, though her eyes flicked curiously to his stepbrother's fiancée standing here held against his chest. When Agnes looked back at his face, not a single hint showed in her expression to say that what she was seeing was a shock.

'Mr Rico keeps ringing, demanding to speak to Miss Moyles,' the housekeeper informed him.

Natasha quivered again. This time he soothed the quiver by tracking a hand down the length of her spine and settling it in the curvy hollow of her lower back. 'We are not here,' Leo instructed. 'And no one gets into this house.'

'Yes, sir.'

The housekeeper left the room again, leaving a silence behind along with a tension that grabbed a tight hold on Natasha's chest. Just totally unable to understand what it was she was feeling any more, she took a shaky step away from him, confused heat warming her cheeks.

'Sh-she's going to think w-we—'

'Agnes is not paid to think,' Leo cut in arrogantly and moved off to pour another brandy while Natasha sank weakly back down into the chair.

'Here, take this…' Coming to squat down in front of her, he handed her another glass. 'Only this time try drinking it instead of throwing it at me,' he suggested. 'It is supposed to be better for you that way.'

His dry attempt at humour made Natasha flick him a brief guilty glance. 'I'm sorry I did that. I don't even know why I did.'

'Don't worry about it.' Leo's smile was sardonic. 'I am used to having my face slapped in car parks and drinks thrown at me. Loathsome guys expect it.'

He added a grimace.

Natasha lowered her eyes to watch his mouth take on that grimacing tilt. It was only as she watched it settle back into a straight line again that she realised it was actually a quite beautifully shaped mouth, slender and firm but—nice.

And his eyes were nice, too, she noticed when, as if drawn by a magnet, she looked back at them. The rich, dark brown colour was framed by the most gorgeous thick, curling black eyelashes that managed to add an unexpected appeal to his face she would never have allowed him before. That pronounced bump in the middle of his nose saved his face from being a bit too perfect. A strong face, she decided, hard hewn and chiselled yet very good-looking—if you didn't count the inbuilt cynicism that was there without her actually knowing *how* it was there.

OK, so he was a lot older than her. Older than Rico by eight years, which made him older than her by a very big ten. And those extra years showed in the blunt opinions he had no problem tossing at people—her especially.

But as for his looks, they weren't old. His skin was a warm honey colour that lay smooth against the bones in his face. No age lines, no smile lines, not even any frown lines, though he did a lot of frowning—around her anyway.

Unaware that she was taking short sips at the brandy as she studied him, Natasha let her eyes track the width of his muscled shoulders trapped inside the smooth fit of his jacket, then let them absorb the fact that his torso was very long and lean and tight. When standing up, he was taller than Rico by several inches and his dark hair was shorter, cut to suit the stronger shape of his face.

She was asking for trouble, Leo thought severely as he watched that lush, pink, generous mouth adopt a musing pout while she looked him over as if he were a prime piece of meat laid out on a butcher's slab.

'How old are you, Natasha?' he asked curiously. 'Twenty-six—twenty-seven?'

Her spine went stiff. 'I'm twenty-four!' she iced out. 'And that is just one more insult you've hit me with!'

'And you're counting.' His eyes narrowed.

'Yes!' she heaved out.

With her blue eyes flashing indignation at him she looked pretty damn fantastic, Leo observed as he knelt there, trying to decide what to do next.

He could leap on her and kiss her—strangely enough she seemed to need him to do that. Or he could gently remove the glass she was crushing between her slender fingers, ease her down on her knees in front of him, then encourage her to just get it over with and use his shoulder to have a good weep.

Something twisted inside him—not sexual this time, but an ache of a different kind. Did she know how badly she was trembling? Did she know her slender white throat had to work like crazy each time to swallow some of the brandy and that her hair was threatening to fall free from its knot?

'I th-think I w-want to go home now,' she mumbled distractedly.

To the apartment she shared with her sister? 'Drink the rest of your brandy first,' Leo advised quietly.

Natasha glanced down at the glass she was holding so tightly between her fingers, then just stared at it as if she was shocked to find it there. As she lifted it to her mouth Leo watched her soft lips take on the warm bloom of brandy and the ache inside him shifted back to a sexual ache.

The doorbell rang.

Rico called her name out.

Natasha's head shot up, the brandy glass falling from her fingers to land with a thunk on the carpet, sending brandy fumes wafting up.

'Natasha—' Leo reached out to her, thinking she was going to keel over into a faint.

But once again Natasha Moyles surprised him. He did not need to pull her to her knees because she arrived there right between his spread thighs with her arms going up and over his shoulders to cling to his neck, those vulnerable blue eyes staring up at him with a helpless mix of pleading and dismay.

'Don't let him in,' she begged tensely.

'I won't,' Leo promised.

'I h-hate him. I never want to see him again.'

'I will not let him in,' he repeated gently.

But Rico called out her name again hoarse with emotion and Leo felt her fingernails dig into the back of his neck while the two of them listened to his housekeeper make some stern response.

'My heart's beating so fast I can't breathe properly,' Natasha whispered breathlessly.

A spark of challenge lit Leo's eyes. He should have contained it—he knew that even as he murmured the challenging, 'I can make it beat faster.'

If he'd said it to distract her attention away from Rico, it certainly worked when her mouth parted on a surprised little gasp. Leo raised a ruefully mocking eyebrow, feeling the buzz, the loin heating, sex-charging, *challenging* buzz.

And he leant in and claimed her mouth.

It was like falling into an electrified pit, Natasha likened dizzily as not a single part or inch of her missed out on the high-voltage rush. She'd never experienced anything like it. He crushed her lips to keep them parted, then slid his tongue into her mouth. The sheer shock feel of that alien wet contact stroking across her own tongue made her shiver with pleasure, then stiffen in shock. He did it again and this time she whimpered.

Leo murmured something, then slid his arms around her

so he could draw her closer to him and deepen the kiss. The next few seconds went by in a fevered hot rush. She felt plastered against his muscled torso. She could hear Rico shouting. Something hard and ridged was pushing against her front. The wildly disturbing recognition of what that something was sent her deaf to everything else as her own senses bloomed with an excited sparkle in response.

It was crazy, she tried telling herself. She didn't even *like* Leo Christakis yet here she was *drowning* in the full on power of his heated kiss! In all of her life she had never kissed anyone like this—never felt even remotely like this! It was like throwing herself against a rock only to discover that the rock had magical powers. His hand skated the length of her spine to her waist, then pressed her even closer, at the same time that he increased the pressure on her mouth, sending her neck arching backwards as he used his tongue to create a warm, thick chain reaction that poured through her entire body like silk.

Natasha heard herself groan something. He muttered a very low, sensual rasp in response. Then Rico called out to her again, harsh and angry enough to pierce into her foggy consciousness, and she wrenched her mouth free.

Trembling and panting with her heart pounding wildly, she stared up at this man while her mind fed her an image of the way Rico had been enjoying Cindy across his desk.

As if her sister knew what she was thinking, her phone began to ring in her purse.

The scald of betrayal burned her up on the inside.

'For God's sake, Natasha, let me *talk* to you!' Rico's rasping voice ground out.

Revenge lit her up.

Leo saw it happen and knew exactly where it was coming from. Sanity returned to him with a gut-crushing whoosh. She was going to offer herself to him, but did he want her like this, bruised and heartbroken and throbbing with a desire for revenge on Rico, who could easily charge in here and catch them?

As they had walked into Rico's office and caught him.

Natasha leant away from Leo and began unbuttoning her jacket with shakily fumbling, feverish fingers.

Leo released a sigh. 'You don't want to do this, Natasha,' he said heavily.

'Don't tell me what I don't want,' she shook out.

The two pieces of fabric were wrenched apart to reveal a white top made of some stretchy fabric that crossed over and moulded the thrusting fullness of her two tight breasts.

Leo looked down at them, then up into her fever-bright eyes, and wanted to bite out a filthy black curse. As she wrenched the jacket off altogether, he reached out to try and stop her, only to freeze when he read the helpless plea that had etched itself on her paper-white face.

If he turned her down now, the rejection was going to shatter her.

Her smooth white throat moved as she swallowed, those kiss-warmed lips parting so she could whisper out a husky little, 'Please…'

And he was lost, Leo knew it. Even as she took the initiative away from him by winding her arms around his neck again, he knew he was not going to stop this. Lifting his hands up to mould her ribcage, he stroked them down the tight white fabric to the sexy indentation of her waist in an exploring act that rolled back the denials still beating an urgent tattoo in his head.

Her mouth was a hungry invite. Leo raked his hands back up her body again and this time covered the full perfect globes of her breasts. She fell apart on a series of gasps and quivers that sent her body into an acute sensual arch, fingernails digging into his neck again, hair suddenly tumbling free in a glorious roll of fine silken waves down her back. She was amazing, a stunningly complicated mix of prim, straight-lace and pure untrammelled passion with her lily-white skin and her lush parted mouth, and her breasts two sensational mounds that filled his hands and…

The front door slammed.

Rico had gone.

If Natasha recognised what the sound meant she did not make a response. Her eyes still burned into him with the fevered invitation she was offering.

Time to make a decision, Leo accepted grimly. Continue this or put a stop to it?

Then her fingernails dug deeper to pull his mouth back down onto hers and the decision was made for him.

Natasha felt his surrender and took it with a leap of triumph that bordered on the mad. She became aware of the power of his erection pressing against her again, instinct made her move against it. He muttered a low, throaty response and he was suddenly tightening his hold of her and drawing her to her feet. Next he was swinging her up into his arms and carrying her, the kiss still a seething hot fuse that frazzled her brain and had her heart pounding to the beat of his footsteps echoing on oak flooring as he headed across the hall and began climbing the stairs.

It was the moment that Natasha saw a small chink of sanity. Her head went back, rending the kiss apart as she opened her eyes to look deep into Leo Christakis's heavily lidded dark eyes before she glanced around her as if she'd been woken up suddenly from a dream.

It was only then that she realised that the hallway was empty. No one was there. No Rico witnessing his betrayed fiancée being carried to bed by her soon-to-be new lover. No housekeeper containing her disapproval and shock.

'Changed your mind now you don't have a witness?' Leo's hard voice swung her eyes back to him again.

He'd gone still on one of the stairs and the look of cold cynicism was back, lashing his skin to the bones in his face.

'No,' Natasha breathed, and she discovered that she meant it. She wanted to do this. She wanted to be carried to bed and made love to by a man who genuinely wanted her—she wanted to lose every single old-fashioned and disgustingly outmoded inhibition she possessed!

'Please,' she breathed softly as she leant in to brush a kiss across the hard line of his mouth. 'Make love to me, Leo.'

There was another moment of hesitation, a glimpse of fury in the depths of his eyes. Then he was moving again, allowing her to breathe again though she had not been aware of holding her breath. He finished the climb up the stairs and carried her into a sultry summer-warmed bedroom with pale walls and big dark pieces of furniture. A red Persian rug covered most of the polished oak floor.

Then he really shocked her by dumping her unceremoniously on the top of a huge soft bed.

As Natasha lay there blinking up at him Leo stood looking down at her, his expression as hard and cynical as hell. 'Stay there and pull yourself together,' was all he uttered before he turned around to walk back to the door.

'Why?' Natasha shook out.

'I will not play substitute to any man,' the cold brute answered.

Natasha sat up. 'Y-you said you wanted me.'

'Strange—' he turned, his kiss-heated mouth taking on a scornful twist '—but seeing you getting off on the possibility of Rico witnessing us together was a real turn off for me.'

Natasha sat up with a jolt. 'I was not getting off on it—!'

'Liar,' he lashed back, then really startled her by striding back to the bed to come and lean over her—close enough to make her blink warily because she just didn't know what was going to come next.

'To keep things clear between us, Natasha,' he murmured silkily, 'if you loved what we were doing downstairs so much you forgot all about Rico, then ask yourself what that tells me about Miss Betrayed and Broken-hearted, hmm—?'

It was as good as a cold, hard slap in the face. Natasha just stared up at him because the worst thing of all was that he had only told it how it was! She *had* been thinking about Rico when she'd invited what she had downstairs. And she had *no* excuse for the way she had begged him to bring her up here!

But had he behaved any better? 'You cruel, h-hateful swine,' she breathed, and pulled up her knees so she could bury her face.

Leo agreed. He was behaving like an absolute beast feeding her all the blame for whatever had erupted in *both* of them downstairs. It was still erupting inside him, he admitted as he turned away again and strode back to the door, wishing that he had stayed in Athens this morning instead of…

Telephones started ringing again, piercing through the high-octane atmosphere—his phone in his jacket pocket and another phone ringing somewhere else in the house. Retrieving his mobile, Leo glared at the display screen, expecting it to show Rico's name.

But it was Juno, his PA. Leo sanctioned the connection. 'This had better be important,' he warned as he stepped out of the bedroom and pulled the door shut.

Natasha lifted her head at the sound of the door snapping into its housing. He'd gone. He'd left her sitting here in a huddle on his bed and just walked away from her—because he could.

On a sudden pummelling punch of self-hatred she scrambled up off the bed, hurt beyond sense that yet another man had humiliated her in the space of one horrible day.

Oh, she had to get out of here! Natasha almost screeched that need at herself as she looked around the floor for her shoes and couldn't find them. Then she remembered the vague echo of them falling off her feet and hitting the floor when Leo had picked her up. Her hair fell forward, tumbling in long waves around her face as if to taunt how she'd been so wrapped up in what she'd been doing with him that she hadn't even noticed before now how her hair had sprung free of its restraints!

Like herself. She shuddered, turning like a drunk not knowing where she was going and heading for the door. She made it out onto the landing and even found her way back down the stairs without coming face to face with anyone else. The door to the living room still hung wide-open and the wretched tears almost broke free when she saw the way her jacket lay in a pale blue swish of fabric on the floor by the chair she had been sitting on before she…

Swallowing, she hurried forward to snatch up the offending garment, pulling it on and fastening it up while she scrambled her feet into her shoes.

He arrived in the doorway, lounging there and filling it with his lean, dark, overbearing presence and…

Her phone started to ring in her purse.

With what tiny bit of control she had left, Natasha bent down to scoop up the purse, then dragged the phone out with trembling fingers and just slammed the wafer-thin piece of shiny black plastic forcefully down on the floor.

It stopped ringing.

The sudden rush of silence throbbed like the beat of a drum in her head, and the tears were really threatening now like hot, sharp shards of flaming glass hitting the backs of her eyes and her throat. She spun towards the door to find Leo was still there, blocking her only exit.

Her mouth began to work, fighting—fighting the tears. 'Please,' she pushed out at him on a thick broken whisper. 'I need you to move out of my way so I can leave.'

Silence. He said nothing. He did not attempt to move. His eyes were half hooded, his lips straight and tight. And there was just enough narrow-eyed insolence in the way he was casually standing there with his arms folded across his front like that to make Natasha realise that something about him had altered dramatically.

'W-what—?' she shook out.

Leo wondered how she would react if he accused her of being a play-acting little thief?

'I am just curious,' he posed very levelly. 'Leave here for where?'

But inside he didn't feel level in any other way. Inside he was feeling so conned he didn't know how he was managing to hold it all in!

Rico's little accomplice—who would have thought it? Apparently Miss Cool and Prim was not so prim when it came to letting her greedy, grasping, slender fingers scoop up the cash Rico had stolen from him!

'To find Rico, perhaps?' he suggested when she didn't say anything.

'No!' She even managed to shudder. 'H-home,' she said, 'to my apartment.'

'You don't have your keys.'

'I'll get the janitor to let me in.'

'Or your loving sister,' Leo provided. 'I predict she is already there, waiting to pounce on you the moment that you arrive.'

Was the other sister in on the scam, too?

And look at this one, he thought as he shuttered his eyes that bit more before running them down her front. She was back to being buttoned up to the throat as if the passionate interlude they'd just shared had never taken place—if you didn't count the flowing hair and the flush on her cheeks and the kiss-swollen bloom on her lips that he had put there.

'What does it matter to you if she is?' Natasha asked. 'This was never your problem,' she informed him stiffly. 'You should not have become involved. I don't even know why you did *or* why you had to bring me here at all!'

'You needed a safe place to recover,' Leo said dryly.

'*Safe?*' Natasha choked out. 'You'd barely dragged me through your front door before you were coming on to me!'

His careless shrug shot Natasha into movement, wanting, *needing* to get away from the insufferable devil so badly now she was prepared to risk the feeble strength in her shaky legs to walk towards him—aware of the way his eyes followed her every footstep—aware that at any second now she was going to fall down in a screaming hot puddle of tears on the floor.

And *still* he did not move out of her way so she could get out of here, so the closer she came to him, the more her senses went wild, fluttering in protest in case he dared to touch her again—and at the same time fizzing with excitement in the hope that he did!

I don't know myself any more, Natasha thought helplessly. 'Move,' she demanded, resorting to a bit of his own blunt way of speech.

The slight tug his mouth gave was an acknowledgement of it, but he didn't shift. 'You cannot leave,' he coolly informed her.

Was he mad? 'Of course I can go.' Shoulders tense, Natasha tried to push him out of her way by placing her hands on his chest. It didn't happen. It was like trying to move a fully grown tree, and in the end Leo caught up her fingers to lift them away from his chest.

'When I said you cannot leave, Natasha, I meant it,' he informed her very seriously. 'At least not until the police arrive to take you away, that is…'

CHAPTER THREE

Natasha froze for a second. Then, 'The police?' she edged out blankly.

'The Fraud Squad, to be more accurate,' Leo confirmed.

'Fraud…?'

His mouth gave a twitch at the way she kept on echoing him. 'As in swindler and charlatan,' he provided, driving his gaze down her body as if to say the crime was that she looked the way she did yet could turn on so hotly the way she had.

Natasha quivered, her cheeks turning pink with shamed embarrassment. 'I don't usually…'

'Turn on for a man just to pull the wool over his eyes…?'

Untangling her fingers from his, she fell back a couple of steps and really looked at him, catching on at last that he was leading somewhere with this that she was not going to like.

'Since I don't have a single clue what it is you're trying to get at, I think you had better explain,' Natasha prompted finally.

'Does that mean you *do* want to go to bed with me and it is not a sham act?'

Natasha tensed, lips parting then closing again, because the true answer to that taunt was just not going to happen. 'I was in shock when I—'

'In a state of fright, more like,' he interrupted, 'as to what

Rico had done to all your plans, with his crass bit on the desk today.'

'Plans for what?' Lifting a hand into her hair, she pushed the tumbling mass back from her angrily bewildered face. 'I was planning to marry him—well, there's one plan gone down the tubes,' she choked out. 'And as you've just kindly pointed out to me, I caught him having sex with my own sister—so there's my pride gone the same way along with any love for my sister!' The hand dropped to fold along with the other hand tight across her front. 'Then I surrendered to some mad desire to be wanted by *anybody* and you happened to be in the right place at the right time,' she pushed on, 'but that was just another plan sent off down the tubes when you changed your mind about w-wanting me!'

'And now your carefully creamed nest egg is about to go the same way,' Leo added without a hint of sympathy. 'So I would say that you are having a very bad day, today, Natasha. A very bad day indeed.'

'Nest egg?' Natasha picked up. 'What is it you are talking about now?'

Wearing that smile on his lips that she didn't like, Leo levered himself away from the doorframe and moved away, leaving her to turn and watch as he headed for the drinks cabinet.

He needed something strong, Leo decided as he poured neat whisky into a glass. He took a good slug, then turned back to look at her, 'I have just been talking to my PA,' he enlightened. 'Juno has been very busy investigating where Rico stashed the money he stole from me and has managed to trace it to an offshore bank account in your name, so lose the bemused expression, Natasha. I'm on to you….'

Nothing happened. She didn't gasp, she didn't faint, she didn't jump in with a flood of denials or excuses aimed to defend what it was he was talking about now. Instead, Leo stood there and watched while something cold struck into him because there it was, the dawning of *honesty* taking over her lying, cheating, paling face.

That mouth was still a killer though, he observed—and slammed the glass down, suddenly blisteringly angry with himself for being so easily duped by her *challengingly* prim disguise!

'I think you had better sit down before you fall down,' he advised her flatly.

And she did, which only helped to feed his anger all the more. The flowing-haired witch dropped like a stone into the nearest chair, then covered her guilty face with her light-fingered thieving hands!

Rico had *stolen* the money, Natasha was busily replaying over and over. He'd placed *stolen* money in an offshore bank account in *her* name! One of her hands twisted down to cover her mouth as the nausea returned with a vengeance. In the dragging silence blanketing the space separating them she could feel Leo Christakis's ice-cold anger and blistering contempt beating over her in waves.

If he'd made this declaration yesterday, she would not have believed him. But now, with everything else she'd been forced to look at today, Natasha didn't even see a chink of a question glimmering in the nightmare her mind had become as to whether there had been some kind of mistake.

Everything about Rico had been a lie from start to finish. The way he'd used his looks and his charm and his fabulous blinding-white smile to lure her to him, the way he'd poured soft words of love over her too-susceptible head and refused to make love to her because he wanted to protect her innocence, while all the time he'd been cynically planning to turn her into a thief!

Pulling her fingers away from her mouth, 'I'll give you the money back just as soon as I can access it,' she promised.

'Sure you will,' Leo confirmed. 'Once you have recovered your composure, we will go and see to it straight away.'

That brought her face up, whiter than white now so her eyes stood out bluer than blue. 'But you don't understand. I can't touch it yet.'

'Don't play the broken doll with me next, Natasha,' Leo bit out impatiently. 'It won't alter the fact that you are going to give me my money back now—today.'

'But I can't!' Anxiety shot her quivering to her feet. 'I can't touch it until the day before I was supposed to be marrying Rico! He said it was a tax loophole he'd discovered—that *you* had told him about! He said we had to lock the money up under my name in an offshore account until end of business the day before we marry, then transfer it to another account in our m-married name!'

Leo suddenly exploded spectacularly. 'I do not appreciate you trying to involve my name in your filthy scam!' he bit out at her furiously, 'and telling me stupid lies about access to the money is *not* going to get you out of trouble, Miss Moyles! So cough up the cash or watch me call the damn police!'

In a state of nerve-numbing terror, Natasha backed away as he took two long strides towards her with a murderous expression clamped to his face. The backs of her legs hit the chair she'd just vacated and she toppled back into it. He came to stand over her as he'd done in the bedroom, only this time Natasha put up her hands in an instinctive need to keep him at bay.

Watching her cower in front of him sent Leo into an even bigger rage. 'I don't hit women,' he rasped, then turned on his heel and walked away—right out of the room.

The police—he's going to call the police! Out of her mind with fear now, Natasha scrambled upright and chased after him, terrified of going anywhere near him but even more terrified of what would happen if she didn't stop him from carrying out his threat! He'd crossed the hall and entered a room opposite, which turned out to be a book-lined study.

Coming to a jerky halt in the doorway, she stared as he strode up to the desk and picked up the phone.

Panic sent her heart into overdrive. 'Leo, please…' The pleading quaver in her voice made him go still, wide shoulders taut. 'You have got to believe me,' she begged him. 'I didn't know the money was stolen! Rico conned me into banking it for him as much as he conned you out of it in the first place!'

The last part didn't go down too well because he began stabbing numbers into the telephone with a grim resolve that sent Natasha flying across the room to grab hold of his arm.

Warm, hard muscles bunched beneath her clutching fingers, anger and rejection pouring into his muscular frame. 'He s-said it was to ensure our f-future,' she rushed on unsteadily, 'He said it was a bequeath to him from your father *you* had been holding in trust! He s-said you…'

'Wanted to see the back of him so badly I was prepared to break the law to do it?' Leo suggested when her scramble of words dried up.

'Something like that,' Natasha admitted. Then— Oh, dear God, what had she let Rico do to her? 'Now you are telling me he lied, which means he lied to me about absolutely everything and I—'

The phone went down. Leo turned on her so suddenly Natasha was given no chance to react before she found herself trapped in his arms. His mouth arrived. It took hers with an angry heat that offered nothing but punishment yet she responded—responded to him like a crazy person, clinging and kissing him back as if she'd die if she didn't! When he pulled away again she was limp with shock at her own dizzying loss of control!

'Take my advice,' he rasped. 'Keep with the seduction

theme; it works on me a whole lot better than the innocent pleading does.'

Then his fingers gripped her arms like pincers, which he used to thrust her right away from him, and he was re-establishing his connection with the phone.

Natasha's heart lodged like a throbbing lump of fear in her throat. 'Please,' she begged him, yet again having to swallow to be able to speak at all. 'I did not know that Rico had stolen your money, Leo! I can give you back every penny in six weeks if you'll only wait, but, please—*please* don't ring the police—think of the effect it will have on Rico's mother if you have him arrested! She will—'

'You love the bastard,' Leo bit out roughly. Cutting into what she had been trying to say and making Natasha blink.

'At first, y-yes,' she admitted it. 'He flattered me and...' she swallowed again '...and I know it sounds pathetic but I fell for it because...'

Oh, because she'd been a blind fool! She knew it—probably *everyone* knew it!

'Because things were becoming really bad between me and Cindy and I think I was unconsciously searching for a way out.'

Rico had provided it. It was easier to believe she'd fallen in love with him than to admit to herself that she was so un-happy with her life that she'd grabbed the first opportunity handed to her to get out of it without having to cause ructions within her family. It had been so easy to turn blind eyes to what Rico was really like.

She was a coward, in other words, unwilling to take control of her own life without a nice acceptable prop with which to lean upon as she did.

'I'd already realised Rico wasn't w-what I wanted,' she forced herself to go on. 'I was on my way to tell him so today when we—when we caught him with Cindy. It was—'

'Juno…'

Natasha blinked as Leo's voice cut right through what she had been trying to tell him.

'Put a stop on your investigation of Miss Moyles,' he instructed. 'There has been a—mistake. Have my plane for Athens put on standby and add Miss Moyles's name to the passenger list.'

The phone went down. Natasha tugged in a tense breath. 'Why did you say that?'

'Why do you think?' He turned a hard look on her. 'I want my money back and since you've just told me it will be six weeks before you can give it back to me, I am not letting you out of my sight until you do.'

'But I don't want to go to Athens!' Natasha shrilled out. 'I don't want to go anywhere with you!'

'In your present situation that was not the cleverest thing you could say to me right now, Natasha,' Leo said dryly.

'W-what did you mean by that?'

'Sex,' Leo drawled as if that one shocking word were the answer to everything. 'It is your only bargaining chip, so telling me you don't want me is not going to get you out of this sticky situation, is it?'

A sudden dawning as to where he was going with this shot Natasha's trembling shoulders back, sending her loosened hair flying around her face. 'I am not paying you back with sex!' she protested.

'I should think not,' the cold devil answered. 'No woman, no matter how appealingly she presents herself to me, is worth a cool two million to bed.'

'No…' Yet again Natasha found herself sinking into a thick morass of confusion, the intended insult floating right over her as this new revelation struck a blow to her head. 'F-Five hundred thousand pounds,' she insisted through lips so paper dry now it stung to move them. 'Rico opened the account w-with…'

Her voice trailed away when she saw the expression of mocking contempt that carved itself into this man's face. 'Four separate instalments of five hundred thousand adds up to a cool two million—your arithmetic is letting you down,' Leo spelled out the full ugly truth for her.

'Are you sure?' she breathed.

'Grow up, Natasha,' Leo derided the question. 'You are dealing with a real man now, not the weak excuse for a man you fell in love with—'

'I *don't* love him!'

'So here is the deal.' He kept going as if she hadn't made that denial. 'Wherever I go from now on, you will come with me. And to make the pill sweeter for me to take, you will also share my bed as I wait out the six long weeks until you can access *my* money, when you will then hand it back to me before you get the hell out of my life!'

Real skin-crawling panic had to erupt some time because Natasha had been struggling for so long to keep it in. But now the wild need to get away from this ruthless man and the whole situation sent her spinning around and racing out of the room and back across the hall.

Once again she found herself searching for her bag.

'Going somewhere?' that cruel voice mocked her—again.

'Yes.' She dived on the offending article that kept getting away from her without her knowing it had. 'I'm going to find Rico. He's the only person who can tell you the truth.'

'You think I would believe anything he said to me?'

Swinging around, Natasha almost threw her bag at him! 'I will give you back—every single penny of your rotten two million pounds if it kills me trying!' she choked out.

'Euros…'

Leo's smooth drawl sent her still with her blue eyes relaying her next complete daze as to what he was talking about!

'The money will have been converted into Euros,' he pointed out helpfully, then he named the new figure in Euros, freezing Natasha where she stood. 'Of course it means the same when converted back into pounds sterling so long as the exchange rate remains sound, but…' His shrug said the rest for him—that the figure was growing and growing by the minute in the present financial climate. 'And then there is the interest I will charge you for the—loan.'

'I hate you,' was all she could manage to whisper.

'Fortunate for you, then, that you fall apart so excitingly when I kiss you.'

'I need to speak to Rico,' Natasha insisted.

'Still hoping the two of you can escape from this?'

'No!' She shot up her chin, eyes flashing, hair fascinatingly wild around her tense face. 'I need him to tell you the truth even if you do refuse to believe it!'

Leo observed her from an outwardly calm exterior that did not reflect what was crawling around his insides. He was blisteringly angry—with himself more than anyone because he would have been willing to swear that the prim, cool and dignified Natasha Moyles he'd believed he knew had been the genuine article.

No sign of her now, he observed.

'You will have to catch him first,' he told her dryly. 'Juno tells me that Rico has already left the country. He hitched a ride on a friend's private plane out of London airport. He was quicker than you were at realising what was going to come out of his fevered love fest today, you see. A one-minute telephone conversation with Juno after he left here and he knew he'd been sussed. He's left you to carry the can for him, Natasha.' He spelled it out for her in case she had not worked that out for herself.

Feeling as if the whole weight of the world had just dropped onto her shoulders, 'Then you might as well shop me to the Fraud Squad,' she murmured helplessly.

Leo grimaced. 'That is still one way for me to go, certainly,' he agreed, and watched the telling little flinch that she gave up. 'However, you do still have the other way to pull this around, Miss Moyles…' She even flinched at the formal Miss Moyles now. 'You could still try utilising the only asset you have as far as I am concerned and make me an offer I won't want to refuse?'

He was talking sex again. Natasha went icy. 'The money is peanuts to you, isn't it?'

He offered a shrug. 'The difference between the two of us being that I am wealthy enough to call it peanuts, whereas you are not.'

That was so very true that Natasha did not even bother to argue the point. Instead she made herself look at him. 'So you want me to pay the money back with—favours—' for the life of her she could not bring herself to call it *sex* '—and in return you will promise me you will not take this to the police?'

Leo smiled at the careful omission of the word *sex* and for once the smile actually hit the dark of his eyes. 'You do the prim stuff exceptionally well, Natasha,' he informed her lazily as he began to walk towards her, putting just about every defence mechanism she possessed on stinging alert. 'Shame that your hair is floating around your face like a siren's promise and your lips are still pumped up and hot from my kisses, because it forces me to remember the real you.'

Fighting not to flinch when he reached out to touch her, 'I want your promise that if I do what you w-want me to do, you won't go to the police,' she insisted.

His fingers were drifting up her arms. 'You do know you don't have anything left to bargain with, don't you?'

Pressing her lips together, Natasha nodded, her heart pounding in her chest when his fingers reached her shoulders and gripped. 'I'm relying on your sense of honour.'

'You believe I have one?' He sounded genuinely curious.

She nodded again. 'Yes,' she delivered on a stifled breath. She had to believe it because it was the only way she was going to cope with all of this.

He drifted those light caressing fingers along her shoulders until they reached her smooth skin at her nape, making her jump as a long thumb arrived beneath her chin to tilt up her face. His warm, whisky-scented breath had her lips parting like traitors because they knew what was coming next.

'Then you have my promise,' he said softly.

It was the most soul-shrivelling thing Natasha had ever experienced when she fell into that deal-sealing kiss.

Then her mobile phone started ringing, shocking them apart with Natasha turning to stare down at the phone in surprise because she thought she'd killed it when she'd thrown it to the floor.

Leo went to pick it up, since she didn't seem able to move a single muscle, stepping around her and reminding her of a big, sleek giant cat, the way he moved with such loose-limbed grace. Without asking her permission, he sanctioned the call and put her phone to his ear.

It was some fashion designer wanting to know why Cindy had not turned up for a fitting. 'Natasha Moyles is no longer responsible for her sister's movements,' Leo announced before cutting the connection.

Natasha stared up at him in disbelief. 'What did you say that for?'

He turned a mocking look on her. 'Because it is the truth?'

She went to take her phone back. He snatched it out of her way, then slid it into his jacket pocket. 'Think about it,' he insisted. 'You cannot continue play your sister's doormat while you are in Athens with me.'

And just like that he brought the scene in Rico's office pouring back in. Rico hadn't only involved her in his thieving scam, but he'd been treating her like his doormat, too! Natasha turned away, despising herself for being so gullible—despising Rico for making her see herself like this! And then there was Cindy, her loving sister Cindy playing the selfish, spoiled brat who took anything she felt like because she always had done and been allowed to get away with it!

Then another thought arrived, one that hit her like a brick in the chest. Cindy didn't even need Natasha to keep her life running smoothly because arrangements were already in place to hand her singing career over to a professional agency. One of those big, flashy firms with the kind of high profile Cindy had loved the moment its name was mentioned to her. From as early as next week, Natasha would no longer be responsible for Cindy at all, in effect, to free her up to concentrate on her wedding preparations and her move to Milan!

And she'd just found the reason why Cindy had been doing *that* with Rico. Cindy was about to get everything she'd always wanted—a high-profile management team that was going to fast-track her career and more significantly her absolute freedom from the restraints the sister she resented imposed.

She lifted a hand up to cover her mouth. Her fingers were trembling and she felt cold through to the bone.

'What now?' Leo Christakis shot at her.

She just shook her head because she couldn't speak. Cindy being Cindy, she just could not let Natasha walk off into the sunset with her handsome Italian without going all out to spoil it. *I've had your man, Natasha. Now you can trip off and marry him.* She could hear Cindy's voice trilling those words even though they had not yet been said!

Cindy's little swansong. Her wonderful farewell.

'She set me up,' she managed to whisper. 'She knew I was going to meet Rico today so she made sure she got to his office before I did and set me up to witness her doing—that with him.'

'Why would your own sister want to set you up for a scene like that?'

'Because I'm not her real sister.' Natasha slid her fingers away from her mouth. 'I was adopted…' By two people who'd believed their chances of having a child of their own had long passed them by. Five years later and their real daughter had arrived in their arms like a precious gift from heaven. Everyone had adored Cindy—*Natasha* had adored her!

A firm hand arrived on her arm to guide her down into the chair again, then disappeared to collect a second brandy. 'Here,' he murmured, 'take this…'

Natasha frowned down at the glass, then shook her head. 'No.' She felt too sick to drink anything. 'Take it away.'

Leo put the glass down, but remained squatting in front of her as he'd done once before. Strong thighs spread, forearms resting on his knees. His suit, she saw as if for the first time, was made of some fabulously smooth fabric, expensive and creaseless—like the man himself.

And his mouth might look grim, but it was still a mouth she could taste; she felt as if she already knew it far more intimately than any other man's mouth—and that included Rico.

'Stop looking at me as if you *care* what's happening inside my head!' she snapped at the way he was squatting there studying her as if he were really concerned!

He had the grace to offer an acknowledging grimace and climbed back to his full height. So did Natasha, making herself do it, feeling cold—frozen right through, because it had also just hit her that she was on her own now. No sister. No fiancé. Not even a pair of loving parents to turn to because, although they'd loved her in their own way, they had never loved her in the way they loved Cindy. Cindy was always going to come first with them.

'So what is it you want me to do?' she murmured finally in a voice that sounded as cold as she felt.

Leo threw her a frowning dark look. 'I told you what I want.'

'Sex.' This time she managed to name it.

'Don't knock it, Natasha,' Leo drawled. 'The fact that we find we desire each other is about to keep you out of a whole lot of trouble.'

He turned away then, leaving her to stare at his long, broad back. He was so hard she had to wonder who it was that had made him like that.

Then she remembered Rico telling her that Leo had been married once. From what Rico had said, his wife had been an exquisite black-haired, black-eyed pure Latin sex bomb who used to turn men on with a single look. The marriage had lasted a short year before Leo had grown tired of hauling her out of other men's beds and he'd kicked her out of his life for good.

But he must have really loved her to last a whole year with a faithless woman like that. Had his ex-wife mangled up his feelings so badly she'd turned him into the ruthless cynic she was looking at now?

As if he could tell what she was thinking he glanced round at her, catching the expression on her face. Their eyes maintained contact for a few nerve-trapping seconds as something very close to understanding stirred between them, as if he knew what she was thinking and his steady regard was acknowledging it.

'OK, let's go.' Just that quickly he switched from seeming almost human to the man willing to use her for sex until he could get his precious money back. 'Take it or leave it, Natasha,' he cut into the thrumming thick nub of her silence—

there because she was finding the switch much harder to make. 'But make your mind up, because we have a flight to catch.'

A flight to catch. A life to get on with while she put her own on hold—again.

Natasha answered with a curt nod of her head.

It was all he required to have him reach out and pull her back into his arms. The heat flared between them. She uttered a helpless protest as his mouth arrived to claim hers. And worst thing of all was how the whole heady, hot pleasure of it caught hold of her as fast as it took him to make that sensual stroking movement with his tongue along the centre of hers. By the time he drew back, she was barely focusing. Her lips felt swollen and thick—but deep inside, in the core element where the real Natasha lay hidden, she still felt as cold as death.

Leo thought about just saying to hell with it and taking her back upstairs to bed and forgetting about the rest of this. She had no idea—*none* whatsoever—what that hopeless look on her face teamed with the buttoned-up suit was doing to him.

He turned away from temptation, frowning at his own be-wildering inclinations. How had he gone from being a tough business-focused tycoon to a guy with his brains fixed on sex?

More than his brains, he was forced to acknowledge when he had to stand still for a moment and work hard to bring much more demanding body parts under control.

Then she moved, swinging him back round to look at her, and he knew then exactly why he was putting this woman before his cool business sense. She had been driving him quietly crazy for weeks now, though he had refused to look at the reason why until Rico had ruined his chances with her.

Rico's loss, his gain. Natasha Moyles was going to come so alive with his tutelage she was not going to be able to hide anything from him. And he was going to enjoy every minute of making that exposure take place. Then once their six weeks were over he would get his money back and walk away so he could get on with his life without having her as a distraction that constantly crept into his head.

Maybe it was worth the cool two million to achieve it.

'I need to speak to m-my parents…'

'You can ring them—from Athens. Hit them with a situation they cannot argue with.'

'That wouldn't be—'

'You prefer to relay the full ugly details to their faces?' he cut in on her. 'You prefer to explain to them that you and Rico have been caught thieving and that their other daughter is a man-thieving tramp?'

The tough words were back. The sigh that wrenched from Natasha was loaded down with defeat. 'I will need to get my passport from the apartment,' was all she said.

'Then let's go and get it.' Leo held out his hand to her in an invitation that was demanding yet another surrender—one that sizzled in the short stillness that followed it.

A step on the road to ruin, Natasha recognised bleakly as she lifted her hand and settled her palm against his. His long tanned fingers closed around her slender cold fingers, she felt his warmth strike through her icy skin and his strength convey itself to her as he turned and trailed her behind him into the hallway, then out of the house.

CHAPTER FOUR

OUTSIDE the afternoon sunlight was soft on Natasha's face. The short journey to her apartment was achieved in silence. The first thing she saw when they arrived there was Cindy's silver sports car and her aching heart withered, then sank.

Leo must have recognised the car, too, because, 'I'm coming in with you,' he insisted grimly.

It had not been a request. And anyway Natasha was glad she was not going to have to face Cindy on her own.

Feeling dread crawling across her flesh, she walked into the foyer with Leo at her side. The janitor looked up and smiled. It was all she could do to smile politely back by return.

'I've mislaid my keys,' she told him. 'Do you think I could borrow the spare?'

'Your sister is home, Miss Moyles,' the janitor informed her. 'I can call up and she will let you—'

'No.' It was Leo who put in the curt interruption. The janitor looked up at him and it didn't take a second for him to recognise that he was in the presence of a superior power. 'We will take the spare key, if you please.'

And the key changed hands without another word uttered.

In the lift, Natasha began to feel sick again. She didn't want this confrontation. She would have preferred not to look into Cindy's face ever again.

'Do you want me to go in for you?'

The dark timbre of his voice made her draw in a breath before she straightened her shoulders, pressed her tense lips together and shook her head. The moment she stepped into the hi-tech, ultra-trendy living room, her sister jumped up from one of the black leather chairs.

Cindy's eyes were red as if she'd been crying and her hair was all over the place. 'Where have you been?' she shrilled at Natasha. 'I've been trying to reach you! Why didn't you answer your damn phone?'

'Where I've been isn't any of your business,' Natasha said quietly.

Cindy's fingers coiled into fists. 'Of course it's my business. I employ you! When I say jump you're paid to jump! When I say—'

'Get what you came for, *agape mou*,' a deep voice quietly intruded.

Leo's dark, looming presence appeared in the doorway. Cindy just froze where she stood, her baby-blue eyes standing out as hot embarrassment flooded up her neck and into her face. 'M-Mr Christakis,' she stammered out uncomfortably.

Ah, respect for an elder, Natasha noted, smiling thinly as she walked across the room to open the concealed wall safe where she kept her personal papers.

'I didn't expect you to come here....'

Nor had Cindy expected Leo Christakis to catch her with Rico, thought Natasha, and that was why she was embarrassed to see him again.

Leo said nothing, and Natasha winced at the dismissive contempt she could feel emanating from that suffocating silence. Cindy just wasn't used to being looked at like that. She wasn't used to being ignored. Embarrassment and respect changed to a sulky pout and flashing insolence, which she turned on Natasha.

'I don't know what you think you are doing in my safe, Natasha, but you—'

'Be quiet, you little tramp,' Leo said.

Cindy flushed to the roots of her hair. 'You can't speak to me like that!'

Natasha turned in time to watch the way Leo looked her sister over as if she were a piece of trash before diverting his steady gaze to her. 'Got what you need?' he asked gently.

Gentle almost crucified her, though she was way beyond the point of being able to work out why. Fighting the never-far-away-tears, she nodded and made her shaking legs take her back across the room towards him.

Cindy sent her a frightened look. 'You aren't leaving,' she shot out. 'You *can't* leave. That idiot Rico panicked and phoned the parents looking for you—now they're on their way here!'

Natasha ignored her, her concentration glued to the door Leo was presently filling up. *I just need to get away from her, she told herself. I just need to...*

'You're such a blind, silly, stupid thing, Natasha!' Cindy went back on the attack. 'Do you think I'm the only woman Rico has had while he's been engaged to you? Did you really believe that someone like him was going to fall in love with someone like you—?'

Natasha hid her eyes and just kept on walking.

'What are you but the right kind of stuffed-blouse type his silly mother likes? I did you a favour today. You could have married him still blind to what he's really like! It was time someone opened your eyes to reality. You should be thanking me for doing it!'

Natasha had reached Leo. 'Anything else before we get out of here?' he asked.

'S-some clothes and—things,' she whispered.

'Don't you *dare* ignore me!' Cindy screeched. 'The parents will be here in a minute. I want you to tell them that this was all your own fault! I've got a gig tonight and I just can't perform with all of this angst going on. And you need to get busy with some damage control because you won't like it if I have to do it myself!'

Leo stepped to one side to let Natasha pass by him. The moment she closed her bedroom door, he reacted, stepping right up to Cindy. 'Now listen to me, you spoiled little tart,' he said. 'One false word from you about what took place today and you're finished. I will see to it.'

Cindy's head shot up, scorn pouring out of her bright baby blue eyes. 'You don't have the power—'

'Oh, yes, I do,' Leo said. 'Money talks. Jumped-up little starlets like you come off a conveyer belt. Give me half an hour with a telephone and I can ruin you so quickly you won't see oblivion until you find yourself sunk in it up to your scrawny neck. Pending records deals can be withdrawn. Gigs cancelled. Careers murdered by a few words fed into the right ears.'

Cindy went white.

'I see that you get my drift.' Leo nodded. 'You are not looking into the eyes of a devoted fan now, sweet face, you're looking into the eyes of a very powerful man who can see right through the shiny packaging to the ugly person that lurks beneath.'

'Natasha won't let you do anything to h-hurt me,' Cindy whispered.

'Yes, she will,' Natasha said. She was standing just inside the door with a hastily packed bag at her feet.

As Cindy looked at her Natasha twisted something out of her fingers, sending it spiralling through the air. It landed with a clink on the pale wood floor at Cindy's feet. Looking down, even Leo went still when he saw what it was.

Her ring—her shiny diamond engagement ring. 'That's just something else of mine you haven't tried,' she explained. 'Why don't you put it on and see if it fits you as well as my fiancé did?'

Cindy's appalled face was a picture. 'I didn't want him, and I don't want—that!'

'Well, what's new there?' Natasha laughed, though where the laugh came from she did not have a single clue. 'When have you ever wanted anything once you've possessed it?'

Pandemonium broke out then as their parents arrived, rushing in through the flat door Leo must have left on the latch.

They looked straight at Cindy. They had barely registered that Natasha was even there.

Cindy burst into a flood of tears.

'Oh, my poor baby,' Natasha heard her mother cry out. 'What did that Rico do to you?'

Natasha began to feel very sick again. She stared at the way her two parents had gathered comfortingly around Cindy and felt as if she were standing alone somewhere in outer space.

Then her gaze shifted to Leo standing on the periphery of it all with his steady dark eyes fixed on her painfully expressive face. 'Can we leave now?' she whispered.

'Of course.'

And he was stooping to pick her bag up. As he straightened again his hand made a proprietary curl of her arm and Natasha heard Cindy quaver, 'He's been stalking m-me for weeks, Mummy. I went to see him to tell him to stop it or I would tell Natasha. The next thing I knew he…'

Leo closed the door on the rest. Neither said a single word to each other as they walked out of the apartment and headed for the lift. All the way down to the foyer they kept their silence, all the way out to his car. He drove them away in that same tense silence until Leo clearly could not stand it any longer and flicked a button on his steering wheel to activate his phone.

Natasha recognised the name 'Juno', then nothing as he proceeded to share a terse conversation in Greek.

She kept her eyes fixed on the side window and just let his deep, firm, yet strangely melodious voice wash over her as they drove out of the city and into lush green, rural England. The ugliness of her situation was crawling round her insides, the spin of once-loved faces turning into strangers as they flipped like a rolling film through her head. She didn't know them and, she realised painfully, they did not really know her—or care.

'Do you think they've noticed that you are no longer there yet?'

Realising Leo had finished his telephone conversation and had now turned his attention on her, Natasha lifted a shoulder in an empty shrug. Had they even noticed she was there in the first place? Pressing her pale lips together she said nothing.

A minute later they were turning in through a pair of gates leading to a private airport where, she presumed, Leo must keep his company jet. It took no time at all to get through the official stuff. All the way through it she stood quietly at his side.

So this is it, Natasha told herself as they walked towards a sleek white jet with its famous Christakis logo shining Ionian blue on its side. I'm going to fly off into the sunset to become this man's sole possession.

She almost—almost managed a dry little smile.

'What?' Leo just never missed anything—not even the smallest flicker of a smile.

'Nothing,' she murmured.

'Forget about Rico and your family,' he said harshly. 'You are better off without them. I am the only one you need to think about now.'

'Of course,' Natasha mocked. 'I'm about to become a very rich man's sexual doormat, which has to be quite a hike up from being my family's wimpish doormat and Rico Giannetti's thieving one.'

Leo said nothing, but she could sense his exasperation as he placed his hand on the small of her back to urge her up the flight steps.

The plane's interior gave Natasha an insight into a whole new way of travelling. Breaking free from his touch, she took a couple of steps away from him, then stopped, tension springing along her nerve-ends when she heard the cabin door hiss as someone sealed it into its housing and the low murmur of Leo's voice speaking to someone, though she did not turn around to find out who it was.

This wasn't right. None of it was right, a sensible voice in her head tried to tell her. She should not be on this plane or tripping off to Athens with Leo Christakis—she should be staying in England and fighting to clear her name!

'Here, let me take your jacket.' He arrived right behind her again, making her whole body jerk to attention when his hands landed lightly on her shoulders.

'I would rather keep it on,' she insisted tautly.

'No, you would not.' Sliding his fingers beneath the jacket collar, he followed it around her slender white throat until he located the top button holding her jacket fastened. 'You will be more comfortable without it.' He twisted the button free.

'Then I can do it.' Snapping up her hands, Natasha grabbed his wrists with the intention of pulling his hands away. He didn't let her.

'My pleasure,' he murmured smoothly as the next button gave.

Her two breasts thrust forward, driving a shaken gasp from her throat. 'I wish you would go and f-find someone else to torment,' she breathed out sharply when his knuckles grazed her nipples on their way to locate the next button, and felt her stomach muscles contract as he brushed across them, too.

He just laughed, low and huskily. 'When did you find the time to stick your hair up again?'

'At the flat,' she mumbled, then went as taut as piano wire when the last button gave way to his working fingers.

'You're too skittish,' he chided.

'And you're too sure of yourself!' Natasha flicked out.

'That's me,' he admitted casually, moving his hands down her sleeves to locate her handbag still clutched in one tense set of fingers. He gently prised it free to toss it aside.

Why the loss of her purse should make her feel even more exposed and under threat, Natasha did not have a clue, but by the time he'd eased the jacket from her shoulders she was more than ready to dissolve into panic. And the worst part about it was that she could not even say for sure any more what it was she was panicking about—Leo and his relentless determination to keep her balanced on the edge of reason, or herself because her senses persisted in responding to him even when her head told them to stop!

His hands arrived at the curve of her slender ribcage over the stretchy white fabric that moulded her so honestly it felt as if he were touching her skin. Natasha closed her eyes and prayed for deliverance when he eased her back against him and she felt his heat and his hard masculine contours.

'Leo, please…' It came out somewhere between a protest and a breathless plea.

It made no difference. He lowered his mouth and brushed his lips across the exposed skin at her nape and for Natasha it was like stepping off a cliff, she fell that easily. She murmured a pathetic little stifled groan and her head tipped downwards, inviting the gentle bite of his teeth. As he began kissing his way round her neck, she rolled it sideways on a slow and pleasurable, sensual stretch to give him greater access. She so loved what he was making her feel.

'Mmm, you feel good, like warm, living silk to touch,' he murmured. 'You have a beautiful body, Natasha,' he added huskily, gliding his hands upwards until he cupped her breasts and gently pressed his palms against their tightly budded peaks. 'I need you to turn your head and kiss me, *agape mou*,' he told her huskily.

And she did. She moved on a restless sigh of surrender when he reached for her hands and lifted them upwards, then clasped them around the back of his neck. The sheer sensual stretch of her body felt unbelievably erotic. She whispered something—even she didn't know what it was—then she was giving in and twisting her head and going in search of his waiting mouth.

Leo gave it to her in a hot, deep, stabbing delivery. Her fingers curled into the black silk of his hair. It was shocking. She didn't know herself like this, all soft and pliable and terribly needy.

'We are cleared for take-off, Mr Christakis,' a disembodied voice suddenly announced.

Leo drew his head back and the whole wild episode just went up in a single puff of smoke. Natasha opened her eyes and found that she couldn't focus. Passion coins of heat burned her cheeks. She became aware of her hands still clinging to his head and slid them away from him, her still-parted mouth closing with a soft burning crush of her warm lips.

'You are quite a bundle of delightful surprises,' she heard Leo mock. 'Once unbuttoned you just let it all flood out.'

And the real horror of it was that he was, oh, so right! Each time he touched her it was the same as losing touch with her common sense and dignity. Acknowledging that had Natasha breaking free of him to wrap her arms tightly around her body, then she just stood there, shaking and fighting to get a grip on herself.

An engine purred into life.

'Take a seat, strap yourself in, relax,' his hatefully sardonic tone invited, and he was stepping around her to stride down the cabin.

Watching him go, Natasha thought she glimpsed a flick of irritation in the way that he moved and kind of understood it. To a man like Leo Christakis the deal had been done, so to have her continue to play it coy annoyed him. From the little she'd heard about his private life, he liked his women with the experience and sophistication to know how to respond positively to his seduction routine, not blow hot then tense and skittish each time he attempted to act naturally with her.

The gap in their ages suddenly loomed. The fact that there was nothing natural at all in the two of them being together picked at her nerves as she chose a seat at random and sat down.

The plane slid into movement. Natasha watched Leo remove his suit jacket to reveal wide, muscled shoulders hugging the white fabric of his shirt. He draped the jacket over the back of the chair in front of the desk, then folded his long body into the seat placed at an angle to her, those muscled shoulders flexed as he locked in his seat belt, then reached out to pull a large stack of papers towards him and sat back to read.

Dragging her eyes away from him, she hunted down her seat belt with the intention of fastening it, but she spied her discarded jacket lying on the seat opposite and on sheer impulse she snatched it up and put it back on, buttoning it shut all the way up to her throat, though she had no idea what, by doing it, she was hoping to prove.

Unless it had something to do with the tight bubble of anger she could feel simmering away inside at the way he was lounging there already steeped in paperwork and putting on a good impression that he had already forgotten she was here, which hit too closely at the way her family had behaved at the apartment.

Ten minutes later they were in the air and his laptop computer was open, his voice that same melodic drone in her ears. A gentle-voiced stewardess appeared at Natasha's side to ask her if she would like something to eat and drink. She knew she wouldn't be able to eat anything right now, but she asked if it was possible for her to have a cup of tea, and the stewardess smiled an, 'of course,' and went away to see to it.

Leo swivelled around in his chair.

He looked at her, narrowing his eyes on the buttoned-up jacket. A new rush of stinging awareness spun through the air.

'It will have to stay off at some point,' he murmured slowly.

Natasha pushed her chin up and just glared.

It was a challenge that made his dark eyes spark and sent Natasha breathless. Then he was forced to turn his attention back to his satellite link, leaving her feeling hot and skittish for a different reason.

For the next three hours he worked at the desk and she sat sipping her tea or reading one of the magazines the stewardess had kindly brought for her. Throughout the journey Leo kept on swinging his chair around to look at her, waiting until she felt compelled to look back at him, then holding her gaze with disturbing dark promises of what lay ahead. Once he even got up and came to lean over her, capturing her mouth with a deep, probing kiss. As he drew away again the top button to her jacket sprang open.

He did it to challenge her challenge, Natasha knew that, but her body still tightened and her breasts tingled and peaked. The next time he turned his chair to look at her the button was neatly fastened again and she refused point blank this time to lift her head up from the magazine.

They arrived in Athens to oven heat and humid darkness. It was a real culture shock to witness how their passage through the usual formalities was so carefully smoothed. And Leo felt different, like a remote tall, dark stranger walking at her side. His expression was so much harder and there was a clipped formality in the way he spoke to anyone. A quiet coolness if he was obliged to speak to her.

Natasha put his changed mood down to the way people constantly stopped to stare at them. When she saw the cavalcade of three heavy black limousines waiting to sweep them away from the airport, it really came down hard on her to realise just how much power and importance Leo Christakis carried here in his own capital city to warrant such an escort.

'Quite a show,' she murmured as she sat beside him in the rear of the car surrounded by plush dark leather while the other two cars crouched close to their front and rear bumpers. Seated in the front passenger seat of this car and shut away behind a plate of thick, tinted glass sat a man Leo had introduced to her as, 'Rasmus, my security chief'. It was only as he made the introduction that Natasha realised how often she'd seen the other man lurking on the shadowy periphery of wherever Leo was.

'Money and power make their own enemies,' he responded as if all of this was an accepted part of his life.

'You mean, you always have to live like this?'

'Here in Athens, and in other major cities.' He nodded.

It was no wonder then that he was so cynical about anyone he came into contact with, it dawned on her. He flies everywhere in his private jet aeroplane, he drives around in private limousines and he has the kind of bank balance most people could not conjure up even in their wildest dreams. And he has so much power at his fingertips he probably genuinely believes he exists on a higher plane than most other beings.

'I never saw it in London,' she said after a moment, remembering that while he'd been in London he had driven himself.

He turned his head to look at her, dark eyes glowing through the dimness of the car's interior. 'It was there. You just did not bother to look for it.'

Maybe she didn't, but... 'It can't have been as obvious there,' Natasha insisted. 'I was used to some measure of security when Cindy was performing but never anything like this—and none at all with Rico.' She then added with a frown, 'Though that seems odd now when I think about who Rico is and—'

He moved, it was barely a shift of his body but it brought Natasha's face around to catch the flash to hit his eyes.

'What?' she demanded.

'Don't ever compare me with him,' he iced out.

Her blue eyes widened. 'But I wasn't—'

'You were about to,' he cut in. 'I am Leo Christakis, and this is *my* life you are entering into with all its restrictions and privileges. Rico was nothing.' He flicked a long-fingered hand as if swatting his stepbrother away. 'Merely a freeloader who liked to ride on my coat-tails—'

Natasha went perfectly pale. 'Don't say that,' she whispered.

'Why not when it is the truth?' he declared with no idea how he had just devastated her by using the same withering words to describe Rico as her sister had used to describe her. 'His name is Rico Giannetti, though he prefers to think of himself as a Christakis, but he has no Christakis blood to back it up and no Christakis money to call his own,' he laid out with contempt. 'He held an office in every Christakis building because it was good for his image to appear as if he was worthy of his place there, but he never worked in it—not in the true meaning of the word anyway.' The cynical bite to his voice sent Natasha even paler as his implication hit home. 'He drew a salary he did little to earn and spent it on whatever took his fancy while robbing me blind behind my back as I picked up the real tabs on his extravagant tastes,' he continued on. 'He is a hard-drinking, hard-playing liar to himself and to everyone connected to him, including you, his betrayed, play-acting betrothed.'

Shaken by his contemptuous barrage, 'Ex-betrothed,' Natasha husked out unsteadily.

'Ex-everything as far as you are concerned,' he pronounced. 'From this day on he is out of the picture and I am the only man that matters to you.'

He had demanded that she put her family out of her head, now he was insisting she put Rico out of her head. 'Yes, sir,' she snapped out impulsively, wishing she could put him out of her head, too!

A black frown scored his hard features at her mocking tone. 'I thought a few home truths at this point will help to keep this relationship honest.'

'Honest?' Natasha almost hyperventilated on the breath she took. 'What you're really doing here is letting me know that you expect to control even my thoughts!'

Impatience hit his eyes. 'I do not expect that—'

'You do expect that!'

Leo raked out an angry sigh. 'I will not have Rico's name thrown in my face by you every five minutes!'

Natasha swung round on him in full choking fury. 'I did not throw his name at you—*you* battered *me* with it!'

'That was not my intention,' he returned stiffly.

Twisting on the seat, she glared at the glazed partition. 'You're no better than Rico, just different than Rico in the way you treat people—women!' she shook out with a withering glance across the width of the seat. 'Since we are driving along here like a presidential cavalcade, your loathsome arrogance is one fault I will let you have, but your—'

'Loathsome—again?' he mocked lazily.

It blew the lid off what was left of her temper. 'And utterly, pathetically jealous of Rico!'

Silence clattered down all around them with the same effect as crashing cymbals hitting the crescendo note and making Natasha's heart begin to race. She could not believe she had just said that. Daring another glance at Leo, she could see him looking back at her like a man-eating shark about to go on the attack, and now she couldn't even breathe because the tension between them was sucking what was left of the oxygen out of the luxury confines of the car.

He reacted with a lightning strike. For such a big man he moved with a lithe, silent stealth and the next thing she knew she was being hauled through the space separating them to land in an inelegant sprawl of body and limbs across his lap. Their eyes clashed, his glittering with golden sparks of anger she hadn't seen in them before. Hers were too wide and too blue and—scared of what was suddenly fizzing in her blood.

She had to lick her suddenly very dry lips just to manage a husky, 'I didn't really m-mean—'

Then came the kiss—the hot and passionate ambush that silenced her attempt to retract what she'd said, and flung her instead into fight with lips and tongues and hands that did not know how to stay still. His breath seared her mouth and a set of long fingers was clamped to the rounded shape of her hip, her own fingers applying digging pressure to whatever part of his anatomy they could reach as their mouths strained and fought. The motion of the car and the fact that they were even *in* one became lost in the uneven fight. She wriggled against him. His hand maintained its controlling clamp. She felt her fingernails clawing at his nape and the rock-solid moulding of his chest so firmly imprinted against his shirt.

He loved it. She caught his tense hiss of pleasure in her

mouth and felt a tight, pleasurable shudder attack his front, the powerful surge of his response making itself felt against the thigh he held pressed into his lap. Then his hand was sliding beneath her skirt and stroking the pale skin at the top of her thigh where her stockings did not reach. If he stroked any higher, he was going to discover that she was wearing a thong and she increased her struggle to get free before he reached there, lost the fight, and a quiver of agonising embarrassment sent her kiss-fighting mouth very still.

'Well, what do we have here?' he paused to murmur slowly, long fingers stroking over a smoothly rounded, satin-skinned buttock and crippling Natasha's ability to breathe. 'The prim disguise is really beginning to wear very thin the more I dig beneath it.'

'Shut up,' she choked, eyes squeezed tight shut now. She was never going to wear a thong ever again, she vowed hectically.

He removed his hand and her eyes shot open because she needed to know what he was going to do next, and found herself staring into his mockingly smiling face. The anger had gone and his lazily, sensual male confidence was firmly back in place.

'Any more hidden treasures left for me to discover?' He arched a sleek, dark, quizzing eyebrow.

'No,' Natasha mumbled, which made him release a dark, husky laugh that shimmered right through her as potently as everything else about him did.

Then he wasn't smiling. 'OK, so I am jealous of Rico where you are concerned.' He really shocked her by admitting it. 'So take my advice and don't bring him into our bed or I will not be responsible for the way I react.'

Before she could respond to that totally unexpected backdown, he was lowering his head again and crushing her mouth. How long this kiss went on Natasha had no idea, because she just lost herself in the warm, slow, heady promise it was offering.

The car began to slow.

Both felt the change in speed but it was Leo who broke away and with a sigh lifted her from him to place her back on the seat. Lounging back into the corner of the car, he then watched the way she concentrated on trying to tidy herself, shaky fingers checking buttons and pulling her skirt into place across her knees.

'Miss Prim.' He laughed softly.

Lifting her fingers to smooth her hair, Natasha said nothing, a troubled frown toying with her brow now because she just could not understand how she could fall victim to his kisses as thoroughly as she did.

'It's called sexual attraction, *pethi mou*,' Leo explained, reading her thoughts as if he owned them now.

Her profile held Leo's attention as it turned a gentle pink. If he did not know otherwise, he would swear that Natasha Moyles was an absolute novice when it came to sexual foreplay. She ran from cold to hot to shy and dignified. She was not coquettish. She did not flirt or invite. She appeared to have no idea what she did to him yet she was so acutely receptive to anything that he did to her.

And she made him ache just to sit here looking at her. It was not an unpleasant condition; in fact, it had been so many years since he'd felt this sexually switched on to a woman, he'd believed he had lost the capacity to feel anything quite this intense.

Gianna had done that to him, scraped him dry of so many feelings and turned him into an emotional cynic. But his ex-wife was not someone he wanted to be thinking of right now, he told himself as he focused his attention back on this woman who was keeping his senses on edge just by sitting here next to him.

'We have arrived,' he murmured, using the information like yet another sexual promise to taunt her with, then watched her slender spine grow tense as she glanced beyond the car's tinted glass to catch sight of the twin iron gates that guarded the entrance to his property.

Natasha stared at the gates as they slid apart to their approach. All three cars swept smoothly through them, then two cars veered off to the left almost immediately while theirs made a direct line for the front of his white-painted, three-storey villa.

Rasmus was out of the car and opening Leo's door the moment the car pulled to a stop at the bottom of the curving front steps. Leo climbed out, ruefully aware that his legs didn't feel like holding him up. Desire was a gnawing, debilitating ache once it buried its teeth in you, he mused ruefully as he turned to watch his driver open the other passenger door so the object of his desire could step out of the car.

She gazed across the top of the car up at his villa with its modern curving frontage built to follow the shape of the white marbled steps. Light spilled out of curving-glass windows offset in three tiers framed by white terrace rails.

'I live at the top,' he said. 'The guest suites cover the middle floor. My staff have the run of the ground floor...what do you think?'

'Very ocean-going liner,' Natasha murmured.

Leo smiled. 'That was the idea.'

Rasmus shifted his bulk beside him then, reminding Leo that he was there. Leo glanced at him, that was all, and both Rasmus and the driver climbed back in the car and firmly shut the doors. Then the car moved away, leaving Leo and Natasha facing each other across its now-empty space. It was hot and it was dark but the light from the building lit up the two of them and the exotic scent of summer jasmine hung heavy in the air.

Natasha watched as Leo ran his eyes over her suit and the bag she once again clutched to her front. He didn't even need to say what he was thinking any more, he just smiled and she knew exactly what was going through his head. He was letting her know how much he was looking forward to stripping her of everything she liked to hide behind.

And the worst part about it was that her insides feathered soft rushes of excitement across intimate muscles in expectant response.

When he held out his hand in a silent command that she go to him, Natasha found herself closing the gap between them as if pulled across it by strings.

CHAPTER FIVE

No MAN had a right to be as overwhelmingly masculine as Leo did, Natasha thought as the feathering sensation increased as she walked. With his superior height, the undeniable power locked into his long, muscled body and that bump on his nose, which announced without apology that there was a real tough guy hiding inside his expensively sleek billionaire's clothes.

He turned towards the house as she reached him, the outstretched hand becoming a strong, muscled arm he placed across her back, long fingers curling lightly against her ribcage just below the thrust of her breasts.

Antagonism at his confident manner began dancing through her bloodstream—fed by a fizzing sense of anticipation that held her breath tight in her lungs. Walking beside him made Natasha feel very small suddenly, fragile, so intensely aware of each curve, each small nuance of her own body that it was as close as she'd ever come to experiencing the truly erogenous side of desire.

Inside, the villa was a spectacular example of modern architecture, but Natasha didn't see it. She was too busy absorbing the tingling sensations created by each step she took as they walked towards a waiting lift.

Once she stepped into it she would be lost and she knew it.

So that first step into the lift's confines felt the same to her as stepping off the edge of a cliff. The doors closed behind them. She watched one of Leo's hands reach out to touch a button that sent the lift gliding smoothly up. He still kept her close to him, and she kept her eyes carefully lowered, unwilling to let him see what was going on inside her head. The lift doors slid open giving them access into a vast reception hallway filled with soft light.

The very last thing Natasha wanted to see was another human being standing there waiting to greet them. It interfered with the vibrations passing between the two of them and brought her sinking back to a saner sense of self.

'*Kalispera*, Bernice,' Leo greeted smoothly, his hand arriving at Natasha's elbow to steady her shocked little backwards step.

'Good evening, *kirios—thespinis*,' the stocky, dark housekeeper turned to greet Natasha in heavy, accented English. 'You have the pleasant flight?'

'I—yes, thank you,' Natasha murmured politely, surprised that she seemed to be expected, then blushing when she realised just what that meant.

Bernice turned back to Leo. 'Kiria Christakis has been ringing,' she informed him.

'Kiria Angelina?' Leo questioned.

'*Okhi...*' Bernice switched languages, leaving Natasha to surmise that her ex-future mother-in-law had left a long message to relay her shock and distress, going by the urgency of Bernice's tone.

'My apologies, *agape mou*, but I need a few minutes to deal with this.' Leo turned to Natasha. 'Bernice will show you where you can freshen up.'

His expression was grim and impatient. And despite his

apology he did not hang around long enough for Natasha to answer before he was turning to stride across the foyer, leaving her staring after him.

'Leo…?' Calling his name brought him to an abrupt standstill.

'Yes?' He did not turn around.

Natasha was tensely aware of Bernice standing beside her. 'W-will you tell your stepmother for me, please, that I am truly sorry ab-about the way that—things have worked out?'

His silent hesitation lasted longer than Natasha's instincts wanted to allow for. Beside her, Bernice shifted slightly and lowered her head to stare down at the floor.

'I l-like Angelina,' she rushed on, wondering if she'd made some terrible faux pas in Greek family custom by speaking out about personal matters in front of the paid staff. 'None of what happened was her fault and I know she m-must be disappointed and upset.'

Still, he hesitated, and this time Natasha felt that hesitation prickle right down to her toes.

Then he gave a curt nod. 'I will pass on your message.' He strode on, leaving her standing there feeling…

'This way, *thespinis*…'

Feeling what? she asked herself helplessly as Bernice claimed her attention, indicating that she follow her into a wide, softly lit hallway that led off the foyer.

Bernice showed her into beautiful bedroom suite with yet more soft light spilling over a huge divan bed made up with crisp white linen. Dragging her eyes away from it, Natasha stared instead at a spectacular curving wall of glass backdropped by an endless satin dark sky.

Bernice was talking to her in her stilted English, telling her where the bathroom was and that her luggage would arrive very soon.

Luggage, Natasha thought as the housekeeper finally left her alone. Did one hastily packed canvas holdall classify as luggage?

Dear God, how did I get to be standing here in a virtual stranger's bedroom, waiting for my luggage? she then mocked herself, and wasn't surprised when her gaze slid back to that huge divan bed, then flicked quickly away again before her imagination could conjure up an image of what they were going to be doing there soon.

Heart thumping too heavily in her chest, Natasha sent her restless eyes on a scan of the remainder of her spacious surroundings, which bore no resemblance at all to Leo's very traditional Victorian London home. Here, cool white dominated with bold splashes of colour in the bright modern abstracts hanging from the walls and the jewel-blue cover she'd spied draped across the end of the bed.

Needing to do something—anything—to occupy her attention if she didn't want to suffer a mad panic attack, she walked over to the curved wall of glass with the intention of checking out the view beyond it, but the glass took her by surprise when it started to open, parting in the middle with a smooth silent glide—activated, she guessed, by her body moving in line with a hidden sensor.

Stepping out of air-controlled coolness into stifling heat caught her breath for a second, then she was dropping her purse onto the nearest surface, which happened to be one of the several white rattan tables and chairs spread around out there, and she was being drawn across the floor's varnished wood surface towards the twinkle of lights she could see beyond the white terrace railing, while still trying to push back the nervous flutters attacking her insides along with the deep sinking knowledge that she really should not be doing this.

A city of lights suddenly lay spread out beneath her, looking so glitteringly spectacular Natasha momentarily forgot her worries as she caught her breath once more. She'd been aware that they'd climbed up out of the city on the journey here from the airport, but she had not realised they'd climbed as high as this.

'Welcome to Athens,' a smooth, dark, warm velvet voice murmured lightly from somewhere behind her.

She hadn't heard him come into the bedroom, and now tension locked her slender shoulders as she listened to his footsteps bring him towards her.

'So, what do you think?'

His hands slid around her waist to draw her against him. 'Fabulous,' she offered, trying hard to sound calm when they both knew she wasn't by the way she grew taut at his closeness. 'Is—is that the Acropolis I can see lit up over there?'

A slender hand pointed out across the city. When she lowered it again, she found it caught by one of his.

'With the told quarters of Monastiraki and the Plaka below it,' he confirmed, taking her hand and laying it against her fluttering stomach, then keeping it there with the warm clasp of his. 'Over there you can see Zappeion Megaron lit up, which stands in our National Gardens, and that way—' he pointed with his other hand '—Syntagma Square…'

The whole thing turned a bit surreal from then on as Natasha stood listening to his quietly melodic voice describing the night view of Athens as if there were no sexual undercurrents busily at work. But those undercurrents *were* at work, like the tingling warmth of his body heat and the power of his masculine physicality as he pressed her back against him. She felt wrapped in him, trapped, surrounded and overwhelmed by a pulse-chasing vibration of intimacy that danced along her nerve-ends and fought with her need to breathe.

'It is very dark with no moon tonight but can you see the

Aegean in the distance lit by the lights from the port of Piraeus.' She had to fight with herself to keep tuned into what he was saying. 'After Bernice has served our dinner I will show you the view from the other terrace, but first I would like you to explain to me, *pethi mou*, what has changed in the last five minutes to scare you into the shakes?'

'Leo…' Impulsive, she seized the moment. 'I can't go through with this. I thought I could but I can't.' Slipping her hand out from beneath his, she turned to face him, 'I need you to understand that this…'

Her words dried up when she found herself staring at his white-shirted front. He'd taken off his jacket and his tie had gone, the top couple of buttons on his shirt tugged open to reveal a bronzed V of warm skin and a deeply unsettling hint of curling black chest hair.

The air snagged in her chest, the important words—this will be my first time—lost in the new struggle she had with herself as her senses clamoured inside her like hungry beasts. She wanted him. She did not understand why or how she had become this attracted or so susceptible to him but it was there, dragging down on her stomach muscles and coiling around never before awakened erogenous zones.

'We have a deal, Natasha,' his level voice reminded her.

A deal. Pressing her trembling lips together, she nodded. 'I know and I'm s-sorry but—' Oh, God. She had to look away from him so she could finish. 'This is too m-much, too quickly and I…'

'And you believe I am about show my lack of finesse by jumping all over you and carrying you off to bed?'

'Yes—n-no.' His sardonic tone locked a frown to her brow.

'Then what do you expect will happen next?'

'Do you have to sound so casual about it?' she snapped out, taking a step back so her lower spine hit the terrace rail. Discomforted and disturbed by the whole situation, she wrapped her arms across her front. 'You might prefer to believe that I do this kind of thing on a regular basis, but I don't.'

'Ah,' he drawled. 'But you think that I do.'

'No!' she denied, flashing a glare up at him, then wished she hadn't when she saw the cynically amused cut to his mouth. 'I don't think that.'

'Good. Thank you,' he added dryly.

'I don't know enough about you to know how you run your private life!'

'Just as I know little about your private life,' he pointed out. 'So we will agree to agree that neither of us is without sexual experience and therefore can be sophisticated enough to acknowledge that we desire each other—with or without the deal we have struck.'

'But I haven't,' she mumbled.

'Haven't—what?' he sighed out.

Too embarrassed to look at him, cheeks flushed, Natasha stared at her feet. 'Any sexual experience.'

There was one of those short, sharp silences, in which Natasha sucked on her lower lip. Then Leo released another sigh and this one kept on going until it had wrung itself out.

'Enough, Natasha,' he censured wearily. 'I did not come out of the womb a week ago so let's leave the play-acting behind us from now on.'

'I'm not play-acting!' Her head shot up on the force of her insistence. All she saw was the flashing glint of his impatience as he reached out and pulled her towards him. Her own arms unfolded so she could use her hands to push him away again, but by then his mouth was on hers, hot, hard and angrily determined. Her fists flailing uselessly, he drew her into his arms and once again she was feeling the full powerful length of him against her body. Without even knowing it happened she went from fighting to clinging to his shoulders as her parted mouth absorbed the full passionate onslaught of his kiss.

There was no in-between, no pause to decide whether or not she wanted to give in to him, it just happened, making an absolute mockery of her agitation and her protests because Leo was right, and she did want him—badly.

This badly, Natasha extended helplessly as he deepened the kiss with that oh-so-clever stroke of his tongue, and she felt her body responding by stretching and arching in sensuous invitation up against the hardening heat of his.

And she knew she was lost even before he put his hands to her hips and tugged her into even closer contact with what was happening to him. When he suddenly pulled his head back, she released a protesting whimper—it shocked even Natasha at the depth of throaty protest it contained.

He said something terse, his eyes so incredibly dark now they held her hypnotised. 'You want me,' he rasped softly. 'Stop playing games with me.'

Before she could answer or even try to form an answer, he was claiming her mouth again and deepening the whole wildly hot episode with a kiss that sealed his declaration like a brand burned into her skin. Her arms clung and he held her tightly against him—nothing, she realised dizzily, was now going to stop this.

And she didn't want it to stop. She wanted to lose herself in his power and his fierce sensuality and the heat of the body she was now touching with greedily restless fingers. She felt the thumping pound of his heartbeat and each pleasurable flinch of his taut muscles as her fingers ran over them. His shirt was in her way—he knew it was in her way and, with a growl of frustration, he stepped back from her, caught hold of her hand and led her back inside.

The bed stood out like a glaring statement of intent. He

stopped beside it, then turned to look at her, catching her uncertain blue stare and leaning in to kiss it away before stepping back again. If there was a chink of sanity left to be had out of this second break in contact, it was lost again by a man blessed with all the right moves to keep a woman mesmerised by him.

He began removing his shirt, his fingers slowly working buttons free to reveal, inch by tantalising inch, his long, bronzed torso with his black haze of body hair and beautifully formed, rippling muscles, which Natasha's concentration became solely fixed on. She had never been so absorbed by anything. Sexual tension stung in the air, quickening her frail breathing as he began to pull the shirt free from the waistband of his trousers. When the shirt came off altogether, she felt bathed in the heady thrill of his clean male scent. He was so intensely masculine, so magnificently built—she just couldn't hold back from reaching out to place her hands on him.

And he let her. He let her explore him as if she was on some magical mystery journey into the unknown, his arms, the glossy skin covering his shoulders, the springy black hair covering his chest. As her hands drifted over him, her tongue snaked out to taste her upper lip, but she knew that really it wanted to taste him.

Leo reached up and gently popped the top button of her jacket and she gasped as if it was some major development, her eyes flicking up to catch his wry smile sent to remind her that this undressing part was a two-way thing. He leant in to kiss her parted lips as he popped the next button, and the whole battle they'd been waging with her jacket took on a power of its own as she just stood there and let him pop buttons between slow, deep, sensuous kisses, until there were no buttons left to pop.

He discarded her jacket in the same way he had discarded it once already that day, without letting up on his slow seduction by making her shiver as he trailed his fingers up her bare arms and over her shoulders, then down the full length of her back, making her arch towards him, making her whisper out a sigh of pleasure, making her eyes drift shut in response. Then he just peeled her stretchy white top up her body and right over her head. Cool air hit her skin and the shock of it made her open her eyes again. He was looking down at her breasts cupped in plain white satin, the fullness of their creamy slopes pushing against the bra's balcony edge. When the bra clasp sprang open and he trailed that flimsy garment away, her hands leapt up to cover her bared breasts. Leo caught her wrists and pulled them away again, his ebony eyelashes low over the intense glow in his eyes now as he watched her nipples form into pink, tight, tingling peaks.

Nothing prepared her for the shot of pleasure she experienced when he drew her against him and her breasts met with his hair-roughened chest.

No turning back now, Natasha told herself hazily as the wriggle of doubts faded away to let in the rich, drugging beauty of being deeply kissed. She felt her skirt give, felt it slither on its smooth satin lining down her legs to pool at her feet. Her bra was gone. The thong was nothing. The fine denier stocking clung to her slender white thighs. Her hair came loose next, unfurling down her naked back like an unbelievably sexy caress.

Leo had all but unwrapped her and she'd never felt so exquisitely aware of herself as a desirable woman. When he drew back from her, she reached for him to pull his mouth back to hers. He murmured something—a soft curse, she suspected—then picked her up and placed her down on the bed. Natasha held on to him by linking her hands around his neck to make sure that the kiss did not break. She wanted him—all of him.

'Greedy,' he murmured softly against her mouth as he stretched out beside her, and she was! Greedy and hungry and caught in the sexual spell he'd been weaving around her for most of the day.

Then one of his hands cupped the fullness of her breast and her breath stalled in her throat as he left her mouth to capture the tightly presented peak. Sensation made her writhe as he sucked gently, her fingers clawing into the thick silk of his hair with the intention of pulling him away—only it didn't happen because his teeth lightly grazed her, and soon she was groaning and clinging as the smooth, sharp feel of his tongue and his teeth and his measured suck drew pleasure on the edge of tight, stinging pain downward until it centred between her thighs.

Maybe he knew, maybe she groaned again, but his mouth was suddenly hot and urgently covering hers. And she could feel the hunger in him, the urgent intent of his desire demanding the same from her and getting it when he kissed her so deeply she felt immersed in its power.

Then he was leaving her, snaking upright and trailing the thong away as he did so. Eyes hooded again, dark features severe now, he removed her stockings, then straightened up to unzip his trousers and heel off his shoes while running his eyes over her possessively.

'You're beautiful,' he murmured huskily. 'Tell me you want me.'

There was no denying it when she couldn't take her eyes off him, no pretending that she was a victim here when her body responded wildly to the sight of his naked power.

'I want you,' she whispered.

It was Natasha who reached for him when he came down beside her again. It was she that turned to press the full length of her eager body into his.

Then he was taking control again, pushing her gently onto her back and rolling half across her. What came next was a lesson in slow seduction. He laid hot, delicate kisses across her mouth, touched her with gentle fingers, caressed her breasts and her slender ribcage, stroking feather-light fingertips over her skin to the indentation of her waist and across the rounded curves of her hips. It was an exploration of the most intense, stimulating agony; her flesh came alive as she moved and breathed and arched to his bidding. When he finally let his hand probe the warm, moist centre between her thighs, she was lost, writhing like a demented thing, clinging to his head and begging for his kiss. And he was hot, he was tense, he was clever with those deft fingers. The new shock sensation of what he was doing to her dropped her like a stone into a whirlpool of hot, rushing uproar.

'Leo,' she groaned out.

Saying his name was like giving him permission to turn up the heat. He appeared above her, big and dark—fierce with burning eyes and sexual tension striking across his lean cheeks. He recaptured her mouth with a burning urgency, shuddering when her fingers clawed into his nape. And still, he kept up the unremitting caresses with his fingers, driving her on while each desperate breath she managed to take made the roughness of his chest rasp torturously against the tight, stinging tips of her breasts.

She could feel the powerful nudge of his erection against her. Her tongue quivered with knowledge against his. A flimsy, rippling spasm was trying to catch hold of her and she whimpered because she couldn't quite seize it.

Leo muttered something thick in his throat, then rose above her like some mighty warrior, so powerfully, darkly, passionately Greek that if she had not felt the pounding thunder of his heartbeat when she sent her hands sliding up the wall of his chest, Natasha could have convinced herself that he just wasn't real.

He eased between her parted thighs with the firm, nude tautness of his narrow hips and the rounded tip of his desire made that first probing push against her flesh. Feeling him there, understanding what was coming and so naïvely eager to receive it, Natasha threw her head back onto the bed, ready, wanting this so very badly she was breathless, riddled by needs so new to her that they held her on the very edge of screaming-pitch.

So the sudden, fierce thrust of his invasion followed by a sharp, burning pain that ripped through her body had her clenching her muscles on a cry of protest.

Leo froze. Her eyes shot to his face. She found herself staring into passion-soaked, burning brown eyes turned black with shock. 'You were a virgin. You—'

Natasha closed her eyes and refused to say anything, while his deriding denial that this would be her first time replayed its cruel taunt across her tense body, and the muscles inside her that were already contracting around him.

'Natasha—'

'No!' she cried out. 'Don't talk about it!'

He seemed shocked by her agonised outburst. 'But you—'

'Please get off me,' she squeezed out in desperation and pushed at his shoulders with her tightly clenched fists. 'You're hurting me.'

'Because you are new to this…' His voice had roughened, the hand he used to gently push her hair away from her face trembling against her hot skin.

But he made no attempt to withdraw from her, his big shoulders bunched and glossed with a fine layer of perspiration, forearms braced on either side of her, and his face was so grave now Natasha knew what was coming before he said it.

'I'm sorry, *agape mou*…'

'Just get off!' She didn't want his apology. Balling her

hands into fists, she pushed at his shoulders, writhing beneath him in an effort to get free, only to flatten out again on a shivering quiver of shock when her inner muscles leapt on his intrusion with an excited clamour that made her eyes widen.

Reading her expression with an ease that pushed a hot flush through her body, 'You are not hurting any more,' he husked out, and lowered his head to adorn her face with soft, light, coaxing kisses—her eyes, her nose, her temples, her delicate ear lobes—that made her quiver and squirm and in the end dig fingers into his bunched shoulders and send her mouth on a restless search for his.

'Oh, kiss me properly!' she ended up begging.

Her helpless plea was all it took to tip a carefully contained, sexually aroused man over the edge. On a very explicit curse, he moulded her mouth to his. A second later and Natasha was lost—flung into a strange new world filled with sensation, piling in on top of sensation, unaware that the whole wild beauty of it was being carefully built upon by a master lover until she felt the first rippling spasm wash through her. She knew that he felt it, too, because he whispered something hot against her cheek, slid his powerful arms beneath her so he could hold her close, then angled his mouth to hers and began to thrust really deep, increasing the pace while maintaining a ferocious grip on his own thundering needs.

The grinding drag of fierce pleasure began to flow through her body. Natasha whimpered helplessly against his mouth. Knotting his fingers into her hair, he muttered tensely, 'Let go, *agape mou.*'

And like a fledgling bird being encouraged to fly, Natasha just opened her sensory wings and dropped off the edge of the world into an acutely bright, scintillating dive straight into the frenzied path of an emotional storm. A moment later she felt him shudder as he made the same mind-shredding leap, while

urging her on and on until two became one in a wildly deliri-
ous, spiralling spin.

It was as if afterwards didn't exist for Natasha; pure shock
dropped her like a rock through a deep, dark hole into an exhausted sleep.

Maybe she did it because she did not want to face what she'd
done, Leo mused sombrely as he sat sprawled in a chair by the
bed, watching her—watching this woman he'd just bedded like
some raving sex maniac while giving himself every excuse he
could come up with to help him to justify his behavior.

A virgin.

His conscience gave him a stark, piercing pinch.

And the guilty truth of it was, he could still feel the sense
of stinging, hot pleasurable pressure he'd experienced when
the barrier gave. A muscle low down in his abdomen gave a
tug in direct response to the memory and he lifted the glass
of whisky he held and grimly took a large sip.

The prim persona had been no lie.

She even slept the sleep of an innocent, he observed as he
ran his eyes over her. No hint of sensual abandon in the
modest curve of her body outlined against the white sheet.

Another slug at the whisky and he was studying her face
next. Perfect, beautiful, softened by slumber and washed pale
by the strain of the day she'd been put through when she
should look…

He took another pull of the whisky, and as he lifted the
glass to his mouth, her eyelids fluttered upwards and her
sleep-darkened blue eyes looked directly at him.

The nagging tug on his loins became a pulsing burn that
made him feel like a sinner.

He lowered the glass, and half hiding his eyes, watched her
catch her breath, then freeze for a second before he said
sombrely, 'We will get married.'

Natasha almost jolted right out of her skin. 'Are you mad?' she gasped, pulling the covering sheet tightly up against her chin. 'We have a deal—'

'You were a virgin.'

As she dragged herself into a sitting position her hair tumbled forwards in a shining, loose tangle of waves around her face and she pushed it out of her way impatiently. 'What the heck difference should that make to anything?'

'It means everything,' Leo insisted. 'Therefore we will be married as soon as I can arrange it. I am honour-bound to offer you this.'

'Stuff your honour.' Heaving in a deep breath, Natasha climbed out of the bed on the other side from where he was sitting, trailing the sheet around her as she went. 'Having just escaped one sleazy marriage by the skin of my teeth, I am *not* going to fall into another one!'

'It will not be a sleazy marriage.'

'Everything about you and your terrible family is sleazy!' she turned on him angrily. 'You're all so obsessed with the value of money, you've lost touch with what's really valuable in life! Well, I haven't.' Tossing her chin up, eyes like blue glass on fire with contempt, she drew the sheet around her. 'We made a deal in which I give you sex for six weeks until I can give you back your precious money. Show a bit of your so-called honour by keeping to that deal!'

With that she turned and strode off to the bathroom, needing to escape—needing some respite from Leo Christakis and his long, sexy body stretched out in that chair by the bed. So he'd pulled a robe on—what difference did that make? She could still see him naked, still visualise every honed muscle and bone, each single inch of his taut, bronzed flesh! And she could still feel the power of his kisses and the weight of him on top of her and the…

'You were innocent,' he fed after her.

Was he talking about her sexual innocence or her being innocent of all of the other rotten charges he had laid against her?

Did she care? No.

'Stick to your first impression of me,' she flung at him over her shoulder. 'Your instincts were working better then!'

On that scathing slice, she slammed into the bathroom.

Leo grimaced into his glass. His first impression of Natasha Moyles had been deadly accurate, he acknowledged. It was only the stuff with Rico that had fouled up that impression.

He heard the shower running. He visualised her dropping the sheet and walking that smooth, curvy body into his custom-built wet room. The vision pushed him to his feet with the grim intention of giving into his nagging desires and going in there to join her. This war they were having was not over yet and would not be over until he won it.

Then something red caught the corner of his eye and he glanced down at the bed.

'Theos,' he breathed as his insides flipped into a near-crippling squirm in recognition.

Proof that he had just taken his first virgin was staring him in the face like a splash of outrage.

Leo flexed his taut shoulders, glanced over at the closed door to the bathroom, then back at the bed. 'Damn,' he cursed, trying to visualise what she was going to feel like when she saw the evidence of her lost virginity, and added a few more oaths in much more satisfying Greek.

Instead of going to join her, he discarded his robe to snatch up his trousers and shirt and pulled them back on. He had no idea where Bernice kept the fresh bedlinen, but he was going to have to find out for himself because the hell if he was going to ask...

CHAPTER SIX

WRAPPED in a spare bathrobe she'd found hanging behind the door, Natasha tugged in a deep breath, then opened the bathroom door and stepped out. Her heart was thumping. It had taken her ages to build up enough courage to leave the sanctuary of the bathroom and her muscles ached, she was so locked on the defensive, ready for her first glimpse of Leo sprawled in the chair by the bed.

It took a few moments for her to realise that she'd agonised over nothing because he wasn't even in the room. And the bed had been straightened so perfectly it looked as if it had never been used. Even her clothes had been picked up and neatly draped over the chair he had been sitting in.

Had Bernice come in here and tidied up after them? The very idea pushed a flush of mortified heat into her cheeks. Natasha dragged her eyes away from the bed and began scanning the room for her holdall, while wishing that someone had bothered to tell her that she was going to feel like this—all tense and edgy and horribly uncertain as to what happened after you jumped into bed with a man you hardly knew!

Then the bedroom door flew open and she spun to face it with a jerk. Half expecting to find Bernice or one of the maids walking in, she was really thrown into a wild flutter when it was Leo standing there.

He was dressed and she definitely wasn't. The way his eyes moved over her turned the flush of mortification into something else.

He swung the door shut behind him, then began striding towards her like some mighty warlord coming to claim his woman for a second round of mind-blowing sex and making her more uptight the closer he came. How could he wear that relaxed smile on his face as if everything in his world was absolutely perfect? Had he never felt awkward or nervous or just plain shy about anything?

Not this man, she concluded with a deep inner quiver when he pulled to a stop right in front of her. He gave off the kind of masculine vitality that made her fingers clutch the collar of the bathrobe close to her throat.

'Your hair is wet,' he observed, lifting a hand up to stroke it across the slicked back top of her head.

'Your state-of-the-art wet room has a w-will of its own,' she answered, still feeling the tingling shock she'd experienced when jets of water had hit her from every angle the moment she'd touched the start button in there.

'I'll find you a hairdryer,' he murmured as he moved his hand to stroke the hectic burn in her cheek. 'But in truth, I think you look adorable just as you are and if I thought you could take more of me right now I would be picking you up and taking you back to bed.'

Natasha shook his hand away. 'I wouldn't let you.'

'Maybe,' he goaded softly, 'you would find yourself with little choice?'

Natasha's startled gaze clashed with his smiling dark eyes. 'You would make me, you mean?'

'Seduce you into changing your mind, beautiful one,' he corrected, then lowered his head to steal a kiss.

And it wasn't just a quick steal. He let his lips linger long enough to extract a response from her before he drew back again.

'Fortunately for you, right now I am starving for real food,' he mocked her smitten expression. 'Find yourself something comfortable to put on while I shower, then we will go and eat.'

With that he strode into the bathroom. Arrogant— arrogant—*arrogant!* Natasha thought as she wiped the taste of his mouth from her lips.

Thoroughly out of sorts with herself for being so susceptible to him, she hunted down her holdall and used up some of her irritation by hauling it up onto the bed and yanking open the zip. For the next few seconds she just stood looking down into the bag with absolutely no clue whatsoever as to what the heck she had packed inside it. She only had this very vague memory of grabbing clothes at random, then dropping them into the bag. Tense fingers clutching the gaping robe to her throat again, she let the other hand rummage inside the bag and pulled out an old pair of jeans and a pale green T-shirt.

Great, she thought as she discarded those two unappealing garments onto the bed. A pair of ordinary briefs—not a thong, thank goodness—appeared next, and she tossed those onto the bed, too. She found another suit styled like the pale blue suit she'd been wearing all day, only this one was in a dull cream colour that made her frown because she could not imagine herself buying it, never mind wearing such an awful shade against her fair skin. Yet she must have bought it or it wouldn't be here.

Or perhaps this new Natasha—the one clutching a robe to her throat after losing her virginity to an arrogant Greek—had developed different tastes. She certainly felt different, kind of aching and alive in intimate places and so aware of her own body it started to tingle even as she thought about it.

No make-up, she discovered. She'd forgotten to pack her make-up bag or even a brush or comb. A couple of boring skirts appeared from the bag, followed by a couple of really boring tops. Frowning now with an itchy sense of dissatisfaction that irritated her all the more simply because she was feeling it, she finally unearthed a floaty black skirt made of the kind of fabric that didn't crease when she pulled it free of the bag. A black silk crocheted top appeared next, which was going to have to go with the skirt whether she liked it or not since she did not seem to have anything else like it in the bag.

Only one spare pair of shoes—and *no* spare bra! she discovered. Sighing heavily, she turned towards the chair where her other clothes were neatly folded, and was about to walk over there to recover her white bra—when Leo strode out of the bathroom.

It was as if she'd been thrown into an instant freeze the way she stood there between the bed and the chair, pinned to the polished wood floor while her busy mind full of what to wear came to a sudden halt.

Other than for the towel he had slung low around his lean waist, he was naked. Beads of water clung to the dark hairs on his chest. Her heart began to race as her eyes dropped lower, over the taut golden brown muscles encasing his stomach that shone warm and glossy and sinewy tight. The towel covered him from narrow hips and long powerful thighs to his knees, and the strength she could see structuring his calf muscles held her totally, utterly breath-shot as she felt the undiluted wash of what true desire really meant suffuse heat into each fine layer of her skin.

Oh, dear God, I want him badly, she acknowledged as those legs came to a sudden standstill and brought her eyes fluttering up to clash with his. It was like being suffocated, she likened dizzily, because she knew by the way he narrowed his eyes that he was reading her responses to him.

'I've forgotten to pack any m-make-up.' The words jumped from her in a panic-stricken leap.

He continued to stand there for a few more seconds just studying her, then he started walking again. 'You will not need make-up for dinner here alone with me,' he responded evenly.

Natasha pulled her eyes away from him to glance at the scramble of clothes she'd thrown onto the bed. 'I don't even have anything here fit to wear for dinner,' she said, trying desperately to sound as calm as he had when calm was the last thing she was feeling.

He came to a stop beside her. 'Wear the cream thing,' he suggested with only the vaguest hint of distaste showing in his voice.

It was enough. Natasha shook her head. 'I hate it.'

Beginning to frown now, he turned to look down at her. 'Natasha, what—'

'W-what are you going to wear?' she heard herself blurt out, then grabbed in a tense breath because—in all her life she had never asked a man such a gauche, stupid question! And his frown was darkening by the second. She could actually *feel* him mulling over what to say next! She wanted to call back her silly question. She *wished* she weren't even here!

She turned to face him. 'Listen Leo, I…'

Then it came—his shockingly unexpected answer to her problem: he dropped the towel from around his waist. 'Let's wear nothing,' he said.

The sheer outrageousness of the gesture completely robbed Natasha of speech. Heat flowed through her body, soaking her groin like hot pins and needles before spreading everywhere else. She tried to breathe. She tried to swallow. She tried to stop staring at him but she couldn't. She tried to back off when he reached across the gap between them, but her legs had turned to liquid and were refusing to move.

He reached for the hand she was using to clutch the bathrobe to her throat and gently prized her fingers free.

'Leo, no…' She mouthed the husky protest with her heart clattering wildly against her ribs because she knew what was coming next.

'Leo—yes,' he interpreted softly.

Two seconds later the bathrobe fell to the floor at her feet and his hands were taking its place. Freshly showered skin met with freshly showered skin and her naked breasts swelled and peaked. Her shaken gasp was captured by the sensual crush of his mouth and her troubled world tilted right out of kilter as the whole sexual merry-go-round spun off again. She didn't even want to stop it, she just threw herself into the dizzying pleasure of the kiss with her hands clutching at his solid biceps and her hips swaying closer to the burgeoning evidence of his desire and its formidable promise. Within seconds she was a quivering mass of nerve-endings, moving against him and kissing him back, her heart racing, her breathing reduced to fevered little tugs at oxygen filled with his intoxicating clean scent.

The sound of the bedroom door being thrown open with enough force to send it slamming back into something solid almost blew the top off her head. She flicked her eyes open. Leo was already lifting up his head. Way too dazed to think for herself, Natasha watched him shift the burning darkness of his eyes away from her to look towards the bedroom door, then copied him to look in that direction, too.

A woman stood there. A tall, reed-slender, staggeringly beautiful woman, wearing a dramatically short and slinky red satin dress. Her flashing black eyes were fixed on Leo, her exquisite face turning perfectly white.

'Gianna,' he greeted smoothly. 'Nice of you to drop in, but, as you can see, we are busy....'

As cool as that, he turned Natasha into a block of ice as his wife—his *ex*-wife—threw herself into a rage of shrill spitting Greek. Leo said absolutely nothing while the tirade poured out. His heart wasn't thundering. His breathing was steady. He just stood holding Natasha close as if trying to shield her nakedness with his own naked length, and let the other woman screech herself out.

It was awful. Natasha wished she could just sink into a hole in the ground. It was so humiliatingly obvious that Gianna felt she had a right to yell at Leo like this or why would she do it? Likening this situation to the one she'd witnessed between Cindy and Rico made her shiver in shame.

Feeling her shiver, Leo flicked a glance at her, then frowned as with a smooth grace he bent and scooped up the robe she had been wearing and draped it around her shoulders. 'Shut up now, Gianna,' he commanded grimly. 'You sound like a shrieking cat.'

To Natasha's surprise the shouting stopped. 'You were supposed to be at Boschetto's tonight,' Gianna switched to condemning English. 'I waited and waited for you to arrive and I felt the fool when you did not turn up!'

'I made no arrangement to meet up with you,' Leo said, bending a second time to pick up his towel, which wrapped back around his hips. 'So if you made a fool of yourself, you did it of your own volition.'

'You were expected—'

'Not by you,' Leo stated. 'Here, let me help you...'

Trying to push her arms into the robe sleeves, Natasha found Leo taking over the task, but, 'I'll do it myself,' she breathed tautly, and pushed his hands away.

She couldn't look at him—did not want to look at his ex-wife. Embarrassment was crawling around her insides and she felt so humiliated she was trembling with it.

Speaking earned Natasha Gianna's attention; she felt the other woman scythe a skin-peeling look over her. 'So you like them short and fat now?' she said to Leo.

Fat? Natasha burned up inside with indignation, huddling her size-ten figure into the all-encompassing bathrobe.

'Much better than a rake-thin whore with a sluttish heart,' Leo responded, reaching out to stroke one of his hands down Natasha's burning cheek as if in an apology for his witch of an ex-wife's insult. 'Now behave, Gianna, or I will have Rasmus throw you out of here. In fact,' he then drawled curiously, 'I will be very interested to hear how you got in here at all?'

Daring a glance at the other woman, Natasha saw that she was standing there with her slender arms folded across her slender ribs. She had to be six feet tall and the way she'd been poured into that red satin dress said everything there was to say about the differences between the two of them.

No wonder she still claimed super-model status, she concluded, flicking her eyes up to Gianna's fabulous bone-structure to see that her almond-shaped, Latin black eyes were gleaming defiance at Leo, her lush red mouth set in a provoking pout.

Leo released a soft, very cynical laugh as if he understood exactly what the look was conveying.

'So, who is she?' Gianna flicked another snide look at Natasha. 'Yet another attempt you make to find a substitute for me?'

Natasha flinched. Leo drew her back into his arms again and ignored her when she tried to pull back. 'Never in a thousand years could anyone substitute you, my sweet-tongued angel,' he mocked dryly. Then he looked down at Natasha and, with the silken tone of a man about to rock her world off its axis, 'In the form of a heartfelt apology to you, *agape mou,*' he murmured soft to Natasha, 'I must introduce you to Gianna, my ex-wife.'

'I am your ex-nothing!' Gianna erupted.

'Gianna.' He spoke right across the shrill protest. 'Nothing in this world has ever given me greater pleasure than to introduce you to Natasha, my very beautiful *future* wife.'

As a cool, slick way of dropping a bombshell, it was truly impressive. Staring up at his totally implacable face, Natasha almost fell backwards in shock.

The beautiful Gianna turned deathly white. 'No,' she whispered.

'You wish,' Leo responded.

'But you love *me!*' Gianna cried out in pained anguish.

'Once upon a time you were worth loving, Gianna. Now…?' He gave a shrug that said the rest, then apparently committed the ultimate sin in Gianna's eyes and leant down to capture Natasha's shock-parted lips with a kiss.

Without any warning it was about to happen, fresh pandemonium broke out with a keening wail that spliced up the atmosphere, then Gianna was coming at Natasha like a woman with murder in mind. Natasha jumped like a terrified rabbit. Leo spat out a curse and stepped right in front of her, taking the brunt of Gianna's fury upon himself.

It was horrible, the whole thing. Natasha could only stand there behind him, shocked into shaking while Leo contained his ex-wife's wrists to stop her long nails from clawing his face.

Then he bit out a terse, 'Excuse us…' to Natasha, and he was manhandling the screaming woman out of the bedroom.

The door thudded shut in his wake. Natasha found that her legs couldn't hold her up a moment longer and she sank in a whooshing loss of energy down onto the edge of the bed.

Beyond the door, Rasmus was just stepping out of the lift.

Leo sent him a glancing blow of a look and his security chief paled. 'I'm sorry, Leo,' he jerked out. 'I don't know—'

'Get her out of here,' Leo gritted. 'Take her home and sober her up.'

Gianna had stopped fighting and screeching now and was sobbing into his chest and clinging instead. Disgust flayed Leo's insides when it took the controlled strength of both men to transfer her from himself to Rasmus and get her into the lift.

'I don't know how she got in here,' Rasmus said helplessly.

'But you will do,' Leo lanced out. 'Then see to it that who-ever it was on your staff she laid in return for the favour is gone from here,' he instructed, then stabbed the button that shut the lift doors.

Alone in the hallway, he spun round in a full circle, then grabbed the back of his neck. Anger was pumping away inside him, contempt—repugnance. Having taken a telephone call from Gianna when he first arrived here, he'd told her that she had to get the hell off his back!

Her barging in here had been deliberate. Even the angry shrieking had been a put-up job. And the fact that she would not think twice about seducing one of his staff to get what she wanted was just another side to her twisted personality that filled him with disgust!

'*Theos,*' he muttered, long legs driving him through the apartment and pulling him to a halt outside the closed bed-room door, the knowledge that he'd lost the towel again having no effect on him at all.

He wasn't stupid. He knew that Gianna's nicely timed in-terruption had been a set-up, just as he knew the comparison Natasha had drawn from the moment it all kicked off.

Rico with her sister.

A curse ripped from him, followed by another. He paced out the width of the hall trying to clamp down on the anger still erupting inside him because—how the hell did he explain a sex-obsessed feline like Gianna, who only functioned this side of sane while she knew that he was always going to be around to help pick her up when she fell apart?

You didn't explain it. It was too damn complicated, he recognised as he took in a grim breath of air, then threw open the bedroom door.

Natasha was back in the blue suit, and she was stuffing her things back into her bag.

'Don't you pull a hysterical scene on me,' he rasped, closing the door with a barely controlled thud.

His voice sent a quiver down Natasha's tense spinal cord. 'I'm not hysterical,' she responded quietly.

'Then *what* do you call the way you are packing that bag?'

The searing thrust of his anger shocked even Leo as Natasha swung round to stare at him. Miss Cold and Prim was back with a vengeance, Leo saw, and she was stirring him up like…

She saw *it* happen, and lifted a pair of frosty blue eyes to his. 'Is that response due to her by any chance?' And her voice dripped disdain.

Hell, Leo cursed. 'Sorry,' he muttered, not sure exactly what it was he was apologising for—the snarling way he had spoken to her or his uncontrolled…

She spun her back to him again. Snapping his lips together, he strode over to the bank of glossy white wardrobes and tugged open one of the doors. A second later he was pulling a pair of jeans up his legs.

'She's mad,' he muttered.

'Enter the beautiful mad wife—exit the short, fat other woman.' Natasha pushed a pair of shoes into the bag.

'*Ex*-wife,' he corrected, tugging his zip up.

'Try telling her that.'

'I do tell her—constantly. As you saw for yourself, she does not listen—and you are not going anywhere, Natasha, so you can stop packing that bag.'

Straightening up, Natasha meant to spear him with another crushing look, only to find herself lose touch with what they were saying when she saw him standing there with his long legs encased in faded denim and looking like a whole new kind of man. Her heart gave a telling stuttering thud. Her breathing faltered. He was so blatantly, beautifully masculine it took a fight to drag her covetous mind back on track.

'S-so you thought you might as well make her listen by hitting her with that lie about a future wife?'

A frown darkened his lean features and made the bump on his nose stand out. 'It was not a lie, Natasha,' he declared like a warning.

'Oh, yes, it was,' she countered that. 'I wouldn't marry you if my life depended on it.'

'You mean, you are here merely to use me for sex?'

The sardonic quip was out before Leo could stop it.

'Substitute!' she tossed right back at him like the hot sting from a whip. 'And not even that again,' she added, yanking her eyes away from him altogether and zipping up the hastily packed bag with enough violence to threaten the teeth on the zip.

Easing his shoulders back against the wardrobe door, Leo folded his arms across his hair-roughened chest. 'So I was a tacky one-night substitute, then,' he prodded.

'Very tacky.' Pressing her lips together, she nodded in confirmation, then parted her lips to add bitterly, 'God save me from the super-rich class. Everything they do is so tacky it constantly makes me want to be sick.'

'Was that aimed at me, Gianna or Rico?'

'All three,' she said, frowning as she sent her eyes hunting the room for her purse. She couldn't see it anywhere and she couldn't recall when she had last had it in her hand.

'Lost something valuable?' his hatefully smooth voice questioned. 'Like your virginity, perhaps?'

It was as good as a hard slap in the face. Natasha tugged in a hot breath. 'I've just remembered why I dislike you so much.'

His wide shoulders gave a deeply bronzed shrug against the white wardrobe. He looked like some brooding dark male model posing for one of the big fashion magazines, Natasha thought, feebly aware that her eyes refused to stay away from him for more than ten seconds before they dragged themselves back again because he was so bone-tinglingly good to look at. Sexuality oozed out of every exposed manly pore and those jeans should be X-rated. How had she ever thought that he was nothing to look at next to Rico? If Rico dared to stride in here right now and stand next to this man, Natasha knew she wouldn't even see him. Leo won hands down in each single aspect of his dominant masculine make-up—even the bump in his nose yelled sexually exciting unreconstructed male at her!

Oh, what's happening to me? On that helplessly bewildered inward groan, she yanked her eyes away from him—yet again—and *made* them search the room for her purse! In less than a day it felt as if everything she'd ever held firm about herself had been corkscrewed out of her then mixed around violently before being shoved back inside her to form this entirely new perspective on everything!

And the way he was standing there looking at her with his eyes thoughtfully narrowed just wasn't right, either—as if he was considering striding over here and *showing* her the tough way in which this new order of things worked.

A sensation Natasha just did not want to feel spread itself right down her front. Tense upper lip quivering—she just *had* to get out of here.

'Have you seen my purse?'

'What do you need it for?'

Straightening her tense shoulders, she said, 'I'm ready to leave now.'

'By what form of transport?'

'Taxi!' she spat out.

'You have the Euros to pay for a taxi?' her cool tormentor quizzed. 'And a mobile phone handy to call one up? Do you speak any Greek, *agape mou*? Do you even know this address so you can tell the taxi driver where to come to collect you?'

He was deliberately beating her up with blunt logic. 'Y-you have my mobile phone,' she reminded him, hating that revealing quiver in her voice.

He responded to that with yet another of those irritatingly expressive shrugs against the glossy white wardrobe door. 'I must have mislaid it, as you have your purse.'

Deciding the only way to deal with the infuriatingly impossible brute was to ignore him, Natasha started hunting the bedroom.

While Leo watched her do it, his narrowed gaze ran over the way she looked all neat and tidy in every which way she could be—except for the wet hair which lay in a heavy silk pelt down her back. A man could not find a bigger contrast between Natasha's cool dignity and Gianna's reckless abandon, Leo observed grimly. Where Gianna clung to him like a weeping vine, this aggravating woman was preparing to walk out on him!

'Tell me, Natasha,' he asked grimly, 'why are you so eager to leave when only ten minutes ago you were ready to fall back into bed with me?'

'Your wife got in here somehow,' she muttered, checking beneath one of the cushions on the chair to see if her purse had slid behind it.

'Ex-wife—and…?'

'Maybe her claim on you has some justification,' Natasha said with a shrug.

'Like…?' he prompted, and there was no hint whatsoever left of the provoking mockery with which he had started this conversation. He was deadly curious to hear where she was going with this.

'The way you run your life is your own business.' Chickening out at the last second from stating outright the real question that was beating a hole in her head, she gave up on the chair and tossed the cushion back onto it.

But—did he still sleep with his ex-wife when he felt like it? Did Gianna have a genuine right to her grievances when she'd barged in on them as she had? If so, then it made him no better than Rico in the way that he treated women!

Tacky, as she'd already said. She returned to her search with his brooding silence twitching at her nerve-ends as she moved about the room.

'I do not have a relationship with my ex-wife,' he spoke finally. 'I do not sleep with her and I have no wish to sleep with her, though Gianna prefers to tell herself I will change my mind if she pushes long and hard enough… In case you did not notice,' he continued as Natasha turned to look him, 'Gianna is not quite—stable.'

It was the polite way to call it, but Natasha could see by the flick of a muscle at the corner of his mouth that he was holding back from voicing his real thoughts about Gianna's mental health. And what did she do? She stood here eating up every single word like some lovelorn teenager in need of his reassurance.

'In some ways I still feel responsible for her because she *was* my wife and I *did* care for her once—until she pressed the self-destruct button on our marriage for reasons not up for discussion here.' And the tough way he said that warned her not to try to push him on it. 'I apologise that she barged in here and embarrassed you,' he expressed curtly. 'I apologise that she found a way to enter this property at all!' A fresh burst of anger straightened him away from the wardrobe. 'But that's it—that is as far as I am prepared to go to make you feel better about the situation, Natasha. So stop behaving like a tragic bride on her wedding night and take the damn jacket off before *I* take it off!'

'W-what—?' Not quite making the cross-over from his grim explanation about Gianna to the sudden attack on herself, Natasha blinked at him.

Which seemed to infuriate him all the more. 'While you stand here playing the poor, abused victim, you seem to have conveniently forgotten about the money you stole from me!'

The money.

Natasha tensed up, then froze as if he'd reached out and hit her. Leo smothered a filthy curse because her hesitation told him that she *had* forgotten all about the money. Though the curse was aimed at himself for reminding her about it when he would have preferred it to remain forgotten about! Now she was looking so pale and appalled he grimly wondered if she was going to pass out on him.

A tensely gritted sigh had him striding over to her. Lips pinned together, he reached out and began unbuttoning her jacket with tight movements that bore no resemblance whatsoever to the other times he had taken it upon himself to do this.

She didn't even put up a fight, but just stood there like a waxen dummy and let him strip the garment from her body, which only helped to infuriate him all the more! With the muscles across his shoulders bunching, he tossed the jacket aside, then turned to walk back across the room to the wardrobes. Hunting out a white T-shirt, he dragged it on over his head.

When he turned back to Natasha, he found her still standing where he'd left her, giving a good impression of a perfectly pale ghost.

Theos, he thought, wondering why seeing her looking so beaten was making his senses nag the hell out of him to just go over there and apologise yet again—for being such a brute.

'Dinner,' he said, taking another option, keeping up the tough tone of voice because—well, she was a cheating thief even if he wanted to forget that she was!

At last she moved—or her pale lips did. 'I'm not hungry—'

'You are eating,' he stated. 'You have had nothing since you threw up in my London basement.'

And reminding her of that was Leo Christakis well and truly back as the blunt-speaking insensitive brute, Natasha noted.

Even in the T-shirt and chinos.

And his feet bare…

She felt like crying again, though why the sight of his long, bronzed bare feet moving him so gracefully across the room to the door made her want to do that Natasha did not have a clue, but suddenly she just wanted to sit in a huddle in a very dark corner somewhere and…

He pulled the bedroom door open, then stood there pointedly waiting for her to join him. Head lowered, she went because there was no point in continuing to argue with him when all he had to do was to mention the money to devastate her every line of defence.

Hard, tough, unforgivably ruthless, she reminded herself, wondering how she had allowed herself to forget those things about him while she had been giving him free use of her body—as a part of their *deal*.

She didn't look at him as she walked past him and out into the hallway. She kept her head lowered when he stepped in front of her to lead the way through the apartment and into a room lit by flickering candle-light and another glass wall.

Bernice was there, arranging the last pieces of cutlery on a white linen tablecloth intimately set for two. Candles flickered. Beyond the table stood the night view of Athens, making the most romantic backdrop any woman could wish for.

Any romantically hopeful woman, that was.

Friction stung the atmosphere and the housekeeper smiled and said something in Greek to Leo. He replied in the same language as he held out a chair for Natasha to use. After that there was no privacy to speak of anything personal because a maid arrived to serve them. Natasha had a feeling Leo had arranged it that way so he didn't get into yet another dogfight with her, but the tension between them made it almost impossible to swallow anything, though she did try to eat. When she couldn't manage to swallow another beautifully presented morsel, she stared at the view beyond the glass window, or down at the leftover food on her plate, or at the crisp white wine he had poured into the glass she was fingering without drinking—anywhere so long as it wasn't at him.

Then he shattered it. Without any hint at all that one swift glance from his eyes had sent the maid disappearing out of the room, Leo suddenly leant forwards and stretched a hand out across the table and brazenly cupped her left breast.

'I knew it,' he husked. 'You are wearing no bra, you provoking witch.'

Pleasure senses went into overdrive. Natasha shot like a sizzling firework rocket to her feet. He rose up more slowly, face taut, his dark eyes flickering gold in the candle-light.

'Don't ever touch me like that without my permission again,' she shook out in a pressured whisper, then she turned to stumble around her chair and made a blind dash out of the room.

The lift stood there with its doors conveniently open. Natasha did not even have to think about it as she dashed inside and sent the lift sweeping down to the ground floor. Outside in the garden the thick, humid air was filled with the scent of oranges. Soft lighting drew her down winding pathways between carefully nurtured shrubs and beneath the orange laden trees. She didn't know where she was heading for, all she did know was that she needed to find that dark corner she could huddle in so she could finally—finally give in to the tears she'd held back too long.

She found it in the shape of a bench almost hidden beneath the dipping branches of a tree close to the high stuccoed wall that surrounded the whole property. Dropping down onto the bench, she pulled her knees up to her chin, leant her forehead on them, then let go and wept. She wept over everything. She just trawled it all out and took a good look at everything from the moment she'd opened the message on her mobile telephone that morning to the moment Leo had touched her breast across the dinner table—and she wept and she wept and she wept.

Leo leant against a trunk of the tree and listened. Inside he had never felt so bad in his life. The way he had been treating her all day had been nothing short of unforgivable. The way he'd made love to her when he'd known she should have been doing this instead was going to live on his conscience for a long time to come.

But the way he had reached across the dinner table and touched her just now was, without question, the lowest point to which he had stooped.

And listening to her weep her soul into shreds was his deserved punishment. Except that he couldn't stand to listen to it any longer and, with a sigh, he levered away from the tree trunk and went to sit down beside her, then lifted her onto his lap.

She tried to fight him for a second or two, but he just murmured, 'Shh, sorry,' and held her close until she stopped fighting him and let the tears flow again.

When it was finally over and she quietened, he stood up

with her in his arms and took her back inside. He did it without saying a single word, ignoring the dozen or so security cameras he knew would have been trained on them from the moment Natasha ran outside.

She was asleep, he realised when he lay her down on the bed. With the care of a man dealing with something fragile, he slipped off her shoes and her skirt, then covered her with the sheets.

Straightening up again, he continued to stand there for a few seconds looking down at her, then he turned and walked out of the bedroom and into his custom-built office.

A minute later, 'Juno,' he greeted. 'My apologies for the lateness of the hour, but I have something I need you to do....'

CHAPTER SEVEN

NATASHA drifted awake to soft daylight seeping in through the wall of curved glass and to instant recall that sent her head twisting round on her pillow to check out the other side of the bed.

The sudden pound her heart had taken up settled back to its normal pace when she discovered that she was alone, the only sign that she had shared the bed at all through the night revealed by the indent she could see in the other pillow and the way Leo had thrown back the sheets when he'd climbed out.

Then the whispering suggestion of a sound beyond the bedroom door told her what it was that had awoken her in the first place, and she was up, rolling off the bed and running for the bathroom, only becoming aware as she did so that she was still wearing the white top she'd spent most of the day yesterday in.

So he'd shown a bit of rare sensitivity by not stripping her naked, she acknowledged with absolutely no thought of gratitude stirring in her blood. Leo had taken her to pieces yesterday brick by brutal brick, so one small glimpse of humanity in him because he'd put her limp self to bed and had the grace to leave her with some dignity in place did not make her feel any better about him.

She stepped into the wet room, with her hair safely wrapped away inside a fluffy white towel, frowned and at the range of keypads and dials, trying to work out how she could take a shower without having to endure a thorough dousing at the same time. Leo Christakis was one of life's takers, she decided. He saw an opportunity and went for it. He'd wanted her so he just moved in on her like a bulldozer and scooped her up.

Water jets suddenly hit her from all angles, making mockery of the buttons she'd pushed to stop them from doing it. A gasping breath shot from her as the jets stung her flesh. The sensation was so acute it made her look down at her body, half expecting to see that it had altered physically somehow, but all she saw was her normal curvy shape with its pale skin, full breasts and rounded hips with a soft cluster of dusky curls shaping the junction with her thighs.

But she had changed inside where it really mattered, Natasha accepted. She'd become a woman in a single day. One stripped of her silly daydreams about love and romance, then made to face cold reality—that you didn't need love or romance to fall headlong into pleasures of the flesh.

You didn't need anything but the desire to reach out and take it when it was right there in front of you to take.

Rico was like that. So was her sister, Cindy. They saw, they desired, so they took. It was there to take, so why not? Now she might as well accept that she'd joined the ranks of takers because she could stand here letting the shower jets inflict their torture on her and try to convince herself that she'd been blackmailed and bullied into Leo's bed, but it was never going to be the truth.

She'd wanted, she'd let him see it, Leo had taken, now it was done. What a fabulous introduction to the reality of life.

Bernice was walking in from the terrace when Natasha came out of the bathroom back in the bathrobe once again. Feeling a hot wave of shyness wash over her, Natasha felt like diving back into the bathroom and hiding there until the housekeeper had gone but it was already too late.

Bernice had seen her. '*Kalemera, thespinis,*' the housekeeper greeted with a smile. 'It is a beautiful day to eat breakfast outside, is it not?'

'Perfect.' Natasha managed a return smile, 'Thank you, Bernice,' she added politely.

Walking towards the wall of glass as Bernice left the room, she pushed her hands into the deep pockets of her robe and stepped out into a crystal-clear morning bathed in sunlight and the inviting aroma of hot coffee and toast. By the sudden growl her stomach gave she was hungry, Natasha realised, which shouldn't surprise her when she'd barely eaten anything the day—

Her mind and her feet pulled to a sudden standstill. For some crazy reason she just had not expected to find Leo out here seated at the table set for breakfast. However, there he sat, calmly reading a newspaper with a cup of hot coffee hovering close to his mouth.

Her soft gasp of surprise brought his eyes up from the newspaper, his heavy eyelashes folding back from liquid-dark irises that swamped her in heated awareness as they stroked up the length of her from bare toes to the tangling tumble of her unbrushed hair.

'*Kalemera,*' he murmured softly, and he rose to his feet.

It was like being hit head on by all the things she had not allowed herself to think about since she'd woken up this morning—the man in the flesh. Even though he was wearing a conventional business suit a warm tug of remembered intimacy made itself felt between her thighs. She found her eyes doing much the same thing as his eyes had done, feathering up the length of his long legs encased in smooth-as-silk iron-grey fabric, then his torso covered by a pale blue shirt and dark tie. By the time she reached his clean-shaven face with its too-compellingly, strong golden features, she was blushing and annoyed enough by it to push up her chin.

'Good morning,' she returned in cool English.

A half-smile clipped at the corners of his mouth. 'You slept well, I trust?'

He met her challenge with mockery.

'Yes, thank you.' Natasha kept with cool.

Pulling her eyes off him, she dug her hands deeper into her robe pockets, curled them into tense fists, then made herself walk towards the table and slip into the chair opposite him, expecting Leo to return to his seat, but he didn't.

'Bernice was unsure what you preferred to eat for breakfast so she has provided a selection.' A long, lean hand indicated another table standing to one side of the terrace, which was spread with covered dishes. 'Tell me what you would like and I'll get it for you.'

Glancing at it, then away again, 'Thank you, I'm fine with just toast.'

'Juice?' he offered.

A small hesitation, then she nodded. 'Please.'

He went to pour the juice from the jug set on the other table. You couldn't get a more pleasantly generated scene of calm domesticity if you tried, Natasha noted—though there was nothing domesticated in the way her eyes had to follow him or the way they soaked in every inch of his powerful lean frame like greedy traitors.

Looking away quickly when he turned around, she pretended an interest in the daytime view of Athens glistening in a hazy sunlight. Then one of his hands appeared in front of her to set down the glass of juice. Ice chinked against freshly squeezed oranges. He did not move away and another of those hesitations erupted between them sending out vibrating signals Natasha just did not want to read. And he was standing so close she could smell the clean, tangy scent of him, could *feel* the sheer masculine force of his sexuality that to her buzzing mind was barely leashed.

Then he brought his other hand around her to settle a rack of toast next to the glass of juice.

'Thank you,' she murmured.

'My pleasure,' he drawled—and he moved away to return to his seat, leaving Natasha to pull in a breath she had not been aware she had been holding on to.

He picked up his coffee cup and his newspaper.

Tugging her hands out of her pockets, she picked up the glass and sipped the juice. The sun beat down on the gardens below them while the overhang from the roof suspended above the terrace kept them in much pleasanter shade.

She was about to help herself to a slice of toast when she saw her mobile telephone lying on the table and her fingers stilled in midair.

'Bernice found it in my jacket pocket. I had forgotten I had it.' He might give the appearance of being engrossed in his newspaper, but he clearly was not.

Having to work to stop yet another polite thank-you from developing, Natasha pressed her lips together and nodded, then picked the phone up, her fingers stroking the shiny black casing for a few seconds before she flipped the phone open and looked at the screen.

It filled up with voice and text messages from Rico or Cindy. Aware that Leo was watching her, aware of the silence thickening between the two of them, she began to delete each message in turn, gaining a cold kind of pleasure from watching each one disappear from the screen. As the final one disappeared she flipped the phone shut and placed it back on the table before reaching for the slice of toast.

'I need to shop for some clothes,' she said coolly.

Leo said nothing, though Natasha could feel his desire to say *something* about the way she had wiped her phone clean. Had *he* read her messages? Had he expected to find a volley of instructions from Rico instructing her on how to sneak away from here so she could hole up with him somewhere until the six weeks were up and they could get at their stolen stash?

What Leo did do was to reach inside his jacket pocket and come out with a soft leather wallet. 'I will arrange an account for you with my bank,' he said evenly, 'but for now…'

A thick wad of paper money landed on the table next to her phone. Cringing inside, Natasha just stared at it.

'Buy anything you want,' he invited casually. 'Rasmus will drive you into Athens—'

'I don't need a driver,' she whispered tautly. 'I can find my way to the shops by myself.'

'Rasmus will not be there merely to play chauffeur,' his smooth voice returned. 'He will escort you wherever you go while you are here.'

'For what purpose?' Natasha forced herself to look at him—forced herself to keep silent about the phone and the hateful money he'd tossed down next to it. 'To guard me in case I decide to run out on you? Well, I won't run,' she stated stiffly. 'I don't want to be thrown into jail if I get caught.'

'In that case think of Rasmus as protection,' he suggested.

'Which I need because…?'

The attractive black arc of his eyebrows lifted upwards. 'Because it is a necessary evil in this day and age?' he offered.

'For you perhaps.'

'You are an intimate part of me now, which means you must learn to take the bad with the good.'

So where was the good in being his woman? she wondered

furiously. 'People would have to know I'm with you to make a bodyguard necessary for me.'

'But they will know—from tonight,' he countered, calmly folding his newspaper on that earth-rocking announcement. 'We will be dining out with some friends of mine. So while you are shopping buy a dress—something befitting a black-tie event. Something—pretty.'

Pretty? 'I don't do pretty.' Reaching for the pot of marmalade, Natasha began spreading it liberally on the toast.

'Something—colourful, then to—complement your figure.'

'I am not—' the knife worked faster '—going to dress up like some floozy just to help you prove a point to your awful ex-wife!'

'Why? Don't you believe you have the power to compete?'

The challenge hit Natasha blindside, and she felt her breath stick in her throat.

'It seems to me, Natasha, that you're too easily intimidated by conceited bullies like your selfish sister and my ex-wife,' he went on grimly. 'Woman like them can pick a shrinking violet like you out from a hundred feet away as an easy target. But what really gets to me is that you let them. Grow up, *agape mou*,' he advised as he climbed to his feet. 'Toughen up. You are with me now and I have a reputation for high standards in my choice of women.'

Tense as piano wire now, 'Your standard must have slipped when you married Gianna, then,' she hit back at him.

To her further fury he just uttered a dry husky laugh! 'We are all allowed one mistake. Rico was your mistake, Gianna was mine, so now we are quits.'

With no quick answer ready to offset that one, 'Why don't you just go and do—whatever it is you do and leave me alone?' she muttered, and picked up her slice of toast to bite into it.

The next thing she knew he'd moved around the table and was swooping down to capture her marmalade sticky mouth.

'Mmm, nice,' he murmured as he drew away again. 'I think we will try that again…'

Dipping a fingertip into the marmalade pot, he smeared it across the hot cushion of her bottom lip, then bent his dark head to lick the marmalade off. Like a captivated cat Natasha couldn't stop the pink tip of her own tongue from tracing her lip the moment he withdrew again.

'Yes,' he said softly, and she was drowning in a completely new kind of sensual foreplay that made her want to squirm where she sat.

Then he was straightening up to his full height and moving away from her towards the wall of glass with the smooth stride of an arrogantly self-confident male, leaving the rich, low sound of his amused laughter behind in his wake.

'You forgot to add yourself to the list of bullies in my life!' she threw after him, angrily snatching up a napkin to rub the residue of sticky marmalade from her mouth.

'But Miss Cool and Prim quickly slipped her chains, did she not? Think about it, Natasha.'

The glass slid open to allow him to stride through. Natasha stared after him until she couldn't see him any longer and sizzled and simmered—because she knew he was right. She had lost her cool the moment he'd touched her. It just wasn't fair that he could affect her that easily—it wasn't!

Her eyes went back to the wad of money still lying on the table where he'd tossed it down beside her phone. She was not so dumb that she hadn't recognised his criticism of her clothes and her uncompetitive nature for the challenge it was, but it had hurt to hear him say it in that disparaging tone he'd used.

Mr Blunt, she mocked dully, and felt the hurt tremor attack her poor, abused bottom lip.

Her mobile phone started ringing as she sat in the isolated luxury of one of Leo's limousines. Opening her purse—which

Bernice had also found for her this morning languishing on a table out on the terrace—Natasha plucked out her mobile phone and stared at the screen warily, expecting the caller to be Cindy or Rico, but it wasn't.

'How did you get my number?' she demanded.

'I stole it,' Leo confessed. 'Listen,' he then continued briskly, 'I have had an extra meeting dropped on me today so I will not be finished here in time to get back home and change before we go out. I have arranged with a friend of mine to kit you out with everything you might need in the way of clothes. Her name is Persephone Karides. Rasmus is transporting you to her salon right now. Don't turn stiff on her, *agape mou*,' he cautioned smoothly as if he just couldn't stop himself from criticising her! 'Trust her because she has more sense of style in her little fingertip than anyone else I know.'

Natasha drew in a hurt breath. 'You're very insulting,' she said as she breathed out again. 'Do you always have to think with your mouth?'

There was a silence—a short, sharp shock of one that rang in her ears and made her bottom lip quiver again. 'My apologies,' he murmured—earnestly. 'I did not intend what I said to sound like a criticism of you.'

'Well, it did.' Natasha flipped her phone shut and pushed it back in her bag. It rang again almost immediately but she ignored it.

'Oh, goodness me,' Persephone Karides gasped the moment she saw Natasha. 'When Leo told me you were different, I did not think he meant so fabulously different!'

Standing here in her miserable cream suit eyeing the eye-catching, raven-haired, tall, slender model-type standing a good six inches higher than herself—Natasha had to ask herself if Leo had primed Persephone Karides to say that.

'He's desperate I don't show him up by appearing in a sack, so he sent me to you,' she responded—stiffly.

'Are you joking?' Persephone Karides burst out laughing. 'Leo is much more concerned with his own comfort! He instructed me that he wants modest. He wants quietly elegant and refined. He does not want other men climbing over each other to get a better look at your front! I have not had as much fun in a long time as I did listening to a jealously possessive Leo Christakis, of all men, dictate how he wanted me to protect him!'

Natasha flushed at his intervention. Was he throwing down yet another challenge to her here or was Persephone Karides simply telling it as it was?

Whichever, the fact that he'd dared to give out such arrogant orders to the fashion stylist was enough to put the glinting light of defiance in her blue eyes.

Long hours later Rasmus pulled the car to a stop next to a fabulous-looking private yacht tied up against the harbour wall. Natasha gaped at it because the last thing she'd expected was to be dining in a restaurant situated on a luxury yacht.

'The boss owns it,' Rasmus told her as he shut off the car engine. 'The yacht used to belong to his father. When he decided to sell it, the boss objected. His father let him have the boat so long as he turned it into a profit-making enterprise.'

So he came up with the idea of turning the yacht into a restaurant? 'How old was he?' Natasha questioned curiously.

'Nineteen. He gave her a complete refit, then chartered her out and turned in a profit in his first year,' Rasmus said with unmistaken pride in his voice. 'Two years ago, when she was ready for another refit, he decided her sailing days were over and brought her here. Now she's one of the most exclusive restaurants in Athens.'

Here was a pretty horseshoe-shaped harbour tucked away

from the busy main port, Natasha saw when she climbed out of the car into the hot evening air, cooled by the gentle breeze coming in off the sea. The yacht itself had an old-world grandeur about it that revealed a sentimental side to Leo she would never have given him in a thousand years.

Or it reveals his money-making genius, the cynical side to her brain suggested to her as she walked up the gangway. She felt butterflies take flight in her stomach the closer she came to putting on show her day of defiance aided and abetted by an eager Persephone Karides.

Though the way she had allowed the moment to become so important to her came to lie like a weight across her chest when she saw him. He was leaning against a white painted bulkhead waiting for her. Natasha stilled as her spindle-heeled shoes settled onto the deck itself. He looked breath-shatteringly gorgeous in the conventional black dinner suit he was wearing with a black silk bow tie and a shimmering bright white shirt.

Uncertainty went to war against defiance as she waited for him to say something—show smug triumph because he had manipulated her to do what he wanted her to do or reveal his disapproval at the look she had achieved.

He took his own sweet time showing anything at all as he slid his hooded gaze over her from the top of her loose blonde hair tamed into heavy silk waves around her face and her bare shoulders, then took in the creamy, smooth thrust of her breasts cupped in a misty soft violet crêpe fabric held in place by two flimsy straps, which tied together at the back of her neck. The rest of the dress moulded every curving shape of her figure and finished modestly at her knees—though there was nothing remotely modest about the flirty little back kick pleat that gave her slender thighs length and a truly eye-popping—to Natasha anyway—sensual shape.

Sexy… She knew she looked sexy because Persephone had

told her she did and, as she'd learned during the long day in the Greek woman's care, Persephone did not mess around with empty compliments. 'Leo is going to kill me if you wear that,' she'd said.

And, true to Persephone's warning, Natasha saw that Leo was not happy. His growing frown teased her stomach muscles with a tingling surge of triumph. His mouth was flat, his eyes hidden beneath those disgustingly thick, ebony eyelashes. When he lifted a hand to run an absent finger along his bumpy nose, for some unaccountable reason she wanted to breathe out a victorious laugh.

Then she didn't want to laugh because he was lowering the hand and coming towards her, crossing the space separating them without uttering a single word. The expanse of creamy flesh she had on show began to prickle as he came closer, her wide-spaced, carefully made-up eyes with their eyelashes darkened and lengthened by a heavy lick of mascara trying their very best to appear cool. He came to a stop a few inches away, glanced down at her mouth so sensually shaped by a deep rose gloss, then dropped his gaze even lower, to the misty violet framework of the dress where it formed a perfect heart shape across the generous curves of her breasts.

By the time he lifted his eyes back to hers, Natasha felt as if she were standing on pins. She'd stopped breathing, was barely even thinking much beyond the sizzling clash their eyes had made. Then instinct kicked in and she lifted her chin in an outright challenge.

He slid his hands around her nipped-in waist, tugged her hard up against him, then stole her lipstick with a very hot, aggressive kiss.

'Move an inch from my side tonight and you will find

yourself floating in the water.' His eyes burned the threat into her as he drew away.

'It was you that told me to stop playing the shrinking violet,' she reminded him coolly.

Taking a small step back, he took his time looking her over once again. 'The colour of the dress is right anyway,' he observed finally.

Natasha pulled in a breath., 'Do you find it so totally impossible to say anything nice to me?'

She had a point, Leo acknowledged, but if she thought he had not noticed how pleased she was that she'd annoyed him, then—

'Come on,' he sighed, giving up because he'd got exactly what he'd asked for, and to discover only when it was too late that he no longer wanted it was his problem, not Natasha's. 'Let's find out if we can spend a whole evening together without embarking on yet another fight.'

Walking beside him with one of his long fingered hands a possessive clamp around her waist, Natasha wished she knew if it was triumph or annoyance that was sending sparking electrodes swimming in her blood. The moment they stepped inside the main salon she was immediately struggling with a different set of new conflicts when she found herself the instant centre of attention for twenty or so curious looks.

She moved a bit closer to Leo. Her hand slid up beneath his jacket to clutch tensely at his shirt against his fleshless waist. He liked it, she realised as she sensed a kind of quickening inside him as if his flesh had woken up to her presence. She went to snatch her hand back again, shocked that she'd even dared to put it there in the first place.

'Leave it where it is,' Leo instructed.

Her fingers quivered a little before they settled back against his shirt again. He responded with a delicate caress of her waist. Quickly the sensual charge that had been sparking between them from the moment they first kissed at his home in London was relaying its message again.

He began introducing her around his guests as 'Natasha', that was all, because to add the Moyles was bound to give rise to speculation about Rico, since half the people she was being introduced to were also on the wedding invitation list Rico's mother had emailed to her only last week.

And thinking about Rico did not make her feel comfortable about being here. It began to bother her that Leo had brought her into these people's midst at all. In fact, the more she thought about it, the more sure she became that, once these people found out the truth about exactly who she was, they were going to stop treating her with respect. At the moment they were only doing so because she was with Leo Christakis.

It also began to bother her that she needed to stick this close to Leo—touching, feeling his body warmth and his possessive arm across her back, his hand fixed like a clamp to her waist. Putting herself on show had never been her thing and it took only half an hour of being the centre of attention before she was certain she was never going to want to do it again.

Dinner took place in another salon, presided over by one of Athens's top chefs, she was reliably informed by a friend of Leo's seated opposite her. 'Leo likes only the best in everything,' Dion Angelis told her, grinning at the man in question who occupied the place next to Natasha.

Dion Angelis was about Leo's age and wore the same cloak of wealth about him—as all these people did. The beautiful creature sitting beside him was Marina, his very Greek wife.

Greek wives didn't speak to other men's lovers—at least not in this circle of people, Natasha had discovered tonight. And now she knew why as she watched Dion Angelis drift a lazy look over her with his eyelids lowered in a way she would have to be blind to miss what it meant.

Tensing slightly in her seat, Natasha flicked a glance at Marina who tried her best to hide her anger at her husband's blatant interest—but not before she had sent Natasha a scathing look of contempt. Then she slid her dark gaze to Leo.

'Leonadis…' it made Natasha start in surprise because she had not heard anyone call Leo that before '…Gianna expected you at Boschetto's last night. She was really quite upset when you failed to appear.'

Sitting further back into her chair, Natasha turned her expression blank. So even ex-wives rated higher than lovers, she gleaned from Marina's attempt to put her in her place.

'Gianna has already voiced her objection,' Leo returned smoothly. 'Dion, kindly remove your eyes from my future wife's breasts…'

As a softly spoken show-stopper it silenced a room full of chattering voices. The sophisticated Dion turned a dull shade of red. His wife snapped her lips together and turned her widening stare onto Natasha along with everyone else. Natasha was the only one to turn her shocked stare onto Leo while he, the cool, implacable devil, stared down at his wineglass and remained perfectly calm and relaxed with the kind of smile playing with his lips that turned Natasha's flesh to ice.

'Congratulations,' someone murmured, setting off a rippling effect of similar sentiments while Natasha continued to stare at Leo until he lifted his head and looked back at her, his steady, dark gaze silently challenging her to deny what he'd said.

It was on the tip of her tongue to do it. It was right there hovering on that tingling tip that she should just get it all over with and announce to everyone exactly who she was!

With an ease that belied the speed with which he did it and the strength that he used, Leo's hand caught hold of hers and squeezed. 'Don't,' he warned softly.

He was back to reading her mind again—back to playing it tough! Natasha turned to look at Marina, the light of fury like a crystal-blue haze she could barely manage to see through. 'Tacky, other people's relationships, don't you think?' she remarked with a wry smile that beat Leo's hands down in the chilly stakes. 'I can only hope that my marriage to Leo will come to a less volatile ending than his first marriage did and that I accept it with more—grace.'

With that she stood up, shaking inside now but knowing that she had made her point. She already knew about Gianna. She knew the ex-wife still chased her lost man. And she also knew that Leo had just said what he had because Marina's husband had been eyeing Natasha up and that Dion did it because other men's lovers were clearly fair game around here—which said what about Marina's place in her husband's life?

Leo also came to his feet, his hand still a crushing clamp around her fingers, which kept her pinned to his side. 'Excuse us,' he said dryly to their captive audience. 'It seems that Natasha and I need to find some privacy to discuss her desire to consign our marriage to the divorce courts before it has even begun.'

With that he turned and strode towards the exit, towing her behind him like some naughty child, while leaving a nervously uncertain shimmer of laughter to swim in their wake.

'You always planned to make that announcement, didn't you?' She leapt on the accusation the moment Rasmus closed them inside the car. 'It was the reason why you took me into their company, the reason why you sent me to Persephone to make sure I was suitably dressed for the part!'

'You chose your own style makeover, Natasha,' Leo imparted without a single hint of remorse for what he had just done. 'I recall warning Persephone that I wanted quietly elegant.'

The look she flicked him should have seared off a layer of his skin. 'Before or after you challenged me to put it all out on show?'

A muscle along his jaw flexed. 'I changed my mind about that.'

'Why?' she demanded.

Leo released an irritated sigh. 'Because I feel safer when you play it prim!'

The fact that he was actually admitting it was enough to stop Natasha's breath in her throat.

'Why does this surprise you?' he asked when he caught her expression. 'Your modest mystique was the first thing to attract me to you. Having come to know you a little better, I now realise that I prefer it if you remain mysterious—to everyone else but me.'

'That is just so arrogant I can't believe you even said it!'

All he offered was an indifferent shrug. 'Marina attacked you tonight because she believes you are merely my current lover. Now she knows that my intentions are honourable she will not dare to treat you like that again.'

'Until she finds out who I really am, then she will see the dangerous woman again—the kind that drops one brother to take up with the richer one!'

'Well, that puts Dion out of the frame,' Leo drawled with cool superiority. 'And as for Marina, she will make sure he keeps his wandering eyes to himself from now on.'

'I'm still not marrying you,' Natasha shook out, 'so it's up to you how you get out of the mess you made for yourself.'

Leo met that with silence. Natasha turned to look directly ahead and let the silence stretch. But she could feel his eyes on her, *feel* him trying to decide if she possessed enough determination against his relentless push to get her to agree to marry him, and she could feel the fizz in her insides—as if her newly awakened senses found it stimulating to be constantly sparring with him like this!

Leo was silent because he was considering whether to tell her that he never declared anything without a fault-free strategy already worked out. But he let that consideration slide away in favour of wondering what she would do if he leapt on her instead. She was already expecting it to happen, he could tell by the way she was sitting there tense, clutching her fingers together on her lap and with that invitingly curvy upper lip trembling in readiness of a full on sensual attack.

But it could wait—as *she* could wait until they were within reach of their bed. Though that did not mean he wasn't prepared to up the sensual ante a little. 'So you still only offer me the sex.'

'*Yes!*' Natasha insisted.

And only realised the trap she'd fallen into when he murmured softly, 'Good, because you look so beautiful tonight I ache to slide you out of that dress.'

His intentions declared, Leo left her to sizzle in her own strategic error as they arrived at his house. The heavy gates swung open. The car pulled to a stop at the bottom of the front steps. They both climbed out of it under their own steam, leaving Rasmus to slide the car out of their way so Natasha could cross the gap to Leo's side. He did not attempt to touch her as they walked up the steps and into the house. He let the stinging stitch of anticipation spin separate webs of expectation around both of them as they crossed the foyer and into the lift.

The moment they achieved the privacy of his floor Leo gave up on the waiting and reached for her—only Natasha took a swift step back.

'Tell me why you told everyone we are getting married,' she insisted.

His sigh was filled with irritation that she was persisting

with the subject. 'Because a formal announcement of our intention to marry will appear in all the relevant newspapers tomorrow, so I saw no reason to keep quiet about it,' he answered, and watched her delectable mouth drop.

'But you can't have done that without my say-so!'

'Well, I did.' He strode off, tugging impatiently at his bow tie.

Natasha hurried anxiously after him. 'But you can't have it both ways, Leo. You can't keep my relationship to Rico a secret to your friends *and* announce my name in the press at the same time!'

'You don't have a relationship with Rico.' The bow tie slid free of his shirt collar and was discarded onto a chair.

'Excuse me?' Natasha choked out. 'Aren't you the one who insists I'm Rico's thieving accomplice?'

He turned a steady look on her. 'Are you—his accomplice?'

Sheer angry cussedness made Natasha want to spit out a very satisfying *yes!* Then her innate honesty got the better of her. 'Not intentionally, no,' she answered wearily.

'Then do us both a favour and drop the subject.' As if he was bored with it, he shrugged out of his jacket. 'You were attacked tonight by a woman who cannot keep her husband in check and who is also a good friend of my ex-wife. I defended you. You should be feeling grateful, not screeching at me.'

It was the inference that she had been screeching that snapped Natasha's ready lips shut. Gianna was a screecher. Not in any way, shape or form did Natasha want to be compared with her!

It was only as she watched his hands move to the top button of his shirt that Natasha realised where they were standing in the bedroom and the need to keep fighting him withered right there.

She glanced at the bed, all neat and tidy with its corners turned down ready for them to slide between the cool white sheets. Her heart gave a flutter and she turned her gaze back onto Leo, who was calmly unbuttoning the rest of his shirt while he watched the telling expressions trip across her face.

'You led me in here deliberately,' she murmured.

His acknowledging smile was as lazily amused as hell. 'I am a natural tactician, *agape mou*. You should already know this.'

He was also the most sensuously beguiling man to watch undress. Natasha lost the thread of the conversation when her eyes fixed on the ribbon of hair-matted, bronzed flesh now on show down his front.

'You want to touch me?' The husky question in his voice made her lips tremble and part.

She couldn't even deny it with a shake of her head.

'Then come over here and touch me.' It was a soft-toned invitation—a darkly compelling masculine command.

And it tugged her towards him as if she were attached to him by invisible strings. She didn't even hate herself for giving in to it so easily, she just *wanted*—with a mind-blocking, sense-writhing need that brought her fingers up and reaching for him. He helped by taking hold of them and guiding them to his chest before he sank her into the warm, dark luxury of pleasure with the power of his kiss.

He peeled her out of her dress as promised. He stroked each satin curve of her body as if he were consigning each detail of her to memory, and eventually sank her down onto the bed.

'I shouldn't let you do this to me,' she groaned at one point when he made her feel as if she had molten liquid moving through her veins.

'You think I feel less than you do?' Catching one of her hands, he laid it against the pounding of his heart in his chest.

The rest of the night turned into long—long hours of slow loving. If Natasha had ever let herself wonder if there were really men out there that could sustain the flowing peaks of pleasure so often, then by the time they drifted into sleep she knew she need wonder no more.

Then the morning came, as bright and blue and glittering as the day before had been—only this morning Leo was tipping her unceremoniously out of the bed and pushing her into the bathrobe before dragging her out onto the terrace.

'What do you think you are doing?' Her sleep-hazed brain made her feel dizzy.

He made no answer, and there was no sign of the wonderfully warm and sensual man who'd loved her into oblivion the night before, just a cold, hard, angry male who pushed her down into a chair, then stabbed a finger at the newspaper he had folded open on the table in front of her.

'Read,' he said.

Read, Natasha repeated silently while still trying to get her muddy brain to work. He'd woken her up. He hadn't even let her use the bathroom. She could barely get her eyes to focus, never mind read a single thing!

Then she had no choice but to focus because the headline was typed in such bold black lettering it stabbed her with each soul-shattering, nerve-flaying word.

CHAPTER EIGHT

LOVE CHEAT CHOOSES RICHES OVER RAGS! it yelled at her.

In an intriguing love triangle, Natasha Moyles—sister of Cindy Moyles, the new singing sensation everyone is talking about—has dumped the man she was supposed to be marrying in six weeks to run off with his Greek billionaire stepbrother, Leo Christakis, in a riches over rags love scandal that leaves the poorer Italian playboy Rico Giannetti out in the cold.

Cindy Moyles claims that she didn't see it coming. 'I had no idea that Natasha was seeing Leo Christakis behind Rico's back. I'm as shocked as everyone,' she insisted today as she sat with her new management team, who are about to launch her career with a new single predicted to clean up when it's released.

Rico Giannetti was not available for comment. His mother is said to be very upset. The Christakis PR department is denying there is anything untoward between their employer and his stepbrother's fiancée. However the picture below tells it all…

There was more—lots of it—but Natasha's eyes had stuck on the photograph showing her standing in a heated clinch with Leo right here on the balcony of this house. She was wrapped around him like a sex-hungry feline. There wasn't a hope that anyone was going to call it an innocent clinch.

'The beauty of power-zoom lenses,' Leo mocked from his lounging posture in the chair on the other side of the table.

With her face going white with shock to horror then heart-clutching dismay, she asked, 'But—how did they find out I was here with you?'

'Your sister,' he provided grimly. 'This is a very good example of damage limitation. Cindy's new management team is clearly on the ball. She must have gone straight to them with what happened and they got their heads together and decided to take the initiative by getting in her side of the story first. Fortunately for her I managed to gag Rico before she did or your dear sister placed herself at risk of coming out of this looking like the manipulative little whore that she is.'

'Don't say that.' Natasha felt stifled by the ugly picture he was painting. The truth was bad enough, but this made it all so much worse!

'Look at the evidence, Natasha,' he advised harshly. 'Look at the free publicity she is getting from this. Even her new management team has made sure their company name is printed.'

His angry tone made her shiver. 'Is there anything you can do to—?'

'Plenty of things,' he clipped in. 'I could strangle your sister, but I suspect it is already too late to do that. Or I could kick you out and allow myself the small satisfaction of knowing I will be painted as one hell of a ruthless bastard to have stolen you from beneath Rico's nose for the pleasure of a two-night stand! Being seen as that ruthless is good for my business image—the rest I don't give a toss about.'

Stung right through by his angry barrage, 'Or I could walk away under my own steam,' Natasha retaliated. 'I could play the true slut by making it known that I've had *both* brothers and neither were worth it!'

Across the table Leo's eyes darkened dangerously. Natasha didn't care. 'Well, think of it from my point of view,' she suggested stiffly. 'Miss Cool and Prim isn't quite as cool and prim as people like to think! I could make a small fortune selling my story—a juicy kiss-and-tell about the sexual antics of a billionaire tycoon and the poor Italian playboy!'

'Not worth it?' He picked up on the only part of what she'd thrown at him that seemingly mattered.

'I hate you,' she breathed, hunching inside her bathrobe. 'This was always going to get nasty. You carried me away on a cloud of assurances, but when I think back, you needed only half a minute once you'd got me into your house in London before you were flipping my head by telling me that you wanted me for yourself! What kind of man does that to a woman who'd just witnessed what I had witnessed? What kind of man picks her up and takes her to bed? What kind of man, Leo,' she thrust out furiously, 'propositions a woman, then carries through, knowing she was in no fit state to know what she was doing?'

'What kind of woman falls in love with a useless piece of pampered flesh like Rico and is too blind to notice he's still putting it out there with every female he can lay his hands on?'

Strike for strike, Leo cut deeper than anything she'd stabbed him with. Natasha tugged in a shuddering breath. 'I suppose next you're going to remind me that Rico didn't even want me.'

'So you can accuse me of accepting his unwanted cast offs?'

Natasha pushed to her feet on a daze of trammelled feelings. 'Is that how you see me?' she choked as last night's long loving strangled itself to death.

'No,' his voice rasped like coarse sandpaper across her ragged senses. 'I do not see you like that.'

'They why say it?' she shrilled out. 'Do you think I am

proud of the way I jumped into bed with you? Do you think I hadn't already worked out for myself that I was going to be labelled gold-digging tart for doing it?'

'Then why did you do it?'

He just didn't know when to leave something alone! Natasha's whole body quivered on the deep breath she took. 'Because you wanted me and I needed to be wanted.' And the devil himself couldn't tempt her to add that she'd been lost to reason from the moment their mouths had first touched. 'You get what you ask for,' she then mocked with weak tears thickening it. 'So, thank you, Leo, for taking such great care to teach me I am a normal sexual woman. I really do appreciate it.'

'My absolute pleasure,' he grimly silked out. 'But—to bring this discussion back to its original problem—there is one other option open to me that would save my face and your face.'

'W-what?' she couldn't resist prompting.

He laughed, low and deep and as sardonic as hell. 'A wedding,' he said as he picked up another newspaper, then leant forwards to place it on top of the other one. Instead of a tabloid, this one was a respected UK broadsheet, also conveniently folded at the right place.

It was the announcement of their forthcoming marriage. Natasha had forgotten all about it. Pressing her tense lips together, she made herself sit down and read it.

'It feels quite good to know that my instincts were working so well when I placed that in the papers,' Leo's dry voice delivered.

'I will still always look like a gold-digging tart with or without this.'

'Everyone loves a passionate romance, *agape mou*—so long as we do marry and make ourselves respectable, that is. It convinces the doubters that we cannot live without each other, you see. Of course,' he then added, 'you will have to agree to a gagging clause written into the prenuptial contract you are going to sign once my lawyers have drawn it up.'

And that, Natasha heard, was payback because she had just threatened to involve him in a kiss-and-tell exposé.

'Did you *know* about this tabloid article last night when we were dining with your friends?' she flashed out suddenly, though why the suspicion entered her head was beyond her capability to understand right now.

The velvet dark set of his eyes gave a surprised flicker before he carefully hooded them away. 'I happened to hear of it,' he disclosed coolly.

So he put out a counter-announcement declaring their intention to marry in a bid to make himself look better? Natasha threw herself back into her seat. 'You're as sly and manipulating as Cindy,' she quivered out in shaken dislike. 'God help us all if the two of you ever join up to make a team!'

'Your sister isn't my type. *You* are my type.'

The gullible type that didn't look around corners to see what others were hiding from her? Unable to stop the cold little shiver from tracking her spine, she said, 'A marriage between you and me is never going to work.'

Those sexy, heavy eyelids lifted upwards. 'Did I say I expected it to work?' he silked out.

As an image of the manic Gianna flashed across her eyes Natasha began to understand why the other woman—*wife*—of this man had turned so manic. He just didn't know when to quit with the knives!

'Marriage to Rico is starting to look more appetising by the minute,' she attacked back in muttering derision. 'At least he possessed *some* charm to offset the low-down, sneaky side to his character, whereas you—'

Leo was up out of his chair and looming over her before she could let out a startled shriek. 'You believe so?' he thinned out.

It was then that Natasha caught the glittering gold sparks burning up his eyes and remembered too late what it conveyed. The last time she'd seen that look she'd just accused him of being jealous of Rico, and his reaction then had—

'I was just kidding!' she cried out as his hands arrived around her waist and he hauled her bodily off the chair.

She found herself clamped to his front by a pair of arms that threatened to stop her breathing, her eyes on a level with his.

'I w-was just kidding, Leo,' she repeated unsteadily, forced to push her arms over his shoulders because there was nowhere else she could put them, and it didn't help that she was feeling the buzz, feeling the deep and pulsing, sense-vibrating buzz slink over each separate nerve-end as he held her gaze prisoner with the fierce heat of his next intention, turned with her and started walking them towards the curving glass.

And he didn't say a single word, which made the whole macho exercise even more exciting. He just tumbled her down onto the bed and followed her there, lips flat, face taut, his hands already making light of the belts holding their robes shut.

'Y-you deserved to hear it, though.' Natasha just could not resist adding fire to his anger. 'If—if you think about it, Leo, you're as ruthless ab-about getting what you want as—'

'Say his name again if you dare,' he breathed.

Natasha had the sense to block her tongue behind her teeth and knew she should be feeling alarmed and intimidated by his angry intent, but she didn't. She just lay there and let him part the two robes and waited for him to stretch out on top of her.

Heat by burning heat, their skin melded together at the same moment that his mouth took fierce possession of hers. And like someone who just did not know any better she fell into it all to kiss with every bit of aroused excitement at work inside her, hungry for him, greedy for him, slipping her legs around his waist so she could invite his full driving thrust.

He filled her and she loved it. He still held her eyes total prisoner as he moved in her with the deep and driven plunge of his hips. She loved that, too. Loved it so much she lifted her head to capture his mouth with short, soft, encouraging kisses that pulled a groan from his throat and sent his fingers spearing into her hair so he could hold her back to maintain the electrifying eye contact.

Nothing in her admittedly small experience warned her that the climax she was about to hit would turn her into a trembling state of shimmering static. Or that the man creating it was going to tremble in her arms.

When it was over, he lay heavy on her, his face buried in the heat-dampened hollow of her throat. Her heart was hammering, she could barely draw in her breath. What had just taken place had been so fevered and physical she lay there shell-shocked by the power of it. Every inch of her flesh still trembled, she could feel the same tremors still attacking him. And their limbs were tangled, the white towelling bathrobes generating a cocoon of intimacy all of their own.

When eventually he lifted his head to look down at her, the deep and intense darkness in his eyes snagged her breath all the more.

'I was rough with you,' he murmured unsteadily.

'No.' Natasha drew her hand up to rest it against his mouth. 'Don't say that,' she whispered. 'I—liked it.' And because she simply had to do it, she removed her hand and replaced it with the warm, soft tremor of her mouth.

One kiss led to another. Their robes disappeared. No matter how much angry passion had brought them back to this bed in the first place, this climb back through the senses was slow and deep and breathtakingly intense. He kissed her everywhere and with complete disregard of any shyness she might have had left. She curled herself into him wherever she could do, she kissed and licked and bit his flesh and scored her hands over him, absorbing every pleasurable shudder he gave while whispering his name over and over again.

Afterwards was as if it weren't happening. They drifted with a silent sense of togetherness from the bed to the shower. In the husky deep voice of a man still in the power of what they'd created Leo showed her how to work the wet-room buttons and dials, then handed her a bar of soap and encouraged her to wash him while he stood, big shoulders pressed back against the white tiles with his eyes closed and his lean face stripped of its usual arrogance.

Natasha knew that something crucial had altered between them, though she could not put a name to what that something was.

Then—yes, she could, she thought as she leant in closer and moulded her lips around one of his tightly budded nipples. Somewhere during all of that intense loving, they had both dropped their guard.

Ages later, Leo dressed and went off to work and she—well, Natasha crawled back between the rumpled bedding, curled up on his side of the bed and whispered, 'I love him,' into his pillow.

It was shockingly, horribly that simple. She fell asleep wondering how she could have let it happen—and what the heck she was going to do about it….

That evening he took her out to dinner again. She chose to wear a little black dress that skimmed her curves rather than moulded them. As he ran his eyes over her, he lifted a hand up to absently stroke the bump in his nose and it struck

Natasha that he did that when he was unhappy about something—this time probably the little black dress.

Still, he chose to say nothing. He chose not to comment on the way she had pinned her hair up, leaving her neck and her shoulders bare. He wore a casual, taupe, linen suit and a black T-shirt that made her fingers want to stroke his front. He took her to a small, very select place in the hills outside the city away from the main tourist haunts. They ate food off a tiny candlelit table and drank perfectly chilled white wine. And each time she moved, the luxurious thickness of his eyelashes flowed down low over his eyes and she knew—just knew he was making love to her in his mind.

It was all so heady to be the total centre of his concentration like this. And the knowledge now that she was in love with him tugged and ached inside her so badly she was sure he must be able to tell in the husky quality of her voice and in her body language. Self-awareness became an irresistible drug that made her hold his attention with soft small talk and dark blue, tempting looks she didn't even realize she knew how to do.

Leo was captivated. She was so hooked on what was passing between them she was unaware how she'd drawn an invisible circle around the two of them. People he knew came up to speak to him. Natasha barely noticed. She barely heard the congratulations they were receiving or noticed the interested looks of speculation they sent her way. Whenever his attention was demanded elsewhere, he claimed her slender hand across the table and she even used this contact to keep his senses locked on her with the light brush of her fingers against his.

It was intoxicating to know that this beautiful and tantalising creature revealed herself only for him. To anyone else her responses were quiet and polite, but cool and reserved like the old Natasha. Rico had no idea what it was he had missed out on.

Rico. Leo flicked a hooded, dark glance at her and wondered how often his stepbrother's name crept into her head. Would she prefer to be sitting here with Rico? When she looked at him like this, was she secretly wishing that his face were Rico's face?

On a flick of tension he stood up suddenly and pulled her to her feet. 'Let's go,' he said.

He needed to be alone with her—in his bed.

'What's wrong?' Natasha asked him as Rasmus drove them down the hillside.

Leo didn't even turn his head to look at her, his long body sprawled in the seat beside her so taut she could almost feel the tension plucking at him.

'You are going to marry me whether you want to or not,' he announced coolly.

Silence clattered down around them, increasing the tension holding Leo, while he waited for her to shoot him down with a refusal as she usually did. When nothing came back at him he turned his head. She was sitting beside him with her spine a gentle curve into the leather seat and her eyes were fixed straight ahead. Everything about her was calm and still.

'Did you hear what I said?' he flicked out.

Lips forming the kind of lush, vulnerable profile that made him want to leap on them, she nodded her head.

'Then answer me,' he instructed impatiently.

'I was not aware that you had asked a question,' she responded dryly, 'more a statement of intent.'

'It will still require a *yes* from you when I drag you in front of a priest.'

So it will, Natasha thought with a wry kind of smile altering the contours of her mouth. Yesterday he'd made that shocking announcement to his friends and followed it up this morning with the printed version, tossed at her like a challenge, before coolly informing her that he did not expect a marriage between them to last. Then he'd taken her back to bed and seduced her into falling in love with him. He'd *made love* to her throughout the whole evening. Now the tough-talking man with a marriage ultimatum was back.

'Look at me, Natasha,' he commanded grimly.

She didn't want to look at him—but she still turned her head. It was like drowning in her own newly discovered feelings. Everything about him had become so overwhelmingly important to her in such a short space of time, she'd never felt so hopelessly helpless in her entire life.

'Marry me,' he repeated quietly.

'To help you save face?'

'No,' he denied. 'Because I want you to.'

It was like the final nail in the coffin of her resistance—not just the words he'd spoken, but the deep, dark, husky seriousness with which he had said them—and fed her with an oh-so-weak injection of hope.

'OK—yes,' she said.

OK—yes, he had to live with because, Leo acknowledged frustratingly, OK—yes, was all he was going to get. But he punished her for it later when they hit the bed.

He possessed her body and obsessed her senses, and Natasha let him. She had to because once she'd surrendered the marriage war she found she had no control left over with which to fight him about anything else.

And if this was real love, then it made her hurt like crazy, because, no matter how profoundly she knew she affected him, she also knew deep down inside her that the mind-blowing sex was as deep as it went for him.

Yet he rarely let her leave his side during the next couple of weeks leading up to their marriage. He took her with him wherever he went—even into his office sometimes, where she would stand by the window or sit in a chair and let him throw his weight around with the deeply resonant tone of his voice.

People got to know them as a couple so quickly, it came as no surprise that within days they were being talked about in Athens gossip press. Her betrothal to Rico came out for an airing and the 'riches over rags' label was just too good not to keeping using when they referred to her.

'Do you mind?' Leo asked her when one newspaper in particular did a real character assassination on her.

'It should be me asking you that question, since you don't come out of this any better than I do.'

'How can I mind? You did drop Rico, and you are here with me, and I am most definitely wealthier than Rico will ever be.'

And that was Leo, telling it as it was. Even Natasha couldn't argue with such simplicity and she knew the full truth.

There was no word from Rico. Natasha could find no photograph of him in any newspaper, and no one had tracked him down to get his comments on his broken engagement. He seemed to have dropped off the face of the earth.

Two weeks exactly from the day she had walked onto the Christakis private plane with Leo, Natasha married him in a quiet civil ceremony that took place in a closely guarded, secret location. She wore white—at his insistence—a strapless, French silk, tulle dress with a rouched bodice Persephone had found for her. When she stood beside Leo as they took their vows, he looked so much the tall, dark, sober-faced groom that she almost—almost lost courage and changed her mind.

The announcement of their marriage appeared in the next day's papers. By then they were already in New York. It was being called a honeymoon, but what it actually turned out to be was the beginning of a tour of Leo's business interests, which took them around the world. By day Leo played the powerful and cut-throat businessman, by night he played the suave sophisticate, socialising with business associates, and Natasha learnt to play the game at his side. While in the privacy of their bedroom, whichever country they were in, she played the lover to a man with an insatiably passionate desire for her.

From New York to Hong Kong to Tokyo then Sydney. By the time they landed back on Greek soil two more weeks had gone by and Natasha was such a different person she could barely remember the one she used to be.

But, more than that, she had allowed herself to forget the real reasons why they had embarked on this marriage in the first place.

She received her first jolting reminder as they walked through the airport and passed an English newspaper stand. She saw Cindy's name and face splashed across every magazine, celebrating her first UK number-one hit.

'So she got her dearest wish,' Leo remarked dryly.

'Yes,' Natasha answered, staring at the way Cindy looked so different, more like a beautiful and youthful, blue-eyed blonde with no hint of her old angst or petulance in sight.

Cindy had pulled on a new persona—just as she had, Natasha likened. Whether it went further than skin-deep with her sister was a question she was not likely to find the answer to because Cindy belonged in her past now.

The next stark reminder as to what she'd left behind in England came amongst the stack of congratulation cards they found waiting for them at the house. This particular one stood out from the rest because she recognised the writing and it was addressed only to her. Inside was a traditionally standard greeting card with silver embossed wedding bells on the front and a simple message of congratulations printed inside. It was from her parents, with a brief note written in her mother's hand.

'We wish you every happiness in your marriage,' was all that it said. No loving endearments, no sign that she had ever been their daughter at all.

'Perhaps they know they treated you badly and don't know how to say so,' Leo suggested quietly.

'And perhaps they're just relieved to bring closure to a twenty-four-year-old mistake.' Turning the envelope over, she frowned at it. 'I wonder how they managed to get hold of this address?'

'Angelina,' Leo provided the answer. 'They have been—keeping in touch.'

That brought Natasha's attention up to his face. 'And you knew this but didn't think to tell me?'

'What was there to tell?' he answered with a shrug. 'Angelina needed to ensure her son was not pilloried in the press by an enterprising Cindy. Your parents needed to ensure that Cindy was not pilloried by a bitter Rico out to get his revenge.'

'You mean, Cindy *did* set him up?'

'Whoever made the first move, *agape mou*, it happened.'

And that was Leo at his tell-it-as-it-is best.

Natasha slipped the card back in its envelope and did not look at it again.

Another week went by and Leo was busy with a major takeover he'd been working on while they'd travelled the world. Now they were back in Athens, he was devoting his whole time to it, busy, preoccupied, some nights not coming home at all because he had to fly off to one place or another to meet with people, which meant an overnight stay.

The fact that he didn't take her with him on these occasions didn't worry Natasha at all. She had other things to think about. She might have let Leo pay for all the expensive designer stuff she now wore with such ease and indifference, but she paid for everything else herself. Now her small nest of savings had shrunk so small she needed to find a job.

Anything would do, she wasn't picky. She soon discovered, though, that without even a smattering of Greek in her vocabulary she was pretty much unemployable in a formal office environment. So she started trawling the tourist spots hoping someone would like to employ an Englishwoman with reasonable intelligence and a pleasant speaking voice.

Leo found out about what she was doing. They had their first major row in weeks. He had the overbearing nerve to prohibit *his wife* from working in such menial employment as a tourist shop. He would increase her allowance if she was so strapped for cash, he said.

'Don't you think I *know* I owe you enough money already without letting you shell out even more?'

Saying it out loud like that hit both of them harder than either of them expected. In one week she would have been marrying Rico. In one short week she could access the money locked up in the offshore account.

Leo just stared at her coldly, then spun on his heel and walked away. Natasha felt as if she'd just murdered something special, but the truth was the truth and she had to face up to that.

By telling it as it is, she thought heavily. She'd been taught by a master at it, after all.

The long, swooping dive down into reality began from that moment on. For the next few days they lived in a state of unarmed combat, in which Leo made himself scarce—being busy—and Natasha job-hunted with a grim determination not to let him dictate to her, by working her way along the tourist shops in the Plaka through the stifling heat of a melting July, perfectly aware of the minder Leo had put on her to track her every move.

It had to be the worst luck in the world when she literally bumped right into his ex-wife, Gianna, as she was coming out of one shop, still unemployed, hot, tired and miserable with it. Maybe the meeting had been contrived. How was she to know? But the way Gianna stopped her from walking right past her by clipping her long fingernails to Natasha's arm was enough to make her wonder if the dark beauty had been waiting to pounce.

'I want to talk to you,' Gianna said thinly.

'I don't think so.' Natasha tried to move on, but the nails dug in deeper to keep her still.

'Leo is mine!' Gianna spat at her. 'You think you have him caught with that ring on your finger, but you do not. You think with your cool blonde looks you are the perfect antidote to me, but Leo has always and will always belong to me!'

'Not so anyone would notice,' Natasha responded, refusing to be shaken by the venom in Gianna's voice. 'As you say, I wear his ring now. *I* sleep in his bed. And I *don't* pass myself around his friends!'

Even Natasha could not believe she'd said that. Gianna responded with a laugh that went with the wildly hysterical look in her eyes. She unclipped her fingernails and for a second Natasha thought she was going to score them down her face. She even took a jerky step back, sensed her minder step in closer to her and watched Gianna's top lip curl in scorn.

'You little fool,' she said. 'Where do you think he spends his nights when he is not with you?'

'That's a lie,' Natasha breathed, not even giving the suggestion room to apply its poison and sending Gianna a pitying look. 'Get some help, Gianna,' she advised coldly. 'You desperately need it.'

Then she beat a hasty retreat, with her minder tracking in her shadow as she disappeared into the crowds, angrily refusing to rub her arm where the other woman's fingernails had bit.

Leo was waiting for her when she got back to the house. Grim as anything, he didn't say a single word, but just took possession of her arm and turned it to inspect the angry red crescents embedded in her smooth white skin.

'How did you find out?' Natasha asked as she watched his fingertips lightly stroke the red marks.

'Does it matter?'

'No.' Natasha sighed, remembering the minder by then anyway. 'I think she's stark staring mad and I actually feel very sorry for her.'

'Well, don't,' he said. 'Believe me, it is dangerous to feel sorry for Gianna.'

'Thanks for the warning.' She took her arm back. 'Now you've checked I'm not bleeding to death, you can go back to work.'

It was the way she said it that rang a familiar bell inside Leo's head. He took a step back to look at her. She was *not* looking at him. And if he had been wondering lately if the old Natasha had gone for ever, with that cool remark he discovered that she had not.

He heaved out a sigh. He'd had a lousy week. Several times the takeover had threatened to go stale and he'd had to fly off somewhere at the last minute to affect a recovery. Normally he thrived on the cut-and-thrust challenge of testing deals like this. It was what made his hunter's instincts tick. But it was only now as he stood here listening to Natasha's cool attempt to dismiss him that he realised how much he had missed using his hunter's instinct on her.

'You want to indulge in another argument?' he prompted smoothly.

'No.' She turned her back as if meaning to walk away from him.

'You want to come to bed with me, then, and spend the afternoon showing me how much you wish I did not have to fly to Paris tonight?'

'Paris?' That swung her back to face him. 'But you've only just got back from there yesterday!'

'And now I must go back there tonight.' His elegant shrug made light of the constant travelling his job demanded, but the look in his eyes did not make light of what was now going on in his head.

Natasha folded her arms across her front. 'Is that why you're here—to pack a bag?'

Playing the provoking innocent just flew right over Leo's head because he could read her body language and those folded arms were no protection at all from what he was generating here. 'I was thinking more on the lines of—something different,' he silked out, closing the gap between them like a big, dark and hungry, stalking cat. 'I have this bottle of champagne on ice, you see, no glasses and several novel ways of enjoying it, if you are interested, that is…'

Natasha couldn't help it, she laughed. 'You're shocking—'

'You love me to be shocking.' He took hold of her wrists and gently unlinked her arms. 'It's what makes you give in so easily when I do this…'

And she did give in. She let him possess her mouth and take her to bed and she let him spend the afternoon shocking her, because she wanted him and she'd missed making love with him and…

The power of a poisoned barb, she heard herself think heavily at one point within the sensual haze he'd wrapped her in and knowing that there was a small part of her that let him do this to her because Gianna's comments made her want to send him away to Paris so totally satiated he wouldn't need to look elsewhere for this.

They stayed hidden in the bedroom throughout the afternoon and she could tell that he did not want to go when it was time for him to leave.

'Will you do me a big favour, and take a day off from job-hunting tomorrow?' he requested.

Her stubborn pout was the beginning of a refusal, which he kissed away.

'Please?' he added when he lifted his head again.

'One good reason,' she bargained, slender white fingertips toying with his smoothly shaved face.

Did he remind her that tomorrow was the day she would have been marrying Rico? Leo brooded. And knew it wasn't really a question because the last thing he wanted to do was to leave her here in his bed thinking about his stepbrother instead of him.

'Because I will be back by lunch with a surprise for you…' catching hold of her caressing fingers, he kissed them '…but only if you are right here waiting for me when I get back.'

'Ah,' said Natasha. 'Blackmail is much more your style. It had better be a good surprise, then.'

Leo just smiled as he rose to his impressive six feet four inches of pure arrogant male in a suit. His gaze lingered, though, on the way she was lying there like a fully-fledged siren stretched out on his bed with her tumbled hair and provoking blue eyes and sumptuously kissed, reddened mouth.

'Where did I get the impression that you were a prude?' he mocked as his gaze slid lower over the creamy fullness of her breasts with their tempting pink centres, and the cluster of dusky blonde curls delineating the heart-shaped juncture with her slender white thighs.

Impulse made him lean down again and place a kiss on that cluster, his tongue darting down in a claim of possession that caused one of those delicious quivers of pleasure she was so free with him.

'See you tomorrow,' he murmured, and left the room before he changed his mind about going anywhere, taking with him the confidence that his woman would be thinking only of him until they came together again.

Natasha slept fitfully that night because she missed him beside her. And awoke the next morning with a thick headache that made her decide to take the day off from job hunting as Leo wanted her to do, which should please him—she thought with a smile.

She was lingering over a solitary breakfast when her mobile phone started to ring. So sure it was going to be Leo calling her, she snatched it up and answered it without checking who it was.

So it came as a shock when it was Cindy's voice that jarred her eardrum.

CHAPTER NINE

'WHAT do you want?' Natasha demanded coldly.

She heard her sister's sigh of relief. 'I wasn't sure you still used this mobile number,' Cindy explained the relieved sigh.

Natasha said nothing, just lowered her eyes to watch the way her fingers stroked the frosted dampness from her glass of orange juice and let the silence stretch.

'OK, so you don't want to speak to me,' Cindy acknowledged. 'But I need to talk to you, Natasha, ab-about the parents.'

Natasha's fingers went still. 'Why—what's wrong with them?'

'Nothing—*everything*,' Cindy sighed out. 'Look…I'm in Athens. I flew in this morning without telling anyone I was coming here, and I have to be back in London this afternoon before I'm missed. Will you meet with me to—talk about them? Trust me, Tasha, it's important or I would not be here.'

Which told her that Cindy wanted this contact no more than she did. But if she'd flown all the way just to speak to her, then whatever she needed to say had to be serious.

Her parents—her parents…that weakness called love gave an aching squeeze. 'OK,' she agreed. 'Do you want to come here so we can—'

'Good grief, no,' Cindy shuddered out. 'I have no desire

to bump into Leo, thank you very much. He gives me the heebie-jeebies.'

'He isn't here.'

'I still won't take the risk. I hired a limo at the airport. Just name a location away from your place and I will get my driver to take me there.'

Natasha glanced at her watch, then named a café in Koloniki Square, and heard Cindy consulting with her driver before she said, 'OK. We can be there in an hour.'

It did not occur to Natasha to question the *we* part. It did not occur to her to question why her totally selfish-seeking sister would come all the way here from England to discuss their parents when it would have been so much quicker and easier for her to just say it on the phone. It was only when she sat waiting at a café table beneath the shade of a leafy tree and watched a silver limo pull up at the edge of the square, then a man climb out of it instead of her sister, that she realised just how thoroughly she had allowed herself to be duped.

Natasha stood up, her first instinct being to just walk away! Then curiosity made her go still as she watched Rico pause to look around him, his eyes hidden behind a pair of silver-framed sunglasses as he scanned the whole square until he located Natasha's minder, then took a quick glance at his watch before he continued towards her.

Dressed in a designer casual pale linen suit and a plane white T-shirt, he looked his usual fashion-plate self. His black hair shone like silk in the sunlight and there wasn't a female in the vicinity from the age of nine to ninety that didn't turn and stare.

But then that was Rico, Natasha thought as she watched him. She, too, had fallen instant victim to his amazing good looks and that special aura he carried everywhere with him, so it was no use her pretending it wasn't there. Except—as she looked at him now she felt absolutely nothing. It was like looking at a stranger—a great-looking stranger, she still had to allow, but a total stranger nonetheless.

When he reached her table, Natasha sat back down in her chair and waited for him to take the seat.

'Still hating me, *cara*?' he drawled as his opening volley.

'Isn't Cindy going to join us?' was all she said in return.

'No.' Leaning back in the chair, Rico glanced at Natasha's minder, who was already talking into his mobile phone.

'I would say you have about five minutes to say what you've set me up to say,' Natasha offered up helpfully.

Looking back at her, Rico pulled off his sunglasses and something strange appeared in the dark brown depths of his eyes. 'You look different,' he murmured. 'That dress suits you.'

'Thank you.' Natasha was not in the least bit impressed by the compliment since the dress was a simple coffee-coloured shift thing she had chosen at random and with no intent to impress anyone.

'I think I should…'

'Get straight to the point,' she suggested. 'Since neither of us want to watch Leo appear in his three-car cavalcade.'

Rico grimaced, clearly understanding exactly what it was she was referring to. One of his hands went into his inside jacket pocket and came out with a folded set of documents.

'All I need you to do, Natasha, is put your signature on these, then I will be out of here.'

He laid a set of papers down on the table in front of her, then followed them with a pen. Natasha looked down, understanding instantly what it was he was expecting her to sign.

She looked back at him. 'Would you like to explain to me why you think I should sign these?'

He shifted his wide shoulders. 'Because the money does not belong to you,' he replied with the absolute truth. 'I want it now that it's accessible.'

He didn't know that she knew where the money had come from, Natasha realised. Leo could not have told him, which left her wondering why he hadn't, and what she was supposed to do next.

Her eyes flickered over to where the silver limo was still parked with its tinted windows denying her a glimpse inside. 'Did you convince Cindy to get you this meeting by threatening to give the true story about her involvement with you to the press?'

Rico offered another shrug. 'I lost everything while she gained everything. You tell me if that was fair? Your sister got her record contract and her number-one hit. I got to be laughed at for losing my woman to my big-shot stepbrother.'

'I was never yours in the true sense, Rico,' Natasha reminded him.

He ignored that. 'Leo put me out of a job with no damn reference and I am suddenly persona non grata in every social circle that counts. Even my own mother doesn't like me right now and you sit here looking like a million dollars because Leo likes his women to look worthy of him. But I hope you are happy with him, *cara*, while you share him with his sex-mad ex-wife.'

With a flip of a long, graceful hand, Rico dropped his flashy, state-of-the-art phone down on the table in front of her. 'Take a look,' he invited.

Natasha's eyelashes quivered as she dropped her gaze to the phone. She didn't want to pick it up. She didn't want to look. A cold chill was beginning to freeze her heart muscles because she knew Rico wasn't inviting her to check out his phone for fun, just as he hadn't mentioned Gianna without a reason for doing it.

Even her fingers felt chilled by the time they made a trembling crawl towards the phone and hit the key that would light the screen up. Leo appeared in stark digital clarity with the beautiful Gianna plastered to his front. They were standing outside what looked like a hotel. 'Leo, please,' she heard Gianna's pleading voice arrive in her ears in a near-perfect English speaking voice. 'She does not have to know!'

In full gut-churning colour, she watched Leo smile, watched him run a finger along the lush red contours of Gianna's beautiful mouth. 'OK.' He leant down to kiss that pleading mouth. 'I will come in with you.'

Then they walked up the steps and into the hotel.

'Paris,' Rico answered the question Natasha was trying so hard not to let herself think. 'Last night, to be exact. You can check the date and time if you like,' he indicated to the phone. 'I hung around for two hours waiting for him to come out again, but he didn't. You tell me, *cara*, what you think they were doing with those two hours?'

Natasha didn't answer. She was recalling another scene weeks ago, when she had stood in Rico's office doorway watching *his* betrayal of her drag the blind scales from her eyes. In this case it was Rico's telephone that formed the doorway from which she watched this new betrayal.

Without saying a word she put down the mobile and picked up Rico's pen.

Natasha just scrawled her name on the document, then she got up and walked away.

If she'd looked back she would have seen her minder pausing beside Rico's chair—but she didn't look back. She didn't even offer a sideways glance at the silver limo as she walked past it.

Leo arrived home as she was packing her bag. He came in through the bedroom door like a bullet, a seething mass of barely controlled fury trapped inside a sleek dark business suit.

'What the hell were you doing with Rico?' he bit out.

Natasha didn't answer; she just turned back to her bag.

'I asked you a question!' He arrived at her side and caught hold of her arm to swing her around. It was only as he did so that his eyes dropped to the bag she was packing. Cold fury suddenly lit him up. 'If you think you are leaving me for him you can think it through again,' he raked out.

Natasha just smiled.

The smile hit him as good as a hard slap. 'You bitch,' he choked, tossing her arm aside and reeling away from her. 'I can't believe you could do this to me.'

'Why not?' Natasha let herself speak at last—and the hell if she was going to tell him what she knew about him and Gianna. Let him know what it feels like to have his pride shredded!

It was like watching a mighty rock turn into an earthquake. The shudder that shook him almost shook her, too. 'You signed the money over to him,' he stated hoarsely.

'Yes, I did, didn't I?' she said smoothly. 'Are you going to inform the police?'

His bunched shoulders tensed. 'You're my wife.'

'So I am.'

He swung back, his angry eyes sharpened by the dry tone in her voice. 'What the *hell* is that supposed to imply?'

Natasha offered a shrug. 'Our marriage was just a form of blackmail you used to bring darling Gianna into line, so I don't think it counts as anything much.'

'Don't change the subject. Gianna has nothing to do with this.'

'She has everything to do with it!' Natasha cried out, then took a deep breath and pulled herself together again because she was close to telling him what she knew and she didn't want to do that. She *never* wanted him to know how much he had hurt her today! 'I was there, if you recall. Until she turned up, I was just the little thief you took to your bed to enjoy for six weeks until you got your precious money back. The marriage thing came up as one of your smart-mouthed quips aimed to punish your silly ex-wife for barging in while you were busy with me!'

'That's not true.'

'It is true,' she insisted. 'What was it you said to me before we left London, Leo? Six weeks keeping you sweet in your bed until I could access your money, then I was gone? Well, the six weeks are up. I've accessed the money and now I'm leaving.'

With that she turned back to pick up her holdall. He was at her side before she had touched the strap. The packed bag went flying to the floor. Natasha barely managed a quivering gasp of protest before he was spinning her round to face him again. Black fury was firing from his every skin cell. She had never seen his eyes so hard. He was white—ghost white. He was even shaking as he held her.

'To go back to him?' he shot out.

Eyes like iced-blue glass, she gave him his answer. 'Well, you of all people must know what they say about the devil you know,' she provoked.

She was referring to Gianna and he knew that she was. His eyes gave a blinding bitter flash of instant understanding. 'You know about Paris.'

He was that quick-thinking, the rotten, cruel, heartless swine! 'I hate you, Leo,' she shook out thickly. 'You're a cold and hard, calculating devil. For all his faults, Rico is worth ten of you!'

'You think so?'

'I know so!' Natasha tried to pull free of him.

His fingers tightened. 'Say hello to this devil, then,' he gritted, then his mouth landed on hers like a crushing blow.

They'd kissed in anger before and turned the whole thing into a glorious fight, but this was different. Natasha didn't want this, but her body was not listening. She hated him with every spinning atom of her being but one touch from him lit her up like a torch. And her thin dress was no barrier to help shield her. He dealt with it by the simple method of wrenching the back zip apart so the dress fell in a slither to the ground.

'Get off me!' she choked at him.

'When you stop wanting me so desperately,' he rasped back.

Then he was kissing and touching and caressing and *goading* her to reject what he knew she could not! He knew every weak inch of her. He stripped away her clothes and aroused her with a grim ruthlessness that had her whimpering against his possessing mouth. And when that wasn't enough for him, he lifted her up against him, making her straddle his hips while his mouth maintained the deep, driving possession of her mouth.

Next thing she knew she was being dropped on the bed while he stood over her, holding her still by the sheer power of his angry desire-blackened gaze as he stripped off his clothes. The jacket, the shirt—shoes heeled off and flicked out of his way. When he stripped the last garments away, he was like a menacing threat that completely dominated her every thought and sense, and tingling tight fear cloaked her in sizzling excitement.

'Leo—please...' she begged in an appeal for sanity.

'Leo—please...' he mimicked tautly. 'You have no idea what it does to me when you say that.'

Then he came over her, arriving on the bed. With a bewilderingly slick show of controlled strength Natasha found her thighs smoothly parted and he was lowering his angry dark head. 'Make sure you tell Rico all about this later,' he muttered.

What took place next cast her into an agony of skin-tingling pleasure. She moved and groaned and sobbed and shuddered and he just went on doing it, keeping her finely balanced on the edge of frantic hysterics and a clamouring, desperate need for release. If she tried to protest he snaked up and kissed her. If she tried to get away, he stayed her with the clamp of his hands to her hips. When he finally decided it was time to join them, his first driving thrust made her cry out in soul-crushing relief. Then he was lifting her up and tipping her head back so he could devour her mouth while he rode her like that, with her hair flowing behind her and her fingers clinging to the sinew-tight tension in his neck. The angry glare in his eyes would have been frightening if it weren't for the glaze of hot, urgent desire that matched the quick, deep, thrusting drive of his hips as he brought them both rushing towards the pinnacle of a nerve-screeching release.

When it came, she arched like a slender bow strung so tight she couldn't relax again. The stinging whip-crack of her orgasm played through her in a series of violent, electric shocks as Leo let go with a single powerful quake of his body. The whole wild seduction with its total breakdown of control had taken just a few short dizzying minutes, yet when it was over, Natasha felt as if she'd been scraped clean of energy, exhausted of the strength to even move.

Not so Leo. On a thick growl of contempt he withdrew from her and climbed off the bed. Whether the contempt had been aimed at her or at himself didn't matter. The way he picked up his clothes and left her lying there in a weak, quivering huddle and just strode out of the room riddled her with contempt for herself.

Natasha continued to lie there for ages, trying to come to terms with what had happened—trying to come to terms with the whole barbaric crescendo ending to their relationship. She hated herself for falling victim too easily. She despised him for encouraging it. When she could find the strength to move, she just got off the bed, got dressed in the first clothes that came to hand, then repacked her bag with only the clothes she'd brought with her to Greece.

Then she left. Nobody tried to stop her from going. She didn't even bother to ring for a taxi before she stepped outside and walked down the drive towards the pair of gates. The guard on the gate said absolutely nothing, but just opened them and let her into the street.

Leo stood in front of the curving glass wall and watched her do it. She hadn't even stopped long enough to tidy her hair, he saw, and she was wearing that damn pale blue suit.

He turned away from the window, bitterness warring with an agony that was tightening the muscles lining his throat. He looked at the tangle of sheets on the bed.

Then he saw the manila envelope lying there on top of the bedding. As he walked over to it and saw *'Leo'* scrawled on it he felt his legs turn hollow with dread as he picked the envelope up.

A cruising taxi picked Natasha up and a few minutes later she was heading for the airport without allowing herself a single glance back. It was only when she sat back in the seat that she noticed she was wearing the pale blue suit.

Fitting, she thought bleakly. Maybe the suit should be preserved in a glass case to remind her that she was a fool and all men were lying cheats.

The airport was busy. Trying to get a seat on a flight back to England was impossible, she discovered, beginning to wilt now as that first rush of adrenalin that had carried her this far began to ebb.

'You can only hope for a cancellation, Kyria Christakis,' the booking agent told her. 'Otherwise we have no seat available for the next two days.'

'W-what about a different airport?' Her voice was beginning to shake, Natasha noticed. She could feel a bubble of hysteria fighting to burst free from her throat. 'M-Manchester, perhaps, or Glasgow. I don't really care where I land so long as it is on UK soil.'

What was there in London for her to go back to anyway? she was just asking herself when a hand arrived on her shoulder.

Natasha jumped like a scalded cat as her mind threw up a terrifying image of the hand belonging to the police.

He wouldn't—he *wouldn't*! her mind screamed at her.

Then the voice came. 'That will not be necessary.'

CHAPTER TEN

As Natasha trembled in recognition, Leo's hand became an arm clamping around her shoulders that contained her tense tremor within the power of his grasp. She was engulfed within seconds, by his height, by his strength, by his grim determination and by the cool use of his native language as he spoke to the curious booking agent while Rasmus appeared beside her and calmly bent to claim her bag.

'No…' She tried to stop him. 'I don't w-want—'

'Don't make a fuss, *agape mou*,' Leo murmured levelly. 'We are under surveillance from the Press.'

She was suddenly surrounded by his security men. Before she'd grasped what was happening they were hustling her through the airport like a human bulldozer, which gave her no view as to where they were going, and the tight grip Leo maintained on her kept her clamped against his side.

Gates magically opened for them. Having thought he was taking her back to his apartment, it came as a hard shock to find herself walking across tarmac towards what looked like a helicopter from the brief glimpse she caught of the rotor-blades already beginning to turn as they approached.

Panic erupted. 'I am not getting on that with you!' She pulled to a shuddering halt, causing men to struggle not to bump into her.

Breaking free of his grip, she spun back the way they had come. Leo bit out a command that sent burly men scattering. He hauled her up off her feet and into his arms, then completed the rest of the distance between them and the helicopter with the grim surefootedness of a man happy to dice with death by rotor-blade.

Natasha ducked her head into his shoulder in sheer fright and did not lift it up again until he'd put her down on a seat. The moment he let go of her she hit out at him with her fists.

He chose not to notice as he grimly fastened her into the seat while her angry blows just glanced off him. 'I hate you, *I hate you!*' she kept choking out.

'Save it until later,' he responded, and she'd never seen his face look so tough.

'But why are you doing this?'

He didn't answer, just stepped back to allow six men to pile in the helicopter, swarming like black-suited rats into the seats in front of her and behind. Natasha felt so wretchedly deserted and so terrified that Leo was going to send her off somewhere with his men so that they could deal with her, she couldn't stop herself from crying out, 'Leo—*please* don't leave me with them!'

By then he had his back to her. His wide shoulders gave a tense flex, but he did not turn around. Without offering her a single word of reassurance he just strode round the helicopter and climbed in the seat beside the pilot. In what felt like no time at all they were up in the air and shooting forwards towards the glinting blue of the Aegean. Natasha closed her eyes and tried hard not to let the panic inside her develop any more than it had done already. At least he was in here with her, she told herself fiercely. Whatever else that was happening, *at least* he wasn't leaving her to the care of his horrible men!

Leo dared a brief glance at her via the mirror positioned above the cockpit controls. Her eyes were shut tight, her lips parted and trembling and pale, and she had gone back to clutching her damn purse to her lap as if it were her only lifeline. The blue suit, the purse, the expression—all of them reminded him of the last time he'd virtually abducted her like this.

Except for the hair. The hair was free and tumbling around her stark white beautiful—*beautiful* face!

Hell, damn it. *Theos* help me! he thought angrily as his insides creased up, and he had to look away from her.

His pilot said something. He didn't hear what it was. He was so locked into one purpose it left no room in his head for anything else.

It did not take long to reach their destination. They touched down as the sun was turning everything a warm golden red. Even as they settled onto the ground he could see Natasha struggling to unlock her seat belt and—*hell*, maybe he should just let her escape because he knew he was in no fit state of mind to be safe around her right now.

Rasmus undid the seat belt for her because she couldn't seem to do it. It was from within a dazed state that Natasha stared at her fingers, which seemed to have turned to trembling jelly with no hope of control left. All of her felt that way, when she thought about it.

Rasmus also helped her down onto solid ground with an unusual gentleness for such a tough man. When she glanced up at him to whisper a shaky, 'Thank you,' he sent her the strangest apologetic look.

For some reason that look almost finished her. The tears were suddenly flooding upwards in a hot, raging gush. She turned away from him, not wanting Rasmus to see the tears—not wanting to see his apology! Leo appeared around the nose of the helicopter looking exactly like the tall, dark, tough stranger she used to see him as.

He needed a shave, she noticed hazily. And he was wearing the same clothes he had picked up off the bedroom floor. They looked creased and dishevelled. *He* looked creased and dishevelled.

Her stomach dipped and squirmed but she refused to analyse why.

And she dragged her eyes away from Leo, too.

He didn't touch her.

'Shall we go?' he said, and took an oddly formal step to one side in a silent invitation for her to precede him.

Where to, though? Natasha wondered anxiously as her reluctant feet moved her ahead of him, hating him like poison for doing this to her, and despising him further for bringing her down to the point that she had cried out to him in fear.

They rounded a tall hedge and suddenly she was faced with a rambling two-storey villa with sun-blushed white walls. No housekeeper waited to greet them. Everyone else seemed to have just melted away. Leo stepped in front of her to open the front door, then he led the way across a soft eggshell-blue and cream hallway and into the kind of living room you only usually saw in glossy magazines.

'Wh-what is this place?' Natasha could not stop herself from asking, looking round her new surroundings that were as different again from the two other places Leo taken her to. Not a hint of the old-fashioned heaviness of the London house here, and it was certainly no ultra-modern, urban dwelling aimed to please the eye of the wealthy male.

No, this place was pure classical luxury with stunning artwork hanging on the walls and pieces of handmade furniture that must have cost the earth.

'My island retreat,' Leo answered, removing the jacket to his suit and slinging it over the back of a chair.

His *island* retreat, as in his *whole* island retreat?

In other circumstances Natasha would have been willing to be impressed by that, but she refused to be impressed by anything he said or did from now on—other than to give some answers to the real questions running round in her head.

Standing still just inside the doorway, she clutched her purse in her fingers and lifted up her chin. 'So is this to be my new luxury prison?' she iced out.

'No.' He moved across the room to pour himself a drink.

'You mean, I get to leave it whenever I want to, then?'

She saw his grim mouth flex at her sarcasm. 'No,' he said again.

'Then it's a prison.' She looked away from him.

To her absolute shock, he slammed the glass down and turned to stride back across the room to pull her into his arms and kiss her—hard.

There had never been a kiss like it. This one seemed to rise up from some deep place inside him and flow with a throbbing heat of pure feeling aimed to pour directly into her. It shook Natasha, really shook her. When he put her from him, she could only stare up at him in a bewildered daze.

He turned his back on her. 'Sorry,' he muttered. 'It was not my intention to—'

Like a woman living in some kind a surreal alternative life, Natasha could only stumble into the nearest chair.

'I don't understand what's going on here,' she whispered when he just stood there like a stone pillar. 'You kidnap me from the airport and hustle me like a piece of cattle onto your helicopter and scare me out of my w-wits. Then you bring me in here and *dare* to kiss me like that!'

He didn't speak. He didn't turn. His hands clenched into

fists, then disappeared into his trouser pockets. She noticed that his shirt cuffs were hanging open around his wrists.

'What else do you want from me, Leo?' she cried out in a thick voice.

'Nothing,' he said, his big shoulders flexing. 'I don't want anything else from you. I just don't want you to leave me.'

Then he really bewildered her by striding towards a pair of French windows and throwing them open so he could go outside.

Natasha stared after him and wished she understood him. Then on a sudden rush of angry hot blood she decided that she didn't *want* to understand a man like Leo, she just wanted him to explain that last remark!

Getting up on legs that did not want to carry her anywhere, she followed him outside and found herself stepping onto a deep terrace. The sun was hanging so low in the sky now it blinded her eyes. But she could see enough to know that Leo wasn't here. Casting her gaze out wider, she caught sight of his white shirt moving down through a garden towards the ocean gleaming a deep silken blue not far away.

By the time she reached a low wall that kept the beach back from the gardens, he was standing at the water's edge, hands still pushed into his pockets, staring out to sea.

'What is it with you?' she demanded. 'Why are you doing this to me? If it's because of the money, you only—'

'I don't want the money.'

Natasha paused several feet away from him. 'You found the envelope, then?' He just nodded. She let out a sigh. 'Then what do you want?' she asked helplessly.

Still he made no answer and the tears started coming again. Any second now he was going to succeed in completely breaking her control. Maybe that was what he wanted, she thought as she sank down on the low wall because her legs had finally given in.

'You're so arrogant, Leo,' she said unsteadily. 'You're so cynical about everyone and everything. You see no good in anyone. You believe everyone out there is trying to fleece you in one way or another. Y-your ex-wife wants your body, I want your money, Rico wants to stand in your shoes and *be* you. If you want my opinion, you would be better off poor and down-right ugly—then at least you could be happy knowing no one liked you for just being you!'

He laughed when he wasn't meant to. Natasha had to swallow on the lump her throbbing heart had become in her throat. 'You just love it when you think s-someone has proved your every cynical suspicion about them true.'

'Are you referring to what happened this afternoon?'

So he speaks! Natasha glared at him but couldn't see him through the bank of tears misting up her eyes. 'Yes,' she said, though that wasn't all of it. 'You came into our bedroom today expecting to see a cheating wife so you treated m-me like a cheating wife.'

'I thought you had signed the money over to Rico. It—hurt me.'

'Not enough to make you demand a proper explanation before you drew your own conclusions, though.'

Then she tensed warily as he spun on his heel, crunching gravelly sand beneath his shoes as he did.

'What did you sign for Rico?' he asked curiously.

'Permission to access an empty offshore account,' she answered with a shrug. 'I'd already transferred the money over to my private bank account yesterday. I meant to give you the envelope with the banker's draft in it yesterday but we were—sidetracked.'

By Gianna first, she remembered bleakly, then by an afternoon of—

Something dropped onto her lap and made her blink. 'W-what's this?' Warily she picked up the narrow white envelope.

'Take a look.'

Natasha looked at the envelope for what felt like ages before she could get her fingers to slip the seal. Her lips felt so dry she had to moisten them with her tongue as she removed the contents. It was getting really dark out here now, but still light enough for her to recognise what it was she was looking at.

'I d-don't understand,' she murmured eventually.

'Rasmus took it from Rico,' Leo explained. 'You know, Natasha,' he said dryly then, 'you possess more honour than I do. Even when he showed you evidence of my meeting with Gianna in Paris, you still could not take your revenge on me by signing your money over to him.'

She did not want to talk about his betrayal with Gianna. In fact, she began to feel sick just by recalling it. 'I signed for an empty account,' she pointed out.

'But you still signed Natasha *Christakis* instead of Natasha *Moyles*, which meant that Rico could not touch the account, even an empty one.'

'So what are you accusing me of now?' she demanded helplessly.

'Nothing.' Leo sighed.

'So, how did you get Rico to hand this over?' she asked him next.

'Rasmus—persuaded him.'

'Ah, good old Rasmus,' she mocked, recalling the way her minder had had his phone to his ear from the moment that Rico had put in an appearance. It was a shame that Rasmus did not extend his loyalty to her or maybe he would have felt duty-bound to tell her about his employer's night spent in Paris.

And remembering *that* brought Natasha to her feet. 'Does this prison have a bedroom to which I can escape?' she asked stiffly.

'My bedroom,' he confirmed.

'Not this side of hell, Leo,' Natasha informed him coldly. 'I come too expensive even for you from now on.'

'Then name your price….'

Turning on him, Natasha almost threw some obscene figure at him just to see how he would react! But she didn't. In the end she went for blunt honesty. 'A speedy way off this island and an even speedier divorce!' she flicked out, then turned to walk back to the house.

'Deal,' Leo said, bringing her to a taut-shouldered stand-still after only two steps. 'For one more night in my bed,' he extended, 'I will arrange your transport away from here.'

'I can't believe even you dared to say that,' she whispered.

'Why not? I am the world's worst cynic who believes everyone has their price. If escape from here and divorce is your price, *agape mou*, then I am willing to pay it—for my own price.'

Natasha walked on, stiff-backed and quivering with of-fence. Leo followed, feeling suddenly rejuvenated and—more importantly—hungry for the fight. What he had done that afternoon had been pretty much unforgivable. He'd accepted that even before he had watched her take that long walk down his drive. What his beautiful, proud, icy wife had just unwittingly done was to hand him his weapon of salvation and his last chance to put this right between them.

'You just s-stay away from me!' she shrilled when she heard his footsteps closing in on her.

'I'm wildly in love with you—how can I stay away?'

'How *dare* you say that?' Natasha swung around on him,

eyes like glistening blue chips of hurt. 'What do you know about love, Leo? You would not know how to recognise it!'

'And you do?' he threw back. 'You were supposed to be in love with Rico, but where is that broken-hearted love now?'

Pulling in a deep breath, Natasha snapped her lips together. A tense spin of her body and she was continuing up the path and into the house.

Leo followed, more relaxed the more tense that she became. 'You know I'm madly jealous of Rico,' he offered up from the open French windows. 'I have been jealous of him since I first saw you with him. But I refused to recognise what was wrong with me each time I attacked you—'

'With your nasty sarcasms aimed to make me feel small?'

'I wanted you to notice me— What are you looking for?'

'I noticed you, Leo. My purse.'

'On the floor marking the spot where I last kissed you,' he indicated. 'You have to drop the purse, you see, so you can dig your nails into my neck in case I decide to stop.'

Face burning fire now, Natasha went and picked the purse up then walked out of the room.

'Ask yourself, *agape mou*, did you ever see me with another woman from the first night we met?'

She swung around. 'Gianna, in your bedroom, calling me her whoring substitute?' she offered up. 'Gianna, in Paris, coaxing you into a hotel for a cosy—chat?'

Leo sighed. 'I can explain about Gianna. She—'

'Do I look like I *want* an explanation?' Natasha flicked out.

The stairs drew her. She hadn't a clue where she was going, but it suited Leo that she'd taken that direction.

'Middle door on the right,' he offered helpfully. 'My room. My bed. My offer still in place. I will even throw in a candlelit dinner for two on the beach— Damn.'

He should have seen it coming. He had, after all, been

goading her towards some kind of reaction since he'd decided to go on the offensive. But to watch her drop down on one of the stairs and bury her face in her hands, then start weeping, was more than he'd bargained for.

He was up there and squatting in front of her and pulling her into his chest before she had a chance to let out the second sob. 'No,' he roughed out. 'Not the tears, Natasha. You were supposed to fly at me with your fists so I could catch you and kiss you out of your head.'

'I hate you,' she sobbed. 'You're so—'

'Loathsome, I know,' he sighed out. 'I'm sorry.'

'You think I'm a thief.'

'I have never, for one second, believed you were a thief,' he denied. 'I have a split personality. I can go wild with jealousy over Rico and can still recognise that you're the most honest person I know.'

The sobs stopped coming; she replaced them with a forlorn sniff. 'That wasn't what you said when you made me come to Greece with you.'

'I was fighting for my woman. I was prepared to say or do anything.'

'You were *ruthless* this afternoon.'

'Unforgivably so,' he agreed. 'Give me one night in our bed and I will make it up to you.'

'Then let me go tomorrow?'

'Ah.' That was all, just that rueful *Ah*, and Natasha knew she had caught him out.

'And I always believed you spoke only the truth,' she denounced, frowning when she caught the way her fingers were toying with the buttons on his shirt and wondering why she was letting them do that. 'It was your only saving grace as far as I could tell.'

'I thought the fantastic sex was.'

She shook her head, still watching as a section of hair-roughened, bronzed skin appeared close enough for her to kiss. He smelled warm—of Leo, masculine and tempting.

'I need a shower....'

Natasha shook her head as another button gave on the shirt. His hands moved on her back. 'Dangerous, Natasha,' he warned her gently.

Too late. Her tongue snaked out and she licked.

That's it! he might as well have announced as he rose up to his full height, pulling her up with him, then clamping her hard against his body before mounting the rest of the stairs. 'You know what you are,' he bit out at her. 'You are a man-teaser.'

'I am not!' Natasha denied.

'You tell me you hate me then you lick me as if I am the sweetest-tasting thing in your world! If that is not man-teasing, then I don't know what is.'

'I am still not going to bed with you!'

'No?' He opened up his arms and dropped her like a discarded bundle on a bed and was right there with her before she could recover from the drop, his fingers already busy with the buttons on her jacket. 'You pull this blue thing on like a suit of armour...' he muttered.

The jacket flew open to reveal a skimpy lilac silk camisole, then he was reaching round beneath her so he could unzip her skirt. 'When I think of the years I indulged in classy, sophisticated sex with classy, sophisticated women—' he gritted.

'I don't want to hear about your other women,' Natasha protested, trying to stop him from undressing her by wriggling her hips.

'Were you listening to anything I have already said?' he husked out. 'There have been no other women since I met you! Before you is none of your business.'

'Then don't *talk* about them!'

'I was trying to make a point—that sex without all of this mad, wild, crazily emotional stuff is rubbish sex! Not that you are ever going to find that out.'

'I might do—after tonight.'

About to remove her skirt altogether, Leo went still. 'So you are staying here with me tonight?'

'I might do,' she repeated coolly. 'I suppose it depends on what you're going to tell me you were doing with Gianna in Paris and if I decide to believe you.'

'Ah.' There it was again, the *Ah* sound that said— Caught me out again, Natasha. And he rolled away from her to stretch out beside her on the bed. 'It was not a hotel in Paris,' he stated flatly. 'It was at a very exclusive private clinic made to look like a hotel, and Rico knew that when he showed you what he did because Gianna has been there countless times before….'

'A clinic that looks like a hotel? Very convenient,' Natasha said dryly. 'Next thing you will be telling me you accidentally bumped into her on the steps.'

'No. I took her there,' Leo sighed out. 'The way she put her nails into you made me decide that it was time for me to get tough. You have to know something about her past to understand Gianna,' he went on heavily. 'Things I did not know about until after we were married and had to find out the hard way,' he admitted. 'She is not a bad person just a— very sad product of a sick upbringing in the centre of a wealthy but corrupt family who taught her that sex equalled love.'

'Oh, that's awful,' Natasha murmured, catching on to what he meant.

'And it is her story, not mine to tell. So let me just say that we had been lovers for a couple of months when she told me she was pregnant. Of course I married her, why not?' He was almost asking himself. 'She was beautiful, great company and about to become the mother of my first child. I saw no problem being faithful to her. Then two weeks after we married I caught her in bed with another man. She tried to tell me it didn't mean anything—but it meant a hell of a lot to me.'

'So you threw her out?'

'Walked out,' he amended. 'A week later she lost the baby and I've never felt so bad or so guilty about anything in my entire life because I had allowed myself to forget the fragile life growing inside her when I walked out. She suffered her first breakdown, which placed her in the Paris clinic for the first time. It was while she was in there that the truth about her past came out. Because I felt sorry for her and she needed someone to care about her, I took her back into my life.'

'Because you loved her,' Natasha murmured.

He turned his head to look at her, dark eyes glowing in the darkening sunset. 'I am not going to lie to you, Natasha, and say she no longer means anything to me,' he stated flatly. 'I did not go into my marriage with her, expecting it to turn out the way that it did. But as for loving her? No, I never did love her the way that you mean. But I did and do still care for her, and, believe me, she really does not have anyone else that does.'

Moving onto her side so she could watch his expression, 'So you—look out for her?' she questioned carefully.

His chiselled jaw tightened. 'I do not sleep with her.'

'That was not what I asked.'

'But you are still thinking it,' he said, reading her face the same as she was reading his. 'I have not slept with Gianna since I took her back into my life. She had another lover within days of arriving back in Athens anyway.' He shrugged. 'The unpalatable fact that she can't help using sex as a sub-stitute for love and affection is not her fault, but I couldn't live with it, though we struggled on for several months before I finally walked out.'

'OK…' It was crazy of her to think that he needed her to touch him, but that was what Natasha sensed in him while he lay there talking himself out. But not yet. 'So you still care for her. You look out for her. You do not sleep with her,' she listed. 'Are you expecting me to accept her as a part of my life, too?'

'Hell, no.' He was suddenly rising up to lean over her and crushing her mouth with a hot kiss. 'That part is over,' he vowed as he drew away again. 'She finally killed my lingering guilt and my sympathy for her when it hit me that it was very fortuitous that Rico happened to catch me with her on the clinic steps.'

Natasha frowned. 'I don't follow—'

'Gianna is good at seducing people to do what she wants them to do—so is Rico, come to that. She wanted you out of my life and he wanted his money. Put the two together, plus the fact that Rico knows what Gianna is like about me, and you have a great conspiracy plot to get you to sign over the money and have you walk out of my life at the same time.'

'Oh, that is so—sick.'

'That's Gianna and Rico,' Leo acknowledged ruefully. 'Now can we talk about you and me? What do *you* want, Natasha?' he questioned her.

Natasha lowered her eyes to look at his mouth. It wasn't smiling. It wasn't even thinking about smiling, his question was that serious.

So what did she want?

She felt his fingers come to rest lightly on her cheekbones, felt the weight of his thighs pressing hers into the bed. She lifted her hands up to his chest and watched her fingertips curl into dark coils of hair and felt, heard—saw him take a slow and careful intake of breath. She saw the wedding band he'd placed on her finger glow as the last of the sun caught hold of it and set the gold on fire.

Then she looked up at him, into his eyes, his dark—dark,

serious eyes. 'You,' she breathed out whisperingly. 'I just want you.'

Vulnerable, Leo saw, so vulnerable her lips had to tremble as she made herself say it as if she was still scared to open up to him with the truth.

He pulled in a deep breath. 'I've changed my mind about this suit,' he said, not looking into her eyes any more. 'I love it. It reminds me of the woman I first fell in love with—'

'M-miss Buttoned Up, you mean?'

'Miss *Sexily* Buttoned Up,' he extended, then pushed himself away from her so he could button her back up again before he rose up off the bed, pulling her up so he could turn her around and do up her skirt zip.

'Why are you doing that?'

'I had forgotten about something.' Transferring his fingers to his shirt buttons, he fastened those, too. Natasha watched as he hid his bronze, muscled body away from her and felt the sting of disappointment.

Then he was taking possession of one of her hands and trailing her out of the bedroom, back down the stairs, back through the living room and back through the French doors, where Natasha pulled to a breathless stop in surprise.

The darkened terrace had been transformed while they'd been upstairs in the bedroom, and was now a flickering wonderland of soft candle-light.

A table had been laid for two and Bernice was just turning away from it. '*Kalispera*.' She smiled at the two of them. 'You ready to eat now?'

Leo answered in his own language, while trailing a silenced Natasha over to the table, then politely held out her chair.

'What's going on?' she managed in bewilderment.

'When I plan something this carefully, I usually follow through with it,' this unusual, hard-crusted, soft-centred man standing there drawled. 'The surprise I promised you,' he explained. 'You had forgotten about it, I see.'

'Oh,' she murmured, because she had forgotten.

Leo smiled as he sat down. 'I was not expecting to do this with us both dressed like this. However...' He reached across the table to take hold of her hands. 'Natasha, this is my home. My real home. The others are just convenient places I use when I need a place to stay. But this island will always be the place I come home to.'

'Well, that's—very nice,' she said, wondering where this was leading.

'More than nice, it's special.' His dark eyes were focused intently on her face. 'I am madly, wildly, jealously in love with you, *agape mou*. I spoiled that part too by telling you so earlier,' he then acknowledged with a rueful tilt to his mouth. 'But I do— love you. If it was not already too late, I would be sitting here now asking you to marry me. Since I've already done that part, too, all I can ask you is, will you live here with me, Natasha? Share my home with me, have my children and bring them up here with me, and make this cynical Greek a very happy man...?'

Natasha didn't know what to say. She hadn't come here expecting him to say any of this. In fact, she'd come here believing that she hated him and that he hated her.

'And this is your surprise?' she asked finally.

His fingers twitched on her fingers because she clearly was not giving him the response he desired. 'Until I tried my best to murder my chances this afternoon.' He nodded. 'Did I murder them?'

The outright challenge from the blunt speaker, Natasha noticed distractedly.

She shook her head.

'Then say something a bit more—positive,' he prompted impatiently, 'because I feel like I am sinking very fast here....'

Sinking fast…she was sinking fast…beneath his spell. 'Yes, please,' she said.

Leo muttered something she didn't catch, then sat back in his seat. 'It must be the suit.' He laughed, though it wasn't a real laugh. 'Would you like to explain to me what the polite *yes, please* covers exactly?'

Now he was cross. Natasha frowned. 'You're sitting there just *expecting* me to say it back to you, aren't you?'

'*Theos*, if you don't love me, then I've caught myself yet another little liar for a wife because every damn thing you do around me *tells* me you love me!'

'All right—I love you!' she announced on a rush of heat. 'I love you,' she repeated. 'But I'm still angry with you, Leo, so words like that don't come easily!'

'Angry about what?' His eyes flickered red with annoyance in the candle-light. 'I've already apologised for—'

'You scared me half to death when you hustled me at the airport!'

'I scared myself more when I thought I wasn't going to catch you before you flew away.'

'Oh,' she said.

'Oh,' he repeated, then climbed back to his feet. 'We are going back to bed.'

He already had hold of her hand again and was pulling her to her feet. 'We can't,' she quavered. 'Bernice—'

'Bernice!' Leo called out as they hit the hallway. 'Hold the dinner. We are going back to bed!'

'God, why do you have to be so openly *blunt?*' Natasha gasped in hot embarrassment.

'OK…you make the nice babies now…' the calm answer came drifting back towards them.

'Even Bernice knows blunt is best.' Leo turned on the stairs to grin down at her.

'All right!' Natasha pulled to a stop, eyes flashing blue flames of anger and brimming defiance. 'So I love you!' she repeated at the top of her voice. 'I don't understand *why* I should love you because, quite *bluntly*, Leo, you drive me up the wall! But—'

He pulled her towards him and kissed her right there on the stairs. Her fingers shot around his neck to stop her tumbling backwards—and because they couldn't help themselves.

'That is why you love me,' he insisted when he eventually pulled back.

'You could be right,' Natasha conceded with her eyes fixed on his oh-so-kissable mouth before she lifted them up to clash with his eyes. 'Do you think we could check it out some more, please…?'